15 ot

DATE DUE

GRAD MAR 0 8 '88			
CMSU MAY 9 '88			
GAYLORD			PRINTED IN U.S.A.

CENTAUR CLASSICS

GENERAL EDITOR: J. M. COHEN

POEMS

By Walter Savage Landor

Walter Savage Landor: After J. Gibson

National Portrait Gallery

POEMS

BY WALTER SAVAGE LANDOR

SELECTED AND INTRODUCED BY

GEOFFREY GRIGSON

SOUTHERN ILLINOIS UNIVERSITY PRESS

CARBONDALE   ILLINOIS

CONTENTS

THE POEMS

* Dates, unless otherwise indicated, are those of first printing. Titles between brackets have been supplied.

viii

POEMS PUBLISHED IN 1853

x

POEMS PUBLISHED IN DECEMBER 1857

INTRODUCTION

SOMETHING of value may be discovered about Landor's poems from our understanding, or rather our common misunderstanding, of his most famous epigram, which he called *The Dying Speech of an Old Philosopher*, and which he composed on the evening of his seventy-fourth birthday, after entertaining Charles Dickens and John Forster, who wrote his biography. Landor, we all know, was a hefty egotist with a loud laugh and a quick and at times violent temper; and we laugh ourselves, when we recall the first line of this birthday poem, in which he looked back over life and accepted death: we think how singular that of all men, Landor should say

I strove with none, for none was worth my strife,

when his existence seems to have been an intermittent strife from childhood, and school, and university, to his extreme old age in Bath and Florence. But we are wrong, and Landor was right: Landor wrote his epigram, not as the subject of a known biography, but as a poet and as the prose-master of his *Imaginary Conversations*; in that role, though as a man he might be moiled in law suits and libel actions, and might end as a King Lear rejected by his children, this striving with no one, or no other writer, as writer himself, was firmly at the centre of Landor's creed, stated by him again and again. When his friend Southey died, the praise Landor accorded him, in a prose epitaph, was the praise he accorded himself in the epigram: 'Rarely hath any author been so exempt from the maladies of emulation.' To push, to scramble, to emulate, to compete, and lose independence—that was the sin of authorship, the betrayal of talent. 'Authors are like cattle going to a fair;' he makes a character say in one of the *Imaginary Conversations*, 'those of the same field can never move on without butting one another.' He butted no one for self-advancement (to criticize or despise is something else). He wrote neither for acclaim nor for money; and he realized that for this and for other reasons his situation in literature was a lonely one, and would continue to be lonely after his death.

In his life everybody was for ever regretting the contradictions which appeared to exist in Landor's nature. When he was old and still unpredictable—or all too predictable—in a vigour of conduct outside the norm, his friends would acknowledge his literary power, and regret 'that he gives way to such strange tempers and crotchets and waywardness.' Wordsworth (whose tame side was frequently and justly and wittily ridiculed by Landor[1]) spoke of him rather pompously as 'a man so deplorably

---

[1] *Archdeacon Hare.* Wordsworth is guiltless at least of affectation.

Walter Landor. True; but he is often as tame as an abbess's cat, which in kittenhood has undergone the same operation as the Holy Father's choristers.

tormented by ungovernable passion,' whose character 'may be given in two or three words: a madman, a bad-man, yet a man of genius, as many a madman is.' The mark, though, of this madman's genius was its extreme, unromantic sanity. Crotchets, waywardness and tempers—or ungovernable passion—go back to Landor's childhood in Warwick, where he was born in 1775, the eldest son of a well-to-do, and as the years went by, still more well-to-do, physician. 'In my boyhood I was a fierce democrat and extolled the French.' He indeed told his mother (a foolish woman, or a fussy one, partly to blame for his unbalanced up-bringing) that he hoped 'the French would invade England and assist us in hanging George the Third between two such thieves as the Archbishops of Canterbury and York;' in return for which she boxed his ears. His headmaster at Rugby, who admired his skill as a Latin versifier, found him too rebellious to keep in the school, and insisted that he must either be removed by his father, or ex-pelled. At Oxford (where Southey knew of him as a 'mad Jacobin') he fired a gun at the shuttered windows of a priggish undergraduate, and was sent down. So it continued. He quarrelled with his father, he bungled his love affairs, his inheritance, his estates, his marriage to a pretty, twittering, stupid, ill-educated girl, who developed into a bitch with a nasty mouth. He was driven into exile, as a young man by debt, as an old one by fear of damages in a libel action brought against him by a clergyman's wife. In one part of himself reckless, passionate and ungovernable, in his creative part he was the neo-classic champion of depth, bright surface, and composure. The unifying clue to Landor is that the one supported the other: he was the intemperate champion of temperance. Ultra-vigorous support of one cluster of attitudes involved ultra-vigorous disdain of every opposite cluster, in politics as in poetry. Born on the day—January 30th—on which, as he well knew, Charles I had been executed, rejoicing in Waterloo, yet dreading 'from that moment the reaction under which the continent groans,' he hated for life that 'conspiracy of kings, first against all republics, now openly against all constitutions,' which had so much influenced him, Landor said, in writing in the years after Waterloo the first twenty-three of his *Imaginary Conversations*. The constitu-tional opposite of absolutism, oppression and injustice was a state of things akin to Landor's own preferred style, in prose or poetry, of composure, bright surface, and nourishing depth:

> Poet! I like not mealy fruit; give me
> Freshness and crispness and solidity;
> Apples are none the better overripe,
> And prime buck-venison I prefer to tripe.

Reverting to *The Dying Speech of an Old Philosopher*, every state-ment Landor makes in the poem, his life and his writings confirm explicitly. It is Landor's true biography, setting him both in and

apart from his time, as our one eminent neo-classic. 'Nature I
loved'—if he loved nature, that marked him as a man of his time,
whether neo-classic or romantic (not that one would divorce neo-
classic and romantic too absolutely), and one may recall Landor's
delight—for a while—in the red sandstone valley of his Llanthony
estates: 'I have made a discovery, which is, that there are both
nightingales and glowworms in my valley. I would give two or
three thousand less for a place that was without them'; or—for a
while—in his villa garden on the slopes of Fiesole. Or one may
point to many passages in which a modicum of nature finds natural
language—'Now yellowing hazels fringe the greener plain,' or

> Is it no dream that I am he
>   Whom one awake all night
> Rose ere the earliest birds to see,
>   And met by dawn's red light;
>
> Who, when the wintry lamps were spent,
>   And all was drear and dark,
> Against the rugged pear-tree leant
>   While ice crackt off the bark.

'*Nature I loved, and, next to Nature, Art*': art, composure, modera-
tion—'What is there lovely in poetry,' asked Landor, through the
mouth of Boccaccio, in the *Pentameron* of 1837, 'unless there be
moderation and composure? Are they not better than the hot,
uncontrollable harlotry of a flaunting dishevelled enthusiasm?
Whoever has the power of creating, has likewise the inferior power
of keeping his creation in order. The best poets are most impressive
because their steps are regular; for without regularity there is
neither strength nor state.'
As for the last two lines of the epigram—that he warmed 'both
hands before the fire of Life,' that the fire was sinking and that
Landor was ready to depart, they are a true summary of Landor's
acceptance of life and death; of the fact that he neither evaded,
nor substituted, preferring, for example, Wordsworth to Byron
(Gerard Manley Hopkins perciapiently linked Wordsworth and
Landor as members of a school, in which the award for style went
to Landor), nature and natural language to seraglio and seraglio
talk, or faeries and faery talk, or mists, or infinity; preferring
objectivity to autotoxication or autoblabbery, *here and now* to
somewhere else and then—

> Some see but sunshine, others see but gloom,
> Others confound them strangely, furiously;
> Most have an eye for colour, few for form.
> Imperfect is the glory to *create*,
> Unless on our creation we can look
> And see that all is good; we then may rest.[1]

It could be argued, of course, that Landor's classicism was as much

[1] *To the Author of 'Festus' on the Classick & Romantick.*

a substitution or an ideal evasion of here and now as another writer's liking for an ideal mediaevalism or an aery-faeryism derived from Drayton or *A Midsummer Night's Dream*, or border ballads; to which Landor's reply was that his ideal classic ground— Greek rather than Roman—and classic principles, demanded height, depth, severity, clarity, and grace. In long poems his power to construct, and tell, and hold, is seldom sufficient, and his pressure does fall too low; in his short poems he sometimes goes soft, in the manner of other neo-classic poets, architects, and sculptors (such as Flaxman or Thorwaldsen, whom Landor admired). But Landor, like the Greek style architects of his time, wanted, and frequently achieved, what he considered a Greek stiffening of neo-classic sentimentality: the clear and determinate world of Greece was not the misty, indeterminate chaos of the Gothic. There were poets, Landor said, whose books in half a century would be enquired after only for 'cutting out an illuminated letter from the title-page' (Gothicizing poets) 'or of transplanting the willow at the end, that hangs so prettily over the tomb of Amaryllis' (neo-classically sentimental poets). 'If they wish to be healthy and vigorous, let them open their bosoms to the breezes of Sunium; for the air of Latium is heavy and overcharged.'[1]

The Attic, temple-crowned, sun-clear promontory of Sunium was the ideal ground for Landor, as it had been for Hölderlin, Landor's elder by five years:

> Noch dünkt die Welt mir schön, und das Aug entflieht,
> Verlangend nach den Reizen der Erde, mir
> Zum goldenen Paktol, zu Smyrnas
> Ufer, zu Ilions Wald. Auch möcht ich
>
> Bei Sunium oft landen, den stummen Pfad
> Nach deinen Säulen fragen, Olympion![2]

Or, as Landor expressed it again in his poem on the Classick and the Romantick, in the grave, slow line of this poet reflecting, this poet considering ultimates:

> The ancients see us under them, and grieve
> That we are parted by a rank morass,
> Wishing its flowers more delicate and fewer.
> Abstemious were the Greeks; they never strove
> To look so fierce: their Muses were sedate,
> Never obstreperous: you heard no breath
> Outside the flute; each sound ran clear within.
> The Fauns might dance, might clap their hands, might shout,
> Might revel and run riotous; the Nymphs
> Furtively glanced, and fear'd, or seem'd to fear:
> Descended on the lightest of light wings,
> The graceful son of Maia mused apart,
> Graceful, but strong; he listen'd; he drew nigh;
> And now with his own lyre and now with voice
> Temper'd the strain; Apollo calmly smiled.

[1] *The Pentameron.*   [2] From *Der Neckar*

When Landor writes—and ends a poem—'Apollo calmly smiled',
the three words are fact and metaphor; but fact all through. The
god Apollo calmly smiled, the narrow-waisted, almond-eyed god
whom we know in marble, and who is beauty, youth, composure,
strength, civilization. The clear-edged congruence of word and
object in Landor is one of his virtues, more acceptable, since
language allows of less mannerism than stone and stucco, than the
clear-edged 'Greek' architecture of Landor's time, Doric, Ionic,
Corinthian, which we now value in the buildings of London and
elsewhere. But it does not exhaust Landor's value as a poet to
say that there is more of that clear congruence in his longer poems
than we commonly admit, and to emphasize its creativity in his
epigrams and shorter pieces. He is master especially of a calm line
which often begins with short emphatic accented words, and then
lightens; he makes poetry a matter of rhythm and language and
objectivity, not of imagery and metaphysics; and he would certainly
have rejected ambiguity as an evil. He is various, like his own
large personality. He offers occasional perfection; he offers gravity,
strength, delicacy, wit, comedy. He is lyrical, elegiacal, critical;
but convinced also of pleasure—

> The narrow mind is the discontented one.
> There is pleasure in wisdom, there is wisdom in pleasure
> If thou findest no honey in thy cake,
> Put thy cake into honey with thine own right-hand,
> Nor think it defiled thereby.

He can make flickering fun, or knock down a bullock of stupidity.
Criticism, perhaps with interference from the history of literature,
has inclined to make less than it should have done of poems which
are counter, in so many ways, to the 'romantic' flow of poetry and
the other arts during Landor's extremely long, always active
career. In the past many critics and readers seemed unsure or
sure in the wrong way of the voluminous work of a man at times
so boisterous and in some ways so uninhibited, who survived into
a mealy age (when he died in 1864 he was in his ninetieth year).
What was to be thought in such an age of a *poet*—better to think
of the prose-writer—whose appetites and moral taste were suspect,
who could write as he did about Ianthe's shell or red Priapus
rearing his club among the junipers, who could deliver himself of
an epigram so indecorous as

> Exhausted now her sighs, and dry her tears,
> For twenty youths these more than twenty years,
> Anne, turning nun, swears God alone shall have her . . .
> God ought to bow profoundly for the favour;

who was able to contrive poems with as much ease in outmoded
Latin as in English, taking behind that thin veil Catullan liberties—
O solite incesta pueros pervertere verpa Landor began a poem on a
fellow of an Oxford college—which made even Byron wittily

enquire how moral and sedate Southey could consort with the 'edifying Ithyphallics of Savagius'; and who was evidently less of a Christian than an elderly loudmouthed pagan, from Fiesole, who might enjoy the pink and white flowers of the oleander beside a clear stream, or the small yellow-green flowers of the box, but had no very certain convictions of a future life?

In the present, criticism and reading have not caught up. 'Poetry was always my amusement, prose my study and business': take Landor's word for it, continue to insist that the poems are mostly occasional—(however: 'Regarding the occasional in poetry; is there less merit in taking and treating what is before us, than in seeking and wandering through an open field as we would for mushrooms?')—and use Landor's prose as an excuse for neglecting the poet (and the verse perhaps as an excuse for neglecting the prose). At any rate, a glance at the third and supplementary volumes of the *Cambridge Bibliography of English Literature* (which places Landor unfortunately among the essayists, and not the poets) shows that no English writer—no English poet—of equal size and quality has been less attended to in the last fifty years; which is a loss.

'I stand out a rude rock in the middle of a river, with no exotic or parasitical plant on it, and few others. Eddies and dimples and froth and bubbles pass rapidly by, without shaking me. Here indeed is little room for pic-nic and polka.'[1]

Not a bad account of himself, as a poet; though Walter Landor was less a rock, and rough, than a finely shaped structure, graceful, but strong, like his Hermes in the poem, who invented the lyre and was the son of Zeus as well as of Maia. Landor himself had some of the attributes of the herm, he was more of a whole and healthy poet than many of his time; in justified pride he thought of himself in a high eagle's sunshine, as in his poem which begins

> Ye who have toil'd uphill to reach the haunt
> Of other men who lived in other days

and which ends (after he has established that they found nothing but owls hooting and shaking the ivy berries on their heads, and vipers hissing at them, as they crawled down)

> Now, was it worth your while to mount so high
> Merely to say ye did it, and to ask
> If those about ye ever did the like?
> Believe me, O my friends, 'twere better far
> To stretch your limbs along the level sand
> As they do, where small children scoop the drift,
> Thinking it must be gold, where curlews soar
> And scales drop glistening from the prey above.

---

[1] This and the two previous quotations are from *Archdeacon Hare and Walter Landor*.

ACKNOWLEDGMENTS

No selection of Landor's poems could be made without a heavy reliance on Stephen Wheeler's *Poetical Works of Walter Savage Landor*, first published in four volumes, 1933; though paradoxically that great edition damaged Landor's reputation by squashing poems, between historical and textual apparatus, into the un-readability of double columns, and by arranging them monotonously in blocks under such headings as 'Books and Writers', 'History and Politics', 'Humorous and Satirical', 'Town and Countryside'.

Understanding of Landor as a poet must also depend on R. H. Super's sober and detailed biography, *Walter Savage Landor*, which corrects and supplements the fundamental source of information about Landor, i.e. John Forster's *Walter Savage Landor* of 1869. Malcolm Elwin's *Savage Landor*, 1941, lacks either authority or subtlety, advances theories and then takes theory for fact, roman-ticizing the classic, or turning biography, at whiles, into fiction.

In this selection I have not included *Terry Hogan, An Eclogue*, published anonymously in 1836. Though R. H. Super accepts that Landor wrote this mildly indelicate and rather feeble *jeu d'esprit*, the style and manner of the poem seem to me to contradict Landor's authorship.

WALTER SAVAGE LANDOR
SOME CHIEF DATES

1775 Born, January 30th, at Warwick, eldest son and heir of Walter Landor, physician, and Elizabeth, daughter of Charles Savage.

1783 Boarder at Rugby, under the classically minded headmaster Thomas James. Taken away 1791, as too rebellious.

c.1785 Beginning of friendship with Samuel Parr, classical scholar and Whig.

1793 Undergraduate at Trinity College, Oxford. 'Notorious as a mad Jacobin' (Southey). Sent down 1794, for a shooting episode.

c.1793 Beginning of love affair with Nancy Jones (Iöne, of some of his early verses), at Tenby, South Wales. Lived with her at Swansea, till a child was born. She was dead by—and probably before—1806.

1795 *Poems of Walter Savage Landor*, his first publication (English and Latin). Landor aged 20. Meets Alfieri, poet, dramatist and champion of freedom, in London.
Moral Epistle, Respectfully Dedicated to Earl Stanhope

c.1796-1799 Friendship with Hon. Rose Aylmer and her family at Laugharne, Carmarthenshire.

1798 *Gebir; A Poem, in Seven Books.* Landor aged 23.

1800 *Poetry by the Author of Gebir* (printed, but not published till 1802, after cancellation of 47 pp., including prose *Post-script to Gebir*). Lives mainly in London.

1800-1802, and possibly later. Love affair at Bath with Jane Sophia Swift (Ianthe), who married her cousin Godwin Smith.

1802 Visits Paris, after the peace of Amiens.
Iambi, pamphlet of Latin poems, published anonymously, c.1802.

1803 *Gebirus*, Latin version of Gebir.

1805 Death of Landor's father: Landor succeeds to the family estates.

1806 *Simonidea* (English and Latin poems, including first version of *Ah what avails the sceptred race*), published at Bath.

1808 Meets Southey, his admirer and friend and supporter thereafter, at Bristol.

Purchases Llanthony estates, in Monmouthshire, including the ruins of a priory of Augustinian canons.

Goes to Corunna, to aid Spanish rising against Buonaparte.

1810 Southey's *Curse of Kehama* published, with dedication to Landor.

1811 Marries Julia Thuillier, at Bath. Landor aged 36.

1812 *Count Julian: A Tragedy.*

1813 Abandons Llanthony, after amassing troubles, law suits and debts.

1814 Leaves England for France. Stays in Jersey, separating there from his wife, who rejoins him at Tours, 1815.

1815 Moves to Como, Italy, where Southey visits him, June 1817. *Idyllia Nova Quinque Heroum atque Heroidum,* published Oxford.

1818 Birth of his first child, Arnold Landor. Removes to Genoa, then Pisa, 1818.

1820 *Idyllia Heroica Decem* published at Pisa. Corresponds with Wordsworth. Julia, his daughter, born, 1820.

1821 Settles in Florence. Begins composition in earnest of his *Imaginary Conversations.*

1822 Second son, Walter Landor, born.

1823 First *Imaginary Conversation* (Southey and Porson) appears, in *London Magazine.*

1824 *Imaginary Conversations of Literary Men and Statesmen,* 2 vols., published in March. Landor aged 49.

1825 Birth of third son, Charles Landor.

1828 *Imaginary Conversations of Literary Men and Statesmen,* 3rd vol.

1829 *Imaginary Conversations of Literary Men and Statesmen,* two more volumes published.

- Settles in villa at Fiesole, above Florence. Death of Landor's mother, aged 85. 'Ianthe', now the widowed Countess de Molandé, in Florence with her children.

1831 *Gebir, Count Julian and Other Poems.*

1832 Revisits England after 18 years, meeting Southey, Wordsworth, Coleridge, Charles Lamb; and 'Ianthe'.

1834 *Citation and Examination of William Shakespeare.*

1835 Landor aged 60. Leaves his wife, who continues to live in the villa at Fiesole, with their children. Returns to England.

1836 Landor publishes: *Pericles and Aspasia,* 2 vols.; *Letters of a Conservative*; and *A Satire on Satirists.* Meets the young Robert Browning, and Forster (his biographer).

1837 *The Pentameron and Pentalogia.* Settles in Bath.

1839 *Andrea of Hungary, and Giovanna of Naples*; followed in 1840 by *Fra Rupert.*

1840 Beginning of friendship with Charles Dickens.

1843 Death of his lifelong friend Southey.

1846 *The Works of Walter Savage Landor,* 2 vols.

1847 *Poemata et Inscriptiones,* Landor's collected Latin verses. *The Hellenics of Walter Savage Landor.*

Landor aged 72.

1848 *The Italics of Walter Savage Landor.*

1849 Publishes (in *The Examiner*, December 29th) 'To the Author of Festus on the Classick and Romantick'.

1851 Death of 'Ianthe', at Versailles.

1852 Landor genially caricatured as Boythorn in Dickens's *Bleak House.*

1853 *Imaginary Conversations of Greeks and Romans.*
Landor aged 78.
Last Fruit off an Old Tree (prose as well as poems, including eighteen Imaginary Conversations).

1856 *Antony and Octavius. Scenes for the Study.*

1857 Involved in troubles at Bath with Mrs. Yescombe. Publishes *Walter Savage Landor and the Honourable Mrs. Yescombe*; followed by *Mr. Landor Threatened.*

1858 *Dry Sticks, Fagoted by Walter Savage Landor*, containing verses which led to a writ for libel from Mrs. Yescombe. Landor leaves for Italy before the trial of the case, which Mrs. Yescombe wins.

1859 Landor settles again at Florence, rapidly removing himself from his wife and family. Helped by Robert Browning. *Mr. Landor's Remarks on a Suit Preferred Against Him.*

1863 *Heroic Idyls, with additional poems* (Latin as well as English). Landor aged 88.

1864 Dies at Florence, September 17th, aged 89; and buried there in the Protestant Cemetery.

THE POEMS

[LADY GODIVA]

I<small>N</small> every hour, in every mood,
O Lady, it is sweet and good
To bathe the soul in prayer,
And, at the close of such a day,
When we have ceased to bless and pray,
To dream on thy long hair.

VOYAGE TO ST. IVES, CORNWALL, FROM PORT-EINON, GLAMORGAN

How gladsome yet how calm are ye
White birds that dip into the sea!
How sportive those bright fins below
Which through green alga-meadows glow!

How soft the lustrous air around,
And the red sail's is all the sound,
While me my heart's fierce tempest drives
On from Port-Einon to St. Ives.

INVOCATION TO THE MUSE

T<small>HO</small>' Helicon! I seldom dream
Aside thy lovely limpid stream,
Nor glory that to me belong
Or elegance, or nerve of Song,
Or Hayley's easy-ambling horse,
Or Peter Pindar's comic force,
Or Mason's fine majestic flow,
Or aught that pleases one in Crowe—
Yet thus a *saucy-suppliant* bard!
I court the Muse's kind regard.
'O! whether, Muse! thou please to give
My humble verses long to live;
Or tell me *The decrees of Fate
Have order'd them a shorter date*—
I bow: yet O! may every word
Survive, however, George III.

ON A QUAKER'S TANKARD.

Ye lie, friend Pindar! and friend Thales!—
Nothing so good as water? Ale is.

TO TACÆA[1]

Tomorrow, brightest-eyed of Avon's train,
Tomorrow thou art, slavelike, bound and sold,
Another's and another's!—haste away,
Winde thro' the willows, dart along the path—
It nought avails thee! nought our plaint avails!
O happy those before me, who could say
'Short tho' thy period, sweet Tacæa, short
Ere thou art destin'd to the depths below,
Even from thy valley-cradle, saffron-strown,
Thou passest half thy sunny hours with me.'

I mourn not, envy not, what others gain.
Thee, and thy venerable elms I mourn,
Thy old protectors! ruthless was the pride
And gaunt the need that bade their heads lie low!
I see the meadow's tender grass start back,
See from their prostrate trunks the gorey glare.

Ah! pleasant was it once to watch thy waves
Swelling o'er pliant beds of glossy weed;
Pleasant to watch them dip amid the stones,
Chirp, and spring over, glance and gleam along,
And tripping light their wanton way pursue.
Methinks they now, with mellow mournfulness,
Bid their faint breezes chide my fond delay,
Nor suffer on the bridge nor on the knee
My poor irregularly pencil'd page.
Alas, Tacæa, thou art sore deceived!
Here are no foreign words, no fatal seal—
But thou, and all who hear me, shall avow
The simple notes of sorrow's song are here.

VERSES, WRITTEN NEAR THE SEA, IN WALES

I

I wander o'er the sandy heath
    Where the white rush waves high;
Where adders close before me wreath
    And tawny kites sail screaming by.

[1] Tachbrook. The name of a stream and of a village near Warwick.

Alone I wander! I alone
Could love to wander there!
'*But wherefor?*'—let my church-yard stone
Look toward Tawey and declare.

ON A CERTAIN PRINT

THAT cockt-up nose there, shining like the knob
Of greasy plow-boy's hazle switch,
Is a vile woman's.—tho' upon this globe
Few are so high, and none so rich,
A tinker of tin-shavings she would rob,
Or ointment from Scotch pedlar's breech.
Who that comes filching farthings from one's fob
Need ever feel a fouler itch?

[ROSE AYLMER]

AH what avails the sceptred race,
Ah what the form divine!
What every virtue, every grace!
Rose Aylmer, all were thine.
Rose Aylmer, whom these wakeful eyes
May weep, but never see,
A night of memories and of sighs
I consecrate to thee.

[FROM SAPPHO]

MOTHER, I cannot mind my wheel;
My fingers ache, my lips are dry:
Oh! if you felt the pain I feel!
But Oh, who ever felt as I?

No longer could I doubt him true;
All other men may use deceit:
He always said my eyes were blue,
And often swore my lips were sweet.

[A SHELL]

DARLING Shell, where hast thou been,
What far regions hast thou seen;
From what pastimes art thou come:
Can we make amends at home?

Whether thou hast tuned the dance
    To the maids of ocean,
Know I not—but Ignorance
    Never hurts Devotion—

This I know, my darling Shell,
I shall ever love thee well,
Though too little to resound
While the Nereids dance around;

For, of all the shells that are,
    Thou art sure the brightest:
Thou, Ianthe's infant care,
    Most these eyes delightest—

Earlier to whose aid she owes
Teeth like budding snowdrop rows;
Teeth, whose love-incited pow'rs,
I have felt in happier hours.

On my shoulder, on my neck,
    Still the cherisht mark remains,
Well pourtray'd in many a speck
    Round thy smooth and quiet veins.

Who can wonder then, if thou
Hearest breathe my tender vow;
If thy lips, so pure, so bright,
Are dim with kisses, day and night?

TO IANTHE. WITH PETRARCH'S SONNETS

BEHOLD what homage to his idol paid
The tuneful suppliant of Valclusa's shade.
Often his lively fancy tried to cheat
Passion's fixt gaze with some assumed conceit;
Often behind the mould'ring column stood,
And often started from the laureate wood.[1]
His verses still the tender heart engage,
They charm'd a rude, and please a polisht age.
Some are to nature and to passion true,
And all had been so, had he lived for you.

---

[1] He was remarkably fond of playing on the words *Colonna* and *Lauro:* in the one alluding to his patron, in the other to his mistress.

FROM yon far wood, mark blue-eyed Eve proceed:
First through the deep and warm and secret glens,
Through the pale-glimmering privet-scented lane,
And through those alders by the river-side:
Now the soft dust impedes her, which the sheep
Have hollow'd out beneath their hawthorn shade.
But ah! look yonder! see a misty tide
Rise up the hill, lay low the frowning grove,
Enwrap the gay white mansion, sap its sides
Until they sink and melt away like chalk;
Now it comes down against our village tower,
Covers its base, floats o'er its arches, tears
The clinging ivy from the battlements,
Mingles in broad embrace the obdurate stone,
All . . . ocean, and goes swelling on
In slow and silent, dim and deepening waves.

[IANTHE AWAITED]

WHILE the winds whistle round my cheerless room,
And the pale morning droops with winter's gloom;
While indistinct lie rude and cultur'd lands,
The ripening harvest and the hoary sands;
Alone, and destitute of every page
That fires the poet, or informs the sage,
Where shall my wishes, where my fancy rove—
Rest upon past or cherish promist love?
Alas! the past I never can regain,
Wishes may rise and tears may flow—in vain.
Fancy, that shews her in her early bloom,
Throws barren sunshine o'er the unyielding tomb.
What then would passion, what would reason do?
Sure, to retrace is worse than to pursue.
Here will I sit, 'till heaven shall cease to lour,
And the bright Hesper bring the appointed hour;
Gaze on the mingled waste of sky and sea,
Think of my love, and bid her think of me.

[KISS ME]

SOON, O Ianthe! life is o'er,
    And sooner beauty's playful smile:
Kiss me, and grant what I implore,
    Let love remain that little while.

C

TO ZOË

Against the groaning mast I stand,
The Atlantic surges swell,
To bear me from my native land
And Zoë's wild farewell.

From billow upon billow hurl'd
I yet can hear her say,
'And is there nothing in the world
Worth one short hour's delay?'

'Alas, my Zoë! were it thus,
I should not sail alone,
Nor seas nor fates had parted us,
But are you *all* my own?'

Thus were it, never would burst forth
My sighs, Heaven knows how true!
But, though to me of little worth,
The world is much to you.

'Yes,' you shall say, when once the dream
(So hard to break!) is o'er,
'My love was very dear to him,
My fame and peace were more.'

FROM THE BAY OF BISCAY

Afar our stormy vessel flies
From all my heart holds dear,
But thou art yet before my eyes,
And thy far voice I hear.

The Fates then had not frowns enough;
Too happy had we been
Had not the Atlantic, cold and rough,
Roll'd his wide wave between.

Too happy, yes; but ah! how dear
The price we should have paid!
I fear'd no tempest, there or here,
For thee was I afraid.

GEBIR

A POEM IN SEVEN BOOKS

PRINCIPAL CHARACTERS

GEBIR . . . King of GADES	MYRTHYR . . Sister of DALICA
TAMAR . . . his Brother	NYMPH . . betrothed to TAMAR
CHAROBA . . .Queen of EGYPT	EGYPTIAN AMBASSADORS
DALICA . . . her Nurse	

BOOK I

ARGUMENT

GEBIR, his habitation and habits. Alarms of *Charoba*—imparted to *Dalica*—*Dalica's* reply. The Queen's expostulation, and compliance—her interview with *Gebir*. *Gebir* returning, meets his brother *Tamar*—*Tamar* describes his wrestling with a Nymph. *Her* victory, and promise. *His* regret and shame. *Gebir's* sympathy —his determination to remain in *Egypt*, and to restore the city which *Sidad*, his ancestor, had founded.

WHEN old Silenus call'd the Satyrs home,
Satyrs then tender-hooft and ruddy-horn'd,
With Bacchus and the Nymphs, he sometimes rose
Amidst the tale or pastoral, and shew'd
The light of purest wisdom; and the God
Scatter'd with wholesome fruit the pleasant plains.
　　Ye woody vales of Cambria! and ye hills
That hide in heaven your summits and your fame!
Your ancient songs, and breezes pure, invite
Me from my noon-tide rambles, and the force　　　　10
Of high example influences my lay.
　　I sing the fates of Gebir! how he dwelt
Among those mountain-caverns, which retain
His labours yet, vast halls, and flowing wells,
Nor have forgotten their old master's name,
Though sever'd from his people: how, incens'd
By meditating on primeval wrongs,
He blew his battle-horn, at which uprose
Whole nations: how, ten thousand, mightiest men,
He call'd aloud; and soon Charoba saw　　　　　　20
His dark helm hover o'er the land of Nile.
　　What should the damsel do? should royal knees
Bend suppliant? or defenceless hands engage
Men of gigantic force, gigantic arms?
For, 'twas reported, that nor sword sufficed,
Nor shield immense, nor coat of massive mail;
But, that upon their tow'ring heads they bore
Each a huge stone, refulgent as the stars.
This told she Dalica—then earnest cried
'If, on your bosom laying down my head,　　　　　30
I sobb'd away the sorrows of a child;

If I have always, and Heav'n knows I have,
Next to a mother's held a nurse's name,
Succour this one distress! recall those days;
Love me; though 'twere because you lov'd me then.'
  But, whether confident in magic rites;
Or touch'd with sexual pride to stand implored,
Dalica smiled; then spake: 'Away those fears.
Tho' stronger than the strongest of his kind,
He falls; on me devolve that charge; he falls.   40
Rather than fly him, stoop thou to allure,
Nay, journey to his tents; a city stood
Upon that coast, they say, by Sidad built,
Whose father Gad built Gades; on this ground
Perhaps he sees an ample room for war.
Persuade him to restore the walls himself,
In honor of his ancestors, persuade—
But wherefor this advice? young, unespoused,
Charoba want persuasions! and a queen!'
  'O Dalica!' the shudd'ring maid exclaim'd,   50
'Could I encounter that fierce frightful man?
Could I speak? no, nor sigh!' 'And canst thou reign?'
Cried Dalica; 'yield empire or comply.'
  Unfixt, though seeming fixt, her eyes down-cast,
The wonted buz and bustle of the court
From far, through sculptur'd galleries, met her ear;
Then lifting up her head, the evening sun
Pour'd a fresh splendor on her burnish'd throne,—
The fair Charoba, the young queen, complied.
  But Gebir, when he heard of her approach,   60
Laid by his orbed shield, his vizor-helm,
His buckler and his corslet he laid by,
And bade that none attend him: at his side
Two faithful dogs that urge the silent course,
Shaggy, deep-chested, crouched: the crocodile,
Crying, oft made them raise their flaccid ears,
And push their heads within their master's hand.
There was a bright'ning paleness in his face,
Such as Diana rising o'er the rocks
Shower'd on the lonely Latmian; on his brow   70
Sorrow there was, yet nought was there severe.
But when the royal damsel first he saw,
Faint, hanging on her handmaids, and her knees
Tott'ring, as from the motion of the car,
His eyes looked earnest on her; and those eyes
Shew'd, if they had not, that they might have lov'd,
For there was pity in them at that hour.
With gentle speech, and more, with gentle looks,
He sooth'd her; but, lest Pity go beyond,

And crost Ambition lose her lofty aim,
Bending, he kiss'd her garment, and retir'd.
He went: nor slumber'd in the sultry noon,
When viands rich, and generous wines persuade,
And slumber most refreshes; nor at night,
When heavy dews are laden with disease;
And blindness waits not there for lingering age.
Ere morning dawn'd behind him, he arrived
At those rich meadows where young Tamar fed
The royal flocks, entrusted to his care.
Now, said he to himself, will I repose   90
At least this burden on a brother's breast:
His brother stood before him: he, amaz'd,
Rear'd suddenly his head, and thus began.
'Is it thou, brother! Tamar, is it thou!
Why, standing on the valley's utmost verge,
Lookest thou on that dull and dreary shore
Where many a league Nile blackens all the sand.
And why that sadness? when I passed our sheep
The dew-drops were not shaken off the bar,
Therefor if one be wanting 'tis untold.   100
    'Yes! one is wanting, nor is that untold,'
Said Tamar, 'and this dull and dreary shore
Is neither dull nor dreary at all hours.'
Whereon, the tear stole silent down his cheek.
Silent, but not by Gebir unobserv'd:
Wondering he gazed awhile, and pitying spake:—
'Let me approach thee: does the morning light
Scatter this wan suffusion o'er thy brow,
This faint blue lustre under both thine eyes?'
'O, brother, is this pity or reproach,'   110
Cried Tamar,—'cruel if it be reproach,
If pity—O how vain!'
                            'Whate'er it be
That grieves thee, I will pity; thou but speak,
And I can tell thee, Tamar, pang for pang.'
    'Gebir! then more than brothers are we now!
Every thing—take my hand—will I confess.
I neither feed the flock, nor watch the fold;
How can I, lost in love? But, Gebir, why
That anger which has risen to your cheek?
Can other men? Could you? What, no reply!   120
And still more anger, and still worse conceal'd!
Are these your promises; your pity this?'
    'Tamar, I well may pity what I feel—
Mark me aright—I feel for thee—proceed—
Relate me all.' 'Then will I all relate.'
Said the young shepherd, gladden'd from his heart.

' 'Twas evening, though not sun-set, and spring-tide
Level with these green meadows, seem'd still higher;
'Twas pleasant: and I loosen'd from my neck
The pipe you gave me, and began to play.   130
O that I ne'er had learnt the tuneful art!
It always brings us enemies or love!
Well, I was playing—when above the waves
Some swimmer's head methought I saw ascend;
I, sitting still, survey'd it, with my pipe
Awkwardly held before my lips half-clos'd.
Gebir! it was a nymph! a nymph divine!
I cannot wait describing how she came,
How I was sitting, how she first assum'd
The sailor: of what happened, there remains   140
Enough to say, and too much to forget.
The sweet deceiver stept upon this bank
Before I was aware; for, with surprize
Moments fly rapid as with love itself.
Stooping to tune afresh the hoarsen'd reed,
I heard a rustling; and where that arose
My glance first lighted on her nimble feet.
Her feet resembled those long shells explored
By him who to befriend his steeds' dim sight
Would blow the pungent powder in their eye.—   150
Her eyes too! O immortal Gods! her eyes
Resembled—what could they resemble—what
Ever resemble those! E'en her attire
Was not of wonted woof nor vulgar art:
Her mantle shew'd the yellow samphire-pod,
Her girdle, the dove-color'd wave serene.
'Shepherd,' said she, 'and will you wrestle now,
And with the sailor's hardier race engage?'
I was rejoiced to hear it, and contrived
How to keep up contention;—could I fail   160
By pressing not too strongly, still to press.
'Whether a shepherd, as indeed you seem,
Or whether of the hardier race you boast,
I am not daunted, no: I will engage.'
'But first,' said she, 'what wager will you lay?'
'A sheep,' I answered, 'add whate'er you will.'
'I cannot,' she replied, 'make that return:
Our hided vessels, in their pitchy round,
Seldom, unless from rapine, hold a sheep.
But I have sinuous shells, of pearly hue   170
Within, and they that lustre have imbibed
In the sun's palace porch; where, when unyoked,
His chariot wheel stands midway in the wave.
Shake one, and it awakens; then apply

Its polished lips to your attentive ear,
And it remembers its august abodes,
And murmurs as the ocean murmurs there.
And I have others given me by the nymphs,
Of sweeter sound than any pipe you have.—
But we, by Neptune, for no pipe contend;   180
This time a sheep I win, a pipe the next.'
Now came she forward, eager to engage;
But, first her dress, her bosom then, survey'd,
And heav'd it, doubting if she could deceive.
Her bosom seem'd, inclos'd in haze like heav'n,
To baffle touch; and rose forth undefined.
Above her knees she drew the robe succinct,
Above her breast, and just below her arms:
'This will preserve my breath, when tightly bound,
If struggle and equal strength should so constrain.'   190
Thus, pulling hard to fasten it, she spoke,
And, rushing at me, closed. I thrill'd throughout
And seem'd to lessen and shrink up with cold.
Again, with violent impulse gushed my blood;
And hearing nought external, thus absorb'd,
I heard it, rushing through each turbid vein,
Shake my unsteady swimming sight in air.
Yet with unyielding though uncertain arms,
I clung around her neck; the vest beneath
Rustled against our slippery limbs entwined: 200
Often mine, springing with eluded force,
Started aside, and trembled, till replaced.
And when I most succeeded, as I thought,
My bosom and my throat felt so comprest
That life was almost quivering on my lips,
Yet nothing was there painful! these are signs
Of secret arts, and not of human might,
What arts I cannot tell: I only know
My eyes grew dizzy, and my strength decay'd,
I was indeed o'ercome!—with what regret,   210
And more, with what confusion, when I reached
The fold, and yielding up the sheep, she cried,
'This pays a shepherd to a conquering maid.'
She smil'd, and more of pleasure than disdain
Was in her dimpled chin, and liberal lip,
And eyes that languished, lengthening,—just like love.
She went away: I, on the wicker gate
Lean'd, and could follow with my eyes alone.
The sheep she carried easy as a cloak.
But when I heard its bleating, as I did,   220
And saw, she hastening on, its hinder feet
Struggle, and from her snowy shoulder slip,

(One shoulder its poor efforts had unveil'd,)
Then, all my passions mingling fell in tears!
Restless then ran I to the highest ground
To watch her; she was gone; gone down the tide;
And the long moon-beam on the hard wet sand
Lay like a jaspar column half uprear'd.'
   'But, Tamar! tell me, will she not return?'
'She will return: but not before the moon   230
Again is at the full; she promis'd this;
But when she promis'd I could not reply.'
   'By all the Gods! I pity thee! go on—
Fear not my anger, look not on my shame;
For, when a lover only hears of love,
He finds his folly out, and is ashamed.
Away with watchful nights, and lonely days,
Contempt of earth, and aspect up to heaven,
With contemplation, with humility,—
A tatter'd cloak that pride wears when deform'd—   240
Away with all that hides me from myself,
Parts me from others, whispers I am wise—
From our own wisdom less is to be reaped
Than from the barest folly of our friend.
Tamar! thy pastures, large and rich, afford
Flowers to thy bees, and herbage to thy sheep,
But, battened on too much, the poorest croft
Of thy poor neighbour yields what thine denies.'
   They hastened to the camp; and Gebir there
—Resolved his native country to forego—   250
Ordered, that from those ruins to their right
They forthwith raise a city: Tamar heard
With wonder, though in passing 'twas half-told,
His brother's love; and sigh'd upon his own.

END OF BOOK THE FIRST

THE SECOND BOOK OF GEBIR

ARGUMENT

On the seventh morning the works are miraculously destroyed. *Gebir* exhorts his soldiers to deprecate the wrath of heaven. Proposes to *Tamar*, now the time draws near when the *Nymph* was again to meet him, that he himself should assume the brother's habit, and contend with her thus disguised. *Tamar* reluctant,— misinterprets the motive,—is satisfied,—complies. *Gebir* meets the *Nymph*— contends—conquers. Reasons suggested why the *Nymph* failed. Her astonishment —alarm—indignation—entreaty—reproach—and submission. Consoled—dis- covers to *Gebir* how the city is destroyed—prescribes a ceremony. He performs it. The earth opens—he descends.

THE Gadite men the royal charge obey.
Now fragments, weigh'd up from th' uneven streets,
Leave the ground black beneath; again the sun
Shines into what were porches, and on steps
Once warm with frequentation—clients, friends,
All morning, satchel'd idlers all mid-day,
Lying half-up, and languid, though at games.
   Some raise the painted pavement, some on wheels
Draw slow its laminous length, some intersperse
Salt waters thro' the sordid heaps, and seize   10
The flowers and figures starting fresh to view.
Others rub hard large masses, and essay
To polish into white what they misdeem
The growing green of many trackless years.
Far off, at intervals, the ax resounds
With regular strong stroke, and nearer home
Dull falls the mallet with long labor fringed.
Here, arches are discover'd, there, huge beams
Resist the hatchet, but in fresher air
Soon drop away: there lies a marble, squar'd   20
And smoothen'd; some high pillar, for its base,
Chose it, which now lies ruin'd in the dust.
Clearing the soil at bottom, they espy
A crevice: they, intent on treasure, strive
Strenuous, and groan, to move it: one exclaims
'I hear the rusty metal grate: it moves!'
Now, overturning it, backward they start;
And stop again, and see a serpent pant,
See his throat thicken, and the crisped scales
Rise ruffled; while upon the middle fold   30
He keeps his wary head and blinking eye,
Curling more close, and crouching ere he strike.
Go mighty men, and ruin cities, go—
And be such treasure portions to your heirs.
   Six days they labor'd: on the seventh day
Returning, all their labors were destroyed.
'Twas not by mortal hand, or from their tents
'Twere visible; for these were now removed
Above, where neither noxious mist ascends,
Nor the way wearies ere the work begin.   40
There Gebir, pierced with sorrow, spake these words.
   'Ye men of Gades, armed with brazen shields;
And ye of near Tartessus, where the shore
Stoops to receive the tribute which all owe
To Bœtis, and his banks, for their attire;
Ye too whom Durius bore on level meads!
Inherent in your hearts is bravery;
For earth contains no nation where abounds

The generous horse and not the warlike man.
But neither soldier, now, nor steed, avails!   50
Nor steed nor soldier can oppose the Gods;
Nor is there aught above like Jove himself,
Nor weighs against his purpose, when once fixt,
Aught but, with supplicating knee, the Prayers.
Swifter than light are they; and every face
Though different, glows with beauty: at the throne
Of mercy, when clouds shut it from mankind,
They fall bare-bosom'd; and indignant Jove
Drops, at the soothing sweetness of their voice,
The thunder from his hand. Let us arise   60
On these high places, daily, beat our breast,
Prostrate ourselves, and deprecate his wrath.'
    The people bow'd their bodies and obey'd.
Nine mornings, with white ashes on their heads,
Lamented they their toil each night o'erthrown.
And now the largest orbit of the year,
Leaning o'er black Mocattam's rubied brow,
Proceeded slow, majestic, and serene:
Now seem'd not further than the nearest cliff,
And crimson light struck soft the phosphor wave.   70
Then Gebir spake to Tamar in these words:—
'Tamar! I am thy elder, and thy king,
But am thy brother too, nor ever said,
"Give me thy secret, and become my slave;"
But haste thee not away: I will myself
Await the nymph, disguised in thy attire.'
Then starting from attention, Tamar cried,
'Brother! in sacred truth it cannot be!
My life is your's, my love must be my own.
O surely he who seeks a second love   80
Never felt one; or 'tis not one I feel.'
But Gebir with complacent smile replied,
'Go then, fond Tamar, go in happy hour.
But ere thou goest, ponder in thy breast,
And well bethink thee, lest thou part deceiv'd,
Will she disclose to thee the mysteries
Of our calamity? and unconstrain'd?
When even her love thy strength was to disclose.
My heart, indeed, is full: but witness, heaven!
My people, not my passion, fills my heart.'   90
    'Then let me kiss thy garment,' said the youth,
'And heaven be with thee, and on me thy grace.'
    Him then the monarch thus once more addressed,
'Be of good courage: hast thou yet forgot
What chaplets languished round thy unburnt hair,
In color like some tall smooth beech's leaves

Curl'd by autumnal suns?'—How flattery
Excites a pleasant, sooths a painful shame!
  'These,' amid stifled blushes, Tamar said,
'Where of the flowering raspberry and vine: 100
But ah! the seasons will not wait for love,
Seek out some other now.' They parted here:
And Gebir, bending through the woodlands, cull'd
The creeping vine and viscous raspberry,
Less green and less compliant than they were,
And twisted in those mossy tufts that grow
On brakes of roses, when the roses fade;
And as he pass'd along, the little hinds
That shook for bristly herds the foodful bough,
Wonder, stand still, gaze, and trip satisfied;   110
Pleas'd more if chesnut, out of prickly husk,
Shot from the sandal, roll along the glade.
  And thus unnoticed went he, and untired
Stept up the acclivity; and as he stept,
And as the garlands nodded o'er his brow,
Sudden, from under a close alder, sprang
Th' expectant nymph, and seiz'd him unaware.
He stagger'd at the shock: his feet, not firm'd,
Slipt backward from the wither'd grass short-graz'd;
But, striking out one arm, though without aim,   120
Then grasping with his other, he inclos'd
The struggler; she gain'd not one step's retreat,
Urging with open hands against his throat
Intense; now holding in her breath constrain'd,
Now pushing with quick impulse and by starts,
Till the dust blackened upon every pore.
Nearer he drew her, and still nearer, clasp'd
Above the knees midway; and now one arm
Fell; and her other, lapsing o'er the neck
Of Gebir, swung against his back incurved,   130
The swoln veins glowing deep; and with a groan
On his broad shoulder fell her face reclined.
But ah she knew not whom that roseate face
Cool'd with its breath ambrosial; for she stood
High on the bank, and often swept and broke
His chaplets mingled with her loosen'd hair.
  Whether, while Tamar tarried, came desire,
And she, grown languid, loosed the wings of love,
Which she before held proudly at her will;
And nought but Tamar in her soul, and nought   140
Where Tamar was that seem'd or fear'd deceit,
To fraud she yielded, what no force had gain'd—
Or whether Jove, in pity to mankind,
When from his crystal fount the visual orbs

He fill'd with piercing ether, and endued
With somewhat of omnipotence—ordain'd
That never two fair forms, at once, torment
The human heart, and draw it different ways—
And thus, in prowess like a god, the chief
Subdued her strength, nor soften'd at her charms;   150
The nymph divine, the magic mistress, fail'd.
Recovering, still half resting on the turf,
She look'd up wildly, and could now descry
The kingly brow, arched lofty for command.
   'Traitor!' said she, undaunted—though amaze
Threw o'er her varying cheek the air of fear—
'Thinkest thou thus that with impunity
Thou hast forsooth deceiv'd me? dar'st thou deem
Those eyes not hateful that have seen me fall?
O heaven! soon may they close on my disgrace.   160
Merciless man; what! for one sheep estranged,
Hast thou thrown into dungeons, and of day
Amerst thy shepherd? Hast thou, while the iron
Pierced thro' his tender limbs into his soul,
By threats, by tortures, torn out that offence,
And heard him (O could I) avow his love?
Say, hast thou? cruel, hateful,—ah my fears!
I feel them true! speak, tell me, are they true?'
She, blending thus intreaty with reproach,
Bent forward, as tho' falling on her knee,   170
Whence she had hardly ris'n, and at this pause
Shed from her large dark eyes a shower of tears.
Th' Iberian King her sorrow thus consoled.
'Weep no more, heavenly damsel, weep no more,
Neither by force withheld, or choice estranged,
Thy Tamar lives, and only lives for thee.
Happy, thrice happy, you! 'Tis me alone
Whom heaven, and earth, and ocean, with one hate
Conspire on, and throughout each path pursue.
Whether in waves beneath or skies above   180
Thou hast thy habitation, 'tis from heaven,
From heaven alone, such power, such charms descend.
Then oh! discover whence that ruin comes
Each night upon our city; whence are heard
Those yells of rapture round our falling walls:
In our affliction can the Gods delight,
Or meet oblation for the Nymphs are tears?'
He spake; and indignation sunk in woe.
Which she perceiving, pride refreshed her heart,
Hope wreath'd her mouth with smiles, and she exclaim'd— 190
'Neither the Gods afflict you, nor the Nymphs.
Return me him who won my heart; return

Him whom my bosom pants for, as the steeds
In the sun's chariot for the western wave,
The Gods will prosper thee, and Tamar prove
How Nymphs the torments that they cause assuage.
Promise me this! indeed I think thou hast;
But 'tis so pleasing, promise it once more.'
'Once more I promise,' cried the gladdened king,
'By my right-hand, and by myself, I swear,   200
And ocean's Gods, and heaven's Gods I adjure,
Thou shalt be Tamar's; Tamar shall be thine.'
    Then she, regarding him, long fixt, replied,—
'I have thy promise; take thou my advice.
Gebir, this land of Egypt is a land
Of incantation; demons rule these waves;
These are against thee; these thy works destroy.
Where thou hast built thy palace, and hast left
The seven pillars to remain in front,
Sacrifice there; and all these rites observe.   210
Go, but go early, ere the gladsome Hours
Strew saffron in the path of rising Morn;
Ere the bee, buzzing o'er flowers fresh disclosed,
Examine where he may the best alight
Nor scatter off the bloom; ere cold-lipt herds
Crop the pale herbage round each other's bed;
Lead seven bulls, well pastur'd and well form'd,
Their necks unblemished and their horns unring'd,
And at each pillar sacrifice thou one.
Around each base rub thrice the black'ning blood,   220
And burn the curling shavings of the hoof;
And of the forehead locks thou also burn.
The yellow galls, with equal care preserv'd,
Pour at the seventh statue from the north.'
    He listen'd; and on her his eyes intent
Perceiv'd her not; and now she disappear'd:
So deep he ponder'd her important words.
    And now had morn aris'n, and he perform'd
Almost the whole enjoin'd him;—he had reach'd
The seventh statue, pour'd the yellow galls,   230
The forelock from his left he had releas'd,
And burnt the curling shavings of the hoof,
Moisten'd with myrrh; when suddenly a flame
Spired from the fragrant smoke, nor sooner spired
—Down sunk the brazen fabric at his feet.
He started back, gazed—nor could aught but gaze—
And cold dread stiffen'd up his hair flower-twined:
Then with a long and tacit step, one arm
Behind, and every finger wide outspread,
He look'd and totter'd on a black abyss.   240

He thought he sometimes heard a distant voice
Breathe through the cavern's mouth, and further on
Faint murmurs now, now hollow groans reply.
Therefor suspended he his crook above,
Dropt it, and heard it rolling step by step.
He enter'd; and a mingled sound arose
Like that—when shaken from some temple's roof
By zealous hand, they, and their fretted nest,—
Of birds that wintering watch in Memnon's tomb,
And tell the Halcyons when Spring first returns.   250

END OF BOOK THE SECOND

THE THIRD BOOK OF *GEBIR*

ARGUMENT

Gebir hears his name repeated twice. *Aröar*, who had fought under his fore-fathers, approaches him. *Gebir* enquires with earnestness what power detains *them*. *Aröar* replies evasively—recapitulates the misery that would attend the disembodied Spirits having any intercourse with those on earth—then seriously addresses him, and promises, if he can endure the trial, that he shall gratify his wish. The *Gadite* kings appear—several are described. *Gebir* complains that he cannot see his father—turning to bid adieu, is clasped in his embrace. He briefly tells his son the cause of his suffering, which was the oath exacted of invading Egypt. He disappears—*Gebir* complains—reproved by *Aröar*, who reveals the laws by which these regions are governed—the flaming arch that separates the good from the wicked—once in every hundred years it suddenly starts back and discovers to each state its opposite—the contrast is exemplified in the abode of the ambitious and of the peaceful. *Aröar* teaches that those eternal fires which seem intended only for punishing the vicious, are calculated also to give verdure and pleasantness to the groves of the blest. *Gebir* asks a question on religion—the scene instantly vanishes—he rises, and visits his army.

O FOR the spirit of that matchless man
Whom Nature led throughout her whole domain,
While he, embodied, breath'd etherial air!
   Though panting in the play-hour of my youth,
I drank of Avon, too, a dang'rous draught,
That rous'd within the fev'rish thirst of song—
Yet, never may I trespass o'er the stream
Of jealous Acheron, nor alive descend
The silent and unsearchable abodes
Of Erebus and Night, nor unchastized   10
Lead up long absent heroes into day.
When on the pausing theatre of earth
Eve's shadowy curtain falls, can any man
Bring back the far-off intercepted hills,

Grasp the round rock-built turret, or arrest
The glittering spires that pierce the brow of Heav'n?
Rather, can any, with outstripping voice,
The parting Sun's gigantic strides recall?
  Twice heard was Gebir; twice th' Iberian king
Thought it the strong vibration of the brain   20
That struck upon his ear; but now descried
A form, a man come nearer; as he came
His unshorn hair, grown soft in these abodes,
Waved back, and scatter'd thin and hoary light.
Living, men call'd him Aröar: but no more
In celebration, or recording verse,
His name is heard, no more by Arnon's side
The well-wall'd city, which he rear'd, remains.
Gebir was now undaunted, for the brave
When they no longer doubt, no longer fear,   30
And would have spoken, but the shade began.
  'Brave son of Hesperus! no mortal hand
Has led thee hither, nor without the Gods
Penetrate thy firm feet the vast profound.
Thou knowest not that here thy fathers lie,
The race of Sidad: their's was loud acclaim
When living; but their pleasure was in war:
Triumphs and hatred followed: I myself
Bore, men imagin'd, no inglorious part;
The Gods thought otherwise! by whose decree   40
Depriv'd of life, and more, of death depriv'd,
I still hear shrieking, through the moonless night,
Their discontented and deserted shades.
Observe these horrid walls, this rueful waste!
Here some refresh the vigor of the mind
With contemplation and cold penitence:
Nor wonder, while thou hearest, that the soul
Thus purified, hereafter may ascend
Surmounting all obstruction, nor ascribe
The sentence to indulgence: each extreme   50
Has tortures for ambition; to dissolve
In everlasting languor, to resist
Its impulse, but in vain; to hear, frequent,
Nay, to take counsel from, and seek resource,
Be sooth'd by, or be scoft at by, (O Heaven!)
The vilest of mankind: to be enclosed
Within a limit, and that limit fire:
Sever'd from happiness, from eminence,
And flying, but hell bars us, from ourselves.
  Yet rather all these torments most endure   60
Than solitary pain, and sad remorse,
And tow'ring thoughts on their own breast o'erturn'd,

And piercing to the heart: such penitence,
Such contemplation, theirs! thy ancestors
Bear up against them, nor will they submit
To conquering Time th' asperities of Fate:
Yet, could they but revisit earth once more,
How gladly would they Poverty embrace,
How labour, even for their deadliest foe!
It little now avails them to have rais'd   70
Beyond the Syrian regions, and beyond
Phœnicia, trophies, tributes, colonies:
Follow thou me: mark what it all avails.'
 Him Gebir followed, and a roar confused
Rose from a river, rolling in its bed,
Not rapid—that would rouse the wretched souls—
Nor calmly—that might lull them to repose.
But with dull weary lapses it still heaved
Billows of bale, heard low, but heard afar;
For when hell's iron portals let out Night,   80
Often men start, and shiver at the sound,
And lie so silent on the restless couch
They hear their own hearts beat. Now Gebir breath'd
Another air, another sky beheld.
Twilight broods here, lull'd by no nightingale,
Nor waken'd by the shrill lark dewy-winged,
But glowing with one sullen sunless heat.
Beneath his foot nor sprouted flower nor herb,
Nor chirp'd a grasshopper; above his head
Phlegethon form'd a fiery firmament: 90
Part were sulphurous clouds involving, part
Shining like solid ribs of moulten brass:
For the fierce element which else aspires
Higher and higher, and lessens to the sky,
Below, Earth's adamantine arch rebuffed.
 Gebir, though now such languor held his limbs,
Scarce aught admir'd he, yet he this admir'd;
And thus address'd him then the conscious guide.
'Beyond that river lie the happy fields.
From them fly gentle breezes, which, when drawn   100
Against yon crescent convex, but unite
Stronger with what they could not overcome.
Thus they that scatter freshness thro' the groves
And meadows of the fortunate, and fill
With liquid light the marble bowl of Earth,
And give her blooming health and sprightly force—
Their fire no more diluted, nor its darts
Blunted by passing through thick myrtle bowers,
Neither from odors rising half dissolved,
Point forward Phlegethon's eternal flame: 110

And this horizon is the spacious bow
Whence each ray reaches to the world above.
Fire rules the realms of pleasure and of pain.
Parent and element of elements,
Changing, and yet unchanged, pervading heaven
Purest, and then reviewing all the stars:
All croud around him in their orbits, all
In legions for that radiant robe contend
Allotted them, unseam'd and undefiled:
Then, saturate with what their nature craves,   120
Unite the grateful symphony of guests,
Take short repose, and with slow pace return.
And not the glowing oceans of the sun
Fire fills alone, and draws there smaller streams,
And dashes them on crystal cliffs of hail,
And filters through black clouds and fleecy snows—
But penetrates each cold and blue abyss
Of trackless waves, and each white glimmering gem
That crowns the victim's immolated brow.'
    The hero pausing, Gebir then besought   130
What region held his ancestors, what clouds,
What waters, or what Gods, from his embrace.
'Young man,' said Aröar, 'some indeed declare
That they the spirit, when it is itself,
Have wakened on; and with fixt eyes beheld
Fixt eyes; both stricken speechless, both would speak;
Both stretch'd their kindred arms and would embrace.
That spirit, which thus struggles in its flight
To some one dearest object, with a will
Omnipotent, ne'er, after this returns: 140
Neither can mortal see departed friends,
Or they see mortal: if indeed they could,
How care would furrow up their flow'ry fields,
What asps and adders bask in every beam!
Then oft might faithful fondness from the shades
See its beloved in another's arms,
And curse immoral laws, immodest vows,
Elysium, and the vanity of soul.
She who, evading Modesty, dares take
—With sacrilegious incest most accurst—   150
The lamp of marriage from a husband's tomb,
And beckon up another, to defile
A bed new-litter'd, a mere tavern-stall,
Biting her chain, bays body; and despair
Awakes the furies of insatiate lust.
Others, if worse be any, float immerst
In prisons blackly green with ropy slime,
Where toughens the brown fungus, brittle-stalk'd:

D

Their grosser spirits with the putrid air
Amalgamate, and, in due time, ferment   160
Seed heretofore inert; hence crawls gay-wing'd
The gadfly, hence trails forth the fulsome snake.
Living, they never own'd that Nature's face
Was lovely, never with fond awe beheld
On her parental bosom, Truth repose!'
He paus'd; then sudden, as if rous'd, renew'd.
'But come, if ardor urges thee, and force
Suffices—mark me, Gebir, I unfold
No fable to allure thee—rise, behold
Thy ancestors!' and lo! with horrid gasp,   170
The panting flame above his head recoil'd,
And thunder thro' his heart and life-blood throb'd.
Such sound could human organs once conceive,
Cold, speechless, palsied, not the soothing voice
Of friendship, or almost of Deity,
Could raise the wretched mortal from the dust;
Beyond man's home condition they! with eyes
Intent, and voice desponding, and unheard
By Aröar, tho' he tarried at his side.
'They know me not,' cried Gebir, 'O my sires,   180
Ye know me not!—They answer not, nor hear.
How distant are they still! what sad extent
Of desolation must we overcome!
Aröar, what wretch that nearest us? what wretch
Is that with eyebrows white, and slanting brow?
Listen! him yonder, who, bound down supine,
Shrinks, yelling, from that sword there, engine-hung;
He too amongst my ancestors? I hate
The despot, but the dastard I despise.
Was he our countryman?'
                              'Alas, O King!   190
Iberia bore him, but the breed accurst
Inclement winds blew blighting from north-east.'
'He was a warrior, then, nor fear'd the Gods?'
'Gebir, he fear'd the Demons, not the Gods;
Tho' them, indeed, his daily face adored,
And was no warrior, yet the thousand lives
Squander'd, as stones to exercise a sling!
And the tame cruelty, and cold caprice—
Oh madness of mankind! addrest, adored!
O Gebir! what are men, or where are Gods!   200
Behold the giant next him: how his feet
Plunge flound'ring mid the marshes, yellow-flower'd.
His restless head just reaching to the rocks,
His bosom tossing with black weeds besmear'd,
How writhes he 'twixt the continent and isle!

What tyrant with more insolence e'er claim'd
Dominion? when, from th' heart of Usury
Rose more intense the pale-flamed thirst for gold?
And call'd, forsooth, *Deliverer!* False or fools!
Who prais'd the dull-ear'd miscreant, or who hoped   210
To soothe your folly and disgrace with praise.
  Hearest thou not the harp's gay simpering air,
And merriment afar! Then come, advance—
And now behold him! mark the wretch accurst,
Who sold his people to a rival king.
Self-yoked they stood, two ages unredeem'd.'
'O horror! what pale visage rises there!
Speak Aröar—me, perhaps, mine eyes deceive,
Inured not, yet methinks they there descry
Such crimson haze as sometimes drowns the moon.   220
What is yon awful sight? why thus appears
That space between the purple and the crown?'
  'I will relate their stories when we reach
Our confines,' said the guide; 'for thou, O king,
Differing in both from all thy countrymen—
Seest not their stories, and hast seen their fates.
But while we tarry, lo again the flame
Riseth, and, murmuring hoarse, points straiter; haste!
'Tis urgent; we must on.'
                        'Then, O, adieu,'
Cried Gebir, and groan'd loud; at last a tear   230
Burst from his eyes, turn'd back, and he exclaim'd
'Am I deluded? O ye powers of hell!
Suffer me—O my fathers!—am I torne'—
He spake, and would have spoken more, but flames
Enwrapt him, round and round, intense; he turn'd—
And stood held breathless in a ghost's embrace.
'Gebir, my son, desert me not, I heard
Thy calling voice, nor fate witheld me more.
One moment yet remains: enough to know
Soon will my torments, soon will thine, expire.   240
O that I e'er exacted such a vow!
When dipping in the victim's blood thy hand,
First thou withdrew'st it, looking in my face
Wondering; but when the priest my will explain'd,
Then swarest thou, repeating what he said,
How against Egypt thou wouldst raise that hand
And bruise the seed first risen from our line.
Therefor, in death what pangs have I endured!
Rackt on the fiery centre of the sun,
Twelve years I saw the ruin'd world roll round.   250
Shudder not; I have borne it; I deserved
My wretched fate; be better thine; farewell.'

'O stay, my father! stay one moment more.
Let me return thee that embrace—'tis past—
Aröar! how could I quit it unreturn'd!
And now the gulph divides us, and the waves
Of sulphur bellow through the blue abyss.
And is he gone for ever! and I come
In vain?' Then sternly said the guide, 'In vain!
Sayst thou; what wouldst thou more? alas, O prince,⠀⠀⠀⠀260
None come for pastime here! but is it nought
To turn thy feet from evil—is it nought
Of pleasure to that shade if they are turn'd?
For this thou camest hither: he who dares
To penetrate this darkness, nor regards
The dangers of the way, shall reascend
In glory, nor the gates of hell retard
That man, nor demon's nor man's art prevail.
Once in each hundred years, and only once,
Whether by some rotation of the world,⠀⠀⠀⠀270
Or whether will'd so by some pow'r above,
This flaming arch starts back: each realm descries
Its opposite; and Bliss from her repose
Freshens, and feels her own security.'
⠀⠀'Security!' cried out the Gadite king,
'And feel they not compassion?'
⠀⠀⠀⠀⠀⠀⠀⠀⠀⠀⠀⠀⠀⠀⠀⠀⠀⠀'Child of Earth,'
Calmly said Aröar at his guest's surprize,
'Some so disfigur'd by habitual crimes,
Others are so exalted, so refined,
So permëated by heaven, no trace remains⠀⠀⠀⠀280
Graven on earth: here Justice is supreme;
Compassion can be but where passions are.
Here are discover'd those who tortured Law
To silence or to speech, as pleas'd themselves;
Here also those who boasted of their zeal,
And lov'd their country for the spoils it gave.
Hundreds, whose glitt'ring merchandize the lyre
Dazzled vain wretches, drunk with flattery,
And wafted them in softest airs to Heav'n,
Doom'd to be still deceiv'd, here still attune⠀⠀⠀⠀290
The wonted strings and fondly woo applause;
The wish half granted, they retain their own,
But madden at the mockry of the shades.
While on the river's other side there grow
Deep olive groves: there, other ghosts abide:
Blest indeed they; but not supremely blest.
We cannot see beyond: we cannot see
Aught but our opposite, and here are fates
How opposite to our's! here some observ'd

Religious rites, some hospitality:
Strangers, who from the good old men retired,
Closed the gate gently, lest from generous use
Shutting and opening of it's own accord,
It shake unsettled slumbers off their couch:
Some stopt revenge athirst for slaughter, some
Sow'd the slow olive for a race unborn.
These had no wishes; therefor none are crown'd:
But their's are tufted banks, their's umbrage, their's
Enough of sun-shine to enjoy the shade,
And breeze enough to lull them to repose.'   310
    Then Gebir cried, 'Illustrious host, proceed.
Bring me among the wonders of a realm
Admired by all, but like a tale admired.
We take our children from their cradled sleep,
And on their fancy, from our own, impress
Etherial forms and adulating fates:
But, ere departing for such scenes ourselves,
We seize their hands, we hang upon their neck,
Our beds cling heavy round us with our tears,
Agony strives with agony. Just Gods!   320
Wherefor should wretched mortals thus believe,
Or wherefor should they hesitate to die?'
    Thus while he question'd, all his strength dissolv'd
Within him, thunder shook his troubled brain;
He started; and the cavern's mouth survey'd
Near; and beyond, his people; he arose,
And bent towards them his bewilder'd way.

END OF BOOK THE THIRD

THE FOURTH BOOK OF *GEBIR*

ARGUMENT

In what manner *Charoba* is affected by the report of *Gebir's* visit to the shades.
Collusion of *Love* and *Terror*. Retrospect. The various ways in which *Charoba* is
tormented. Universal alarm. Description of the species of patriotism that is
generated under monarchy. Violence against the *Gadites* meditated. *Dalica*
recommends a festival on their account. *Charoba* unsuspiciously consents—rejoices
at the thought of seeing *Gebir*—hesitates—argues with herself, and is satisfied—
hears tymbrels and cymbals—suspects hostility—exclaims against *Gebir*—finds
that the tumult proceeds from the extravagant merriment of her own people.
Description of an Egyptian holiday—of an embassy—of the *Gadites* reposing in
the evening. Reception of the Egyptian elders at the Iberian tent.

THE king's lone road, his visit, his return,
Were not unknown to Dalica, nor long
The wondrous tale from royal ears delaid.
When the young queen had heard who taught the rites

Her mind was shaken, and what first she asked
Was, whether the sea-maids were very fair,
And was it true that even gods were moved
By female charms beneath the waves profound,
And joined to them in marriage, and had sons . . .
Who knows but Gebir sprang then from the Gods!   10
He that could pity, he that could obey,
Flatter'd both female youth and princely pride,
The same ascending from amidst the shades
Show'd Pow'r in frightful attitude: the queen
Marks the surpassing prodigy, and strives
To shake off terror in her crowded court,
And wonders why she trembles; nor suspects
How Fear and Love assume each other's form,
By birth and secret compact how allied.
Vainly, (to conscious virgins I appeal,)   20
Vainly with crouching tigers, prowling wolves,
Rocks, precipices, waves, storms, thunderbolts,
All his immense inheritance, would Fear
The simplest heart, should Love refuse, assail;
Consent—the maiden's pillowed ear imbibes
Constancy, honor, truth, fidelity,
Beauty, and ardent lips, and longing arms;
Then fades in glimmering distance half the scene,
Then her heart quails and flutters and would fly.
'Tis her beloved! not to her! ye Pow'rs!   30
What doubting maid exacts the vow? behold
Above the myrtles his protesting hand.
Such ebbs of doubt and swells of jealousy
Toss the fond bosom in its hour of sleep
And float around the eyelids and sink thro'.
    Lo! mirror of delight in cloudless days!
Lo! thy reflection: 'twas when I exclaim'd
—With kisses hurried as if each foresaw
Their end, and reckon'd on our broken bonds,
And could at such a price such loss endure—   40
'O what, to faithful lovers, met at morn,
What half so pleasant as imparted fears!'
How many a night serene, shall I behold
Those warm attractive orbits, close inshrined
In ether, over which Love's column rose
Marmoreal, trophied round with golden hair.
Within the valley of one lip, unseen,
Love slumber'd, one his unstrung bow impress'd.
Sweet wilderness of soul-entangling charms!
Led back by Memory, and each blissful maze   50
Retracing, me with magic power detain
Those dimpled cheeks, those temples, violet-tinged,

Those lips of nectar, and those eyes of heav'n!
  Charoba, tho' indeed she never drank
The liquid pearl, or twined the nodding crown;
Or, when she wanted cool and calm repose,
Dream'd of the crawling asp and grated tomb,
Was wretched up to royalty! the jibe
Struck her, most piercing where love pierc'd before,
From those whose freedom centers in their tongue,   60
Handmaids, and pages sleek, and courtiers aged.
Congratulations here, there prophecies,
Here children, not repining at neglect,
While tumult thus sweeps amplest room for play;
Every-where questions, answer'd ere begun,
Every-where groups, for every-where alarm.
Thus, winter gone; nor spring, tho' near, arriv'd,
Urged slanting onward by the bickering breeze
That issues from beneath Aurora's car,
Shudder the sombrous waves; at every beam   70
More vivid, more by every breath impell'd,
Higher and higher up the fretted rocks
Their turbulent refulgence they display.
Madness, which, like the spiral element,
The more it seizes on, the fiercer burns,
Hurried them blindly forward, and involved
In flame the senses, and in gloom the soul.
  Determin'd to protect the country's gods,
Still asking their protection, they adjure
Each other to stand forward, and insist   80
With zeal, and trample under foot the slow;
And disregardful of the Sympathies
Divine, those Sympathies whose delicate hand
Touching the very eyeball of the heart,
Awakens it, not wounds it nor inflames.—
Blind wretches! they with desperate embrace
Hang on the pillar till the temple fall.
Oft, the grave judge alarms religious wealth,
And rouses anger under gentle words.
Woe to the wiser few, who dare to cry   90
'People! these men are not your enemies:
Enquire their errand; and resist when wrong'd.'
Together, childhood, priesthood, womanhood,
The scribes, and elders of the land, exclaim
'Seek they not hidden treasure in the tombs?
Raising the ruins, levelling the dust,
Who can declare whose ashes they disturb!
Build they not fairer cities than our own,
Extravagant enormous apertures
For light, and portals larger, open courts,   100

Where all ascending all are unconfin'd,
And wider streets in purer air than ours?
Temples quite plain, with equal capitals,
They build, nor bearing gods like ours imbost.
O profanation! O our ancestors!'
   Though all the vulgar hate a foreign face,
It more offends weak eyes and homely age,
Dalica most; who thus her aim pursued.
'My promise, O Charoba, I perform.
Proclaim to gods and men a festival   110
Throughout the land, and bid the strangers eat:
Their anger thus we haply may disarm.'
   'O Dalica, the grateful queen replied,
Nurse of my childhood, soother of my cares,
Preventer of my wishes, of my thoughts,
O pardon youth, O pardon royalty!
If hastily to Dalica I sued,
Fear might impel me, never could distrust.
Go then, for wisdom guides thee, take my name,
Issue what most imports and best beseems,   120
And sovranty shall sanction the decree.'
   And now Charoba was alone, her heart
Grew lighter; she sat down, and she arose,
She felt voluptuous tenderness, but felt
That tenderness for Dalica; she prais'd
Her kind attention, warm solicitude,
Her wisdom—for what wisdom pleas'd like her's!
She was delighted: should she not behold
Gebir? she blush'd: but she had words to speak,
She form'd them and reform'd them, with regret   130
That there was somewhat lost with every change:
She could replace them—what would that avail—
Moved from their order they have lost their charm.
While thus she strew'd her way with softest words,
Others grew up before her, but appear'd
A plenteous, rather than perplexing, choice.
She rubb'd her palms with pleasure, heav'd a sigh,
Grew calm again, and thus her thoughts revolv'd.
   —'But he descended to the tombs! the thought
Thrills me, I must avow it, with affright.   140
And wherefor? shews he not the more belov'd
Of heaven, or how ascends he back to day.
Then, has he wrong'd me? Could he want a cause
Who has an army, and was bred to reign?
And yet no reasons against rights he urged.
He threaten'd not; proclaim'd not; I approach'd,
He hasten'd on; I spake, he listen'd; wept,
He pity'd me: he lov'd me, he obey'd;

He was a conqueror, still am I a queen.'
　She thus indulged fond fancies, when the sound
Of tymbrels and of cymbals struck her ear,
And horns, and howlings of wild jubilee.
She fear'd; and listen'd, to confirm her fears;
One breath sufficed, and shook her refluent soul.
Smiting, with simulated smile constrain'd,
Her beauteous bosom, 'O perfidious man,
O cruel foe,' she twice and thrice exclaim'd,
'O my companions equal-aged! my throne,
My people! O how wretched to presage
This day, how tenfold wretched to endure!'　　160
　She ceas'd, and instantly the palace rang
With gratulation roaring into rage:
'Twas her own people. 'Health to Gebir! health
To our compatriot subjects! to our queen
Health and unfaded youth ten thousand years!'
Then went the victims forward crown'd with flowers,
Crown'd were tame crocodiles, and boys white-robed
Guided their creaking crests across the stream.
In gilded barges went the female train,
And, hearing others ripple near, undrew　　170
The veil of sea-green awning, if they found
Whom they desired, how pleasant was the breeze!
If not, the frightful water forced a sigh.
Sweet airs of music ruled the rowing palms;
Now rose they glistening and aslant reclined,
Now they descended, and with one consent
Plunging, seem'd swift each other to pursue,
And now to tremble wearied o'er the wave.
Beyond, and in the suburbs, might be seen
Crouds of all ages; here in triumph passed　　180
Not without pomp, though raised with rude device,
The monarch and Charoba: there a throng
Shone out in sunny whiteness o'er the reeds:
Nor could luxuriant youth, or lapsing age
—Propt by the corner of the nearest street—
With aching eyes and tottering knees intent,
Loose leathery neck and wormlike lip outstretched,
Fix long the ken upon one form; so swift
Through the gay vestures fluttering on the bank,
And through the bright-eyed waters dancing round,　　190
Wove they their wanton wiles, and disappear'd.
　Meanwhile, with pomp august and solemn, borne
On four white camels, tinkling plates of gold,
Heralds before, and Ethiop slaves behind,
Each with the signs of office in his hand,
Each on his brow the sacred stamp of years,

The four ambassadors of peace proceed.
Rich carpets bear they, corn and generous wine;
The Syrian olive's cheerful gifts they bear:
With stubborn goats that eye the mountain-tops   200
Askance, and riot with reluctant horn,
And steeds and stately camels in their train.
The king, who sat before his tent, descried
The dust rise redden'd from the setting sun:
Through all the plains below the Gadite men
Were resting from their labor: some surveyed
The spacious scite, ere yet obstructed, walls
Already, soon will roofs have, interposed.
Nor is the glory of no price, to take
The royal city in, as these presume.   210
Some ate their frugal viands on the steps,
Contented: some, remembering home, prefer
The cot's bare rafters o'er the high gilded dome,
And sing, for often sighs, too, end in song,
'In smiling meads how sweet the brooks repose,
To the rough ocean and red restless sands!
Where are the woodland voices that increast
Along the unseen path on festal days,
When lay the dry and outcast arbutus
On the fane-step, and the first privet-flowers   220
Threw their white light upon the vernal shrine?'
But others trip along with hasty steps,
Whistling, and fix too soon on their abodes:
Haply and one among them with his spear
Measures the lintel, if so great its height
As will receive him with his helm unlower'd.
    But silence went throughout, e'en thoughts were hushed,
When to full view of navy and of camp
Now first expanded the bare-headed train.
Majestic, unpresuming, unappall'd,   230
Onward they marched; and neither to the right
Nor to the left, though there the city stood,
Turn'd they their sober eyes: and now they reach'd
Within a few steep paces of ascent
The lone pavilion of the Iberian king.
He saw them, he awaited them, he rose;
He hail'd them, '*Peace be with you.*' They replied
'King of the western world, be with you peace.'

END OF BOOK THE FOURTH

THE FIFTH BOOK OF *GEBIR*

ARGUMENT

DESCRIPTION of the city *Masar*—occupations of the inhabitants. *Dalica's* journey thither—accosted by a stranger—discovers her sister *Myrthyr*—explains to her the object of her journey—gives an account of *Charoba* from childhood—her sense and courage—enchanted by the spells of *Gebir*—reasons for thinking so—suspects that *Gebir* too is somewhat affected by the exercise of this art—how *Charoba* hates him—resolves his destruction. *Myrthyr* rejoices—takes *Dalica* home—points mysteriously to an incomplete woof. *Dalica* stands amazed. *Myrthyr* dips thrice in a poisonous dye, the garment she had shewn to *Dalica*, and delivers it as a present inevitably fatal to *Gebir*.

ONCE a fair city, courted then by kings,
Mistress of nations, throng'd by palaces,
Raising her head o'er destiny, her face
Glowing with pleasure, and with palms refreshed,
Now, pointed at by Wisdom or by Wealth,
Bereft of beauty, bare of ornaments,
Stood, in the wilderness of woe, Masar.
Ere far advancing, all appear'd a plain.
Treacherous and fearful mountains, far advanced.
Her glory so gone down, at human step   10
The fierce hyæna, frighted from the walls,
Bristled his rising back, his teeth unsheathed,
Drew the long growl and with slow foot retired.
Still were remaining some of ancient race,
And ancient arts were now their sole delight.
With Time's first sickle they had marked the hour
When at their incantation would the Moon
Start back, and shuddering shed blue blasted light.
The rifted rays they gather'd, and immersed
In potent portion of that wondrous wave   20
Which, hearing rescued Israel, stood erect,
And led her armies through his crystal gates.
   Hither—none shared her way, her counsel none—
Hied the Masarian Dalica: 'twas night,
And the still breeze fell languid on the waste.
She, tired with journey long, and ardent thoughts,
Stopt; and before the city she descried
A female form emerge above the sands:
Intent she fix'd her eyes, and on herself
Relying, with fresh vigor bent her way;   30
Nor disappear'd the woman, but exclaim'd—
One hand retaining tight her folded vest—
'Stranger! who loathest life, there lies Masar.
Begone, nor tarry longer, or, ere morn,
The cormorant, in his solitary haunt
Of insulated rock or sounding cove,

Stands on thy bleached bones, and screams for prey.
My lips can scatter them a hundred leagues,
So shrivell'd in one breath, as all the sands
We tread on, could not in as many years.   40
Wretched who die nor raise their sepulchre!
Therefor begone.'
                    But, Dalica, unaw'd,—
Tho' in her wither'd but still firm right-hand
Held up with imprecations, hoarse and deep,
Glimmer'd her brazen sickle, and inclosed
Within its figur'd curve the fading moon—
Spake thus aloud. 'By yon bright orb of Heaven,
In that most sacred moment when her beam
Guided first thither by the forked shaft,
Strikes thro' the crevice of Arishtah's tower—'   50
'Sayst thou?' astonished cried the sorceress,
'Woman of outer darkness, fiend of death,
From what inhuman cave, what dire abyss,
Hast thou invisible that spell o'erheard?
What potent hand hath touched thy quicken'd corse,
What song dissolved thy cearments; who unclosed
Those faded eyes, and fill'd them from the stars?
But if with inextinguished light of life
Thou breathest, soul and body unamerst,
Then, whence that invocation; who hath dared   60
Those hallow'd words, divulging, to profane?'
Then Dalica—
              'To heaven, not earth, addrest,
Prayers for protection cannot be profane.'
   Here the pale sorceress turn'd her face aside,
Wildly, and mutter'd to herself, amazed,
'I dread her who, alone, at such an hour,
Can speak so strangely; who can thus combine
The words of reason with our gifted rites;
Yet will I speak once more—If thou hast seen
The city of Charoba, hast thou marked   70
The steps of Dalica?'
                     'What then?'
                                  'The tongue
Of Dalica has then our rites divulged.'
'Whose rites?'
              'Her sister's, mother's, and her own.'
'Never.'
        'How sayst thou never? one would think,
Presumptuous, thou wert Dalica.'
                                 'I am,
Woman, and who art thou?' with close embrace,
Clung the Masarian round her neck, and cried

'Art thou, then, not my sister? ah I fear
The golden lamps and jewels of a court
Deprive thine eyes of strength and purity: 80
O Dalica, mine watch the waning moon,
For ever patient in our mother's art,
And rest on Heaven suspended, where the founts
Of Wisdom rise, where sound the wings of Power:
Studies intense of strong and stern delight!
And thou too, Dalica, so many years
Wean'd from the bosom of thy native land,
Returnest back, and seekest true repose.
O what more pleasant than the short-breath'd sigh,
When laying down your burden at the gate,   90
And dizzy with long wandering, you embrace
The cool and quiet of a homespun bed.'
    'Alas,' said Dalica, 'tho' all commend
This choice, and many meet with no controul,
Yet, none pursue it! Age, by Care opprest,
Feels for the couch, and drops into the grave.
The tranquil scene lies further still from Youth.
Phrenzied Ambition and desponding Love
Consume Youth's fairest flow'rs; compar'd with Youth
Age has a something something like repose.   100
Myrthyr, I seek not here a boundary
Like the horizon, which, as you advance,
Keeping its form and color, still recedes:
But mind my errand, and my suit perform.
    Twelve years ago Charoba first could speak.
If her indulgent father asked her name,
She would indulge him too, and would reply
'*What? why, Charoba*'—rais'd with sweet surprize,
And proud to shine a teacher in her turn.
Shew her the graven sceptre; what its use?—   110
'Twas to beat dogs with, and to gather flies.
She thought the crown a plaything to amuse
Herself, and not the people, for she thought
Who mimick infant words might infant toys:
But while she watched grave elders look with awe
On such a bauble, she withheld her breath;
She was afraid her parents should suspect
They had caught childhood from her in a kiss;
She blushed for shame, and fear'd—for she believ'd.
Yet was not courage wanting in the child.   120
For I have often seen her with both hands
Shake a dry crocodile, of equal height,
And listen to the shells within the scales,
And fancy there was life, and yet apply
The jagged jaws wide open to her ear.

Past are three summers since she first beheld
The ocean: all around her earnest wait
Some exclamation of amazement wild.
She coldly said, her long-lashed eyes abased,
'Is this the mighty ocean? is this all!'   130
That wond'rous soul Charoba once possessed,
Capacious then as earth or heaven could hold,—
Soul discontented with capacity—
Is gone; I fear, for ever: need I say
She was enchanted by the wicked spells
Of Gebir, whom with lust of power inflamed,
The western winds have landed on our coast.
I since have watched her in each lone retreat,
Have heard her sigh, and soften out the name;
Then would she change it for Egyptian sounds   140
More sweet, and seem to taste them on her lips,
Then loathe them—Gebir, Gebir still return'd.
Who would repine, of reason not bereft!
For, soon the sunny stream of Youth runs down,
And not a gadfly streaks the lake beyond.
Lone in the gardens, on her gather'd vest
How gently would her languid arm recline;
How often have I seen her kiss a flower,
And on cool mosses press her glowing cheek.
Nor was the stranger free from pangs himself.   150
Whether, by spell imperfect, or, while brew'd,
The swelling herbs infected him with foam,
Oft have the shepherds met him wandering
Thro' unfrequented paths, oft overheard
Deep groans, oft started from soliloquies,
Which they believe assuredly were meant
For spirits who attended him unseen.
But when from his illuded eyes retired
That figure Fancy fondly chose to raise,
—For never had she formed so fair an one   160
Herself, till Nature shew'd an architype—
He clasped the vacant air, and stood and gazed.
Then, owning it was folly, strange to tell,
Burst into peals of laughter at his woes:
Next, when his passion had subsided, went
Where from a cistern, green and ruin'd, oozed
A little rill, soon lost; there gather'd he
Violets, and harebells of a sister bloom,
Twining complacently their tender stems
With plants of kindest pliability.   170
These for a garland woven, for a crown
He platted pithy rushes, and ere dusk
The grass was whiten'd with their roots knipt off.

These threw he, finisht, in the little rill,
And stood surveying them with steady smile;
But, such a smile as that of Gebir bids
To Comfort a defiance, to Despair
A welcome, at whatever hour she please.
Had I observ'd him I had pitied him.
I have observ'd Charoba. I have asked   180
If she loved Gebir: '*love him!*' she exclaim'd,
With such a start of terror, such a flush
Of anger, '*I love Gebir? I in love?*'
Then, looked so piteous, so impatient looked—
But burst, before I answer'd, into tears.
Then saw I, plainly saw I, 'twas not love.
For, such her natural temper, what she likes
She speaks it out, or rather, she commands.
And could Charoba say with greater ease
'*Bring me a water-melon from the Nile*'   190
Than, if she lov'd him, '*Bring me him I love.*'
Therefor the death of Gebir is resolv'd.'
    'Resolv'd indeed,' cried Myrthyr, nought surpriz'd,
'Precious mine arts! I could without remorse
Kill, tho' I hold thee dearer than the day,
E'en thee thyself, to exercise mine arts.
Look yonder; mark yon pomp of funeral;
Is this from fortune or from favoring stars?
Dalica, look thou yonder, what a train!
What weeping! O what luxury! come, haste,   200
Gather me quickly up these herbs I dropt,
And then away—hush! I must, unobserved,
From those two maiden sisters pull the spleen;
Dissemblers! how invidious they surround
The virgin's tomb, where all but virgins weep.'
    'Nay, hear me first,' cried Dalica, ' 'tis hard
To perish to attend a foreign king.'
    'Perish! and may not then mine eye alone
Draw out the venom drop, and yet remain
Enough? the portion cannot be perceived.'   210
Away she hasten'd with it to her home:
And sprinkling thrice fresh sulphur o'er the hearth,
Took up a spindle, with malignant smile,
And pointed to a woof, nor spake a word.
'Twas a dark purple; and its dye was dread.
    Plunged in a lonely house, to her unknown,
Now Dalica first trembled; o'er the roof
Wander'd her haggard eyes—'twas some relief—
The massy stones, tho' hewn most roughly, shew'd
The hand of man had once at least been there.   220
But from this object sinking back amazed,

Her bosom lost all consciousness, and shook
As if suspended in unbounded space.
Her thus intranced the sister's voice recall'd,
'Behold it here! dyed once again, 'tis done.'
Dalica stept, and felt beneath her feet
The slippery floor, with moulder'd dust bestrown.
But Myrthyr seized with bare bold-sinew'd arm
The grey cerastes, writhing from her grasp,
And twisted off his horn; nor fear'd to squeeze   230
The viscous poison from his glowing gums:
Nor wanted there the root of stunted shrub
Which he lays ragged, hanging o'er the sands,
And whence the weapons of his wrath are death:
Nor the blue urchin that with clammy fin
Holds down the tossing vessel for the tides.
   Together these her scient hand combined,
And more she added, dared I mention more.
Which done, with words most potent, thrice she dipt
The reeking garb, thrice waved it thro' the air: 240
She ceased; and suddenly the creeping wool
Shrunk up with crisped dryness in her hands.
'Take this,' she cried, 'and Gebir is no more.'

END OF BOOK THE FIFTH

THE SIXTH BOOK OF *GEBIR*

ARGUMENT

TAMAR's nuptials—he appears upon the waves, together with the *Nymph*, and receives with modesty and fear the congratulations of the marine deities. They and their occupations described. *Gebir* and the Egyptian ambassadors—his conduct towards them observed—they return that night. *Tamar* awaked by the *Nymph*—her fondness and delicacy—her exhortations and reflections—prognosticates danger. Courage of *Tamar*—sorrowful at hearing it will fall on *Gebir*—dissuaded from enquiry. Their voyage. Several countries described. *Ætna*. *Corsica*—prediction that hence shall descend 'A mortal man above all mortal praise.' *Tamar's* joy, however, not unmixt on beholding at a distance, and without any hopes of reaching it, his native land—his apostrophe to *Calpe*. The *Nymph's* reflections—assures him that his countrymen will have justice, and Egypt enjoy liberty and equality. The Tuscan coast. Description of the sun setting—of a waterfall under the Apennines. Triumphs of *Tamar's* descendents from the Garonne to the Rhine.

Now to Aurora, borne by dappled steeds,
The sacred gate of orient pearl and gold,
Smitten with Lucifer's light silver wand,
Expanded slow to strains of harmony;
The waves beneath, in purpling rows, like doves
Glancing with wanton coyness tow'rd their queen,

Heav'd softly: thus the damsel's bosom heaves
When, from her sleeping lover's downy cheek,
To which so warily her own she brings
Each moment nearer, she perceives the warmth   10
(Blithe warmth!) of kisses fann'd by playful Dreams.
Ocean, and earth, and heaven, was jubilee.
For 'twas the morning, pointed out by Fate,
When an immortal maid and mortal man
Should share each other's nature, knit in bliss.
    The brave Iberians far the beach o'erspread
Ere dawn, with distant awe: none hear the mew,
None mark the curlew, flapping o'er the field:
Silence held all, and fond expectancy.
Now suddenly the conch above the sea   20
Sounds, and goes sounding thro' the woods profound.
They, where they hear the echo, turn their eyes;
But nothing see they, save a purple mist
Roll from the distant mountain down the shore.
It rolls, it sails, it settles, it dissolves.
Now shines the Nymph to human eye reveal'd,
And leads her Tamar timorous o'er the waves.
Immortals, crowding round, congratulate
The shepherd; he shrinks back, of breath bereft
His vesture clinging closely round his limbs   30
Unfelt, while they the whole fair form admire,
He fears that he has lost it; then he fears
The wave has mov'd it; most to look he fears.
Scarce the sweet-flowing music he imbibes,
Or sees the peopled ocean: scarce he sees
Spio, with sparkling eyes, and Beröe
Demure, and young Ione, less renown'd,
Not less divine, mild-natured, Beauty form'd
Her face, her heart Fidelity; for Gods
Design'd, a mortal, too, Ione loved.   40
These were the Nymphs elected for the hour
Of Hesperus and Hymen; these had strewn
The bridal bed: these tuned afresh the shells,
Wiping the green that hoarsen'd them within:
These wove the chaplets; and at night resolved
To drive the dolphins from the wreathed door.
Gebir surveyed the concourse from the tents,
The Egyptian men around him; 'twas observ'd
By those below how wistfully he looked;
From what attention, with what earnestness   50
Now to his city, now to theirs, he waved
His hand, and held it, while they spake, outspread.
They tarried with him, and they shared the feast.
They stoop'd with trembling hand from heavy jars

E

The wines of Gades gurgling in the bowl,
Nor bent they homeward till the moon appear'd
To hang midway betwixt the earth and skies.
'Twas then that leaning o'er the boy beloved,
In Ocean's grot where Ocean was unheard,
'Tamar!' the Nymph said gently, 'come, awake!   60
Enough to love, enough to sleep, is given,
Haste we away.' This Tamar deem'd deceit,
Spoken so fondly, and he kist her lips;
Nor blushed he then, for he was then unseen.
But she arising bade the youth arise.
'What cause to fly,' said Tamar; she replied
'Ask none for flight, and feign none for delay.'
   'O am I then deceiv'd! or am I cast
From dreams of pleasure to eternal sleep,
And, when I cease to shudder, cease to be!'   70
       She held the downcast bridegroom to her breast,
Look'd in his face and charm'd away his fears.
She said not 'wherefor have I then embraced
You, a poor shepherd, or at least, a man,
Myself a Nymph, that now I should deceive?'
She said not—Tamar did, and was ashamed.
Him overcome her serious voice bespake.
'Grief favours all who bear the gift of tears!
Mild at first sight, he meets his votaries,
And casts no shadow as he comes along: 80
But, after his embrace, the marble chills
The pausing foot, the closing door sounds loud,
The fiend in triumph strikes the vaulted roof,
The uplifted eye sinks from his lurid shade.
Tamar, depress thyself, and miseries
Darken and widen: yes, proud-hearted man!
The sea-bird rises as the billows rise;
Nor otherwise, when mountain floods descend,
Smiles the unsullied lotus glossy-hair'd;
Thou, claiming all things, leanest on thy claim,   90
Till overwhelm'd thro' incompliancy.
Tamar, some silent tempest gathers round!'
   'Round whom,' retorted Tamar; 'thou describe
The danger, I will dare it.'
                              'Who will dare
What is unseen?'
                     'The man that is unblest,'
   'But wherefor thou? It threatens not thyself,
Nor me, but Gebir and the Gadite host.'
   'The more I know, the more a wretch am I,'
Groan'd deep the troubled youth, 'still thou proceed.'
   'Oh seek not destin'd evils to divine,   100

Found out at last too soon! Oh cease the search,
'Tis vain, 'tis impious, 'tis no gift of mine:
I will impart far better, will impart
What makes, when Winter comes, the Sun to rest
So soon on Ocean's bed his paler brow,
And Night to tarry so at Spring's return.
And I will tell, sometimes, the fate of men
Who loos'd from drooping neck the restless arm,
Adventurous, ere long nights had satisfied
The sweet and honest avarice of love: 110
How whirlpools have absorb'd them, storms o'erwhelm'd,
And how amidst their struggles and their prayers
The big wave blacken'd o'er the mouth supine:
Then, when my Tamar trembles at the tale,
Kissing his lips, half-open with surprize,
Glance from the gloomy story, and with glee
Light on the fairer fables of the Gods.
   Thus we may sport at leisure when we go
Where, loved by Neptune and the Naiad, loved
By pensive Dryad pale, and Oread,   120
The spritely Nymph whom constant Zephyr woos,
Rhine rolls his beryl-color'd wave: than Rhine
What River from the mountains ever came
More stately! most the simple crown adorns
Of rushes, and of willows, intertwined
With here and there a flower—his lofty brow,
Shaded with vines, and mistleto, and oak,
He rears; and mystic bards his fame resound.
Or gliding opposite, th' Illyrian gulph
Will harbour us from ill.' While thus she spake,   130
She toucht his eye-lashes with libant lip
And breath'd ambrosial odours; o'er his cheek
Celestial warmth suffusing: grief dispersed,
And strength and pleasure beam'd upon his brow:
Then pointed she before him: first arose
To his astonisht and delighted view
The sacred isle that shrines the queen of love.
It stood so near him, so acute each sense,
That not the symphony of lutes alone,
Or coo serene or billing strife of doves,   140
But murmurs, whispers, nay, the very sighs
Which he himself had utter'd once, he heard.
Next, but long after, and far off, appear
The cloudlike cliffs and thousand towers of Crete:
Still further to the right, the Cyclades.
Phœbus had rais'd, and fixt them, to surround
His native Delos and aërial fane.
He saw the land of Pelops, host of Gods;

Saw the steep ridge where Corinth after stood,
Beck'ning the serious with the smiling Arts   150
Into the sunbright bay: unborn the maid
That, to assure the bent-up hand unskill'd,
Look'd oft; but oft'ner fearing who might wake.
He heard the voice of rivers: he descried
Pindan Peneüs, and the slender Nymphs
That tread his banks, but fear the thundering tide:
These, and Amphrysos, and Apidanus,
And poplar-crowned Spercheios, and, reclined
On restless rocks, Enipeus, where the winds
Scatter'd above the weeds his hoary hair.   160
Then, with Pirenè, and with Panopè,
Evenus, troubled from paternal tears;
And last was Acheloüs, king of isles.
Zacynthus here, above rose Ithaca,
Like a blue bubble, floating in the bay.
Far onward, to the left, a glimm'ring light
Glanced out oblique; nor vanish'd; he inquired
Whence that arose: his consort thus replied.
    'Behold the vast Eridanus! ere night
We shall again behold him, and rejoice.   170
Of noble rivers none with mightier force
Rolls his unwearied torrent to the main.
And now Sicanian Etna rose to view.
Darkness with light more horrid she confounds,
Baffles the breath, and dims the sight, of day.
Tamar grew giddy with astonishment,
And, looking up, held fast the bridal vest.
He heard the roar above him, heard the roar
Beneath, and felt it too, as he beheld,
Hurl, from Earth's base, rocks, mountains, to the skies.   180
    Meanwhile the Nymph had fixt her eyes beyond,
As seeing somewhat; not intent on aught.
He, more amazed than ever, then exclaim'd
    'Is there another flaming isle? or this
Illusion, thus past over unobserved?'
    'Look yonder,' cried the Nymph, without reply,
'Look yonder!' Tamar look'd, and saw two isles
Where the waves whiten'd on the desart shore.
Then she continued. 'That which intervenes
Scarcely the Nymphs themselves have known from Fame: 190
But mark the furthest: there shall once arise,
From Tamar shall arise, 'tis Fate's decree,
A mortal man above all mortal praise.
Methinks already, tho' she threatens Heav'n,
Towering Trinacria to my Corsis yields.'
    Tamar, who listen'd still amidst amaze,

Had never thought of progeny: he clasped
His arms with extasy around his bride,
And pleasure freshen'd her prophetic lips.
He thought too of his ancestors and home.   200
When from amidst grey ocean first he caught
The heights of Calpè, sadden'd he exclaim'd
'Rock of Iberia! fixt by Jove, and hung
With all his thunder-bearing clouds, I hail
Thy ridges, rough and cheerless! what tho' Spring
Nor kiss thy brow, nor deck it with a flower,
Yet will I hail thee, hail thy flinty couch,
Where Valor and where Virtue have reposed.'
    The Nymph said, sweetly smiling, 'Fickle Man
Would not be happy could he not regret!   210
And I confess how, looking back, a thought
Has touched and tuned, or rather, thrill'd my heart,
Too soft for sorrow, and too strong for joy.
Fond foolish maid, 'twas with mine own accord,
It sooth'd me, shook me, melted, drown'd, in tears.
But weep not thou; what cause hast thou to weep.
Weep not thy country: weep not caves abhorr'd,
Dungeons and portals that exclude the day.
Gebir—tho' generous, just, humane—inhaled
Rank venom from these mansions. Rest O King   220
In Egypt thou! nor, Tamar! pant for sway.
With horrid chorus, Pain, Diseases, Death,
Stamp on the slippery pavement of the great,
And ring their sounding emptiness thro' earth.
The Hour, in vain held back by War, arrives
When Justice shall unite the Iberian hinds,
And equal Egypt bid her shepherds reign.
The fairest land dry-lasht could I forego
Rather than crawl a subject; corals, pearls,
Confine me round, if Nymph can be confined,   230
'Twill not console me! Kindness prest by Power
Gives pride fresh tortures, and fresh bars constraint.
And guard me, Heaven! from that paternal care
Which beats and bruises me with iron rods,
Till I embrace them, and with tears protest
That I am happy! rather, when I sin,
Shut me from love and hide me in the deep.'
    Now disappear the Liparean isles
Behind, and forward hang th' Etrurian coasts,
Verdant with privet and with juniper.   240
Now faith is plighted: piled on every hearth,
Crackle the consecrated branches, heard
Propitious, and from vases rough-embost
Thro' the light ember falls the bubbling wine.

And now the chariot of the sun descends!
The waves rush hurried from the foaming steeds:
Smoke issues from their nostrils at the gate;
Which, when they enter, with huge golden bar
Atlas and Calpè close across the main.
They reach th' unfurrow'd Appennines—all hail   250
Clime of unbounded liberty and love!—
And deep beneath their feet, a river flow'd,
Of varied view; yet each variety
So charming, that their eyes could scarce admire
The many beauties that around them throng'd,
Successive as the wave: aspiring elms
O'er the wide water cast a mingled shade
Of tendrils green and grapes of rosy hue.
Among the branches thousand birds appear'd
To raise their little throats, with trilling song   260
Unwearied, but alas their trilling song,
Fast as it flow'd, the roaring torrent drown'd.
Some, unacquainted with the scene, unmoved
By love of tuneful mate, on timid wing
Fly from the eternal thunder of the waves;
But these, content with humid woods, that yield
The choicest moss to warm their callow young,
Brood over them, nor shudder at the damp
That falls for ever round each circled nest.
Here craggy rocks arise; the stream recoils   270
Struggling; but, hurried to the vast abyss
Abruptly, reascends in gloomy rain;
Bespangling in its way the scatter'd herbs
That cling around each lofty precipice,
Of wintry blasts regardless, and the reeds
Which never shall amuse with shrill essay
The valley or the grove, and tender flowers
On virgin bosom never to repose.
But all around them dart the wandering rays
In myriads, and amid the fresh festoons   280
Of pensile vines a hundred arches bend;
Rais'd by the hand of Phœbus and of Jove,
The seats of Iris.—Rise, Iberian Man!
Rise, maid of Ocean! I myself will rise.
Vigorous with youth, with soaring soul endued,
I feel not earth beneath me—lo I snatch
The sunbeam, scorn the thunder, climb the skies!
What force have you inform'd me with! what sight,
Piercing thro' darkness and futurity.
    Yonder, where, sailing slow, the clouds retire,   290
How grand a prospect opens! Alps o'er Alps
Tower, to survey the triumphs that proceed.

There, while Garumna dances in the gloom
Of larches, mid her Naiads, or reclined
Leans on a broom-clad bank to watch the sports
Of some far-distant chamois silken-hair'd,
The chaste Pyrenè, drying up her tears,
Finds, with your children, refuge: yonder, Rhine
Lays his imperial sceptre at their feet.
　　What hoary form so vigorous vast bends there?　　　300
Time,—Time himself throws off his motly garb
Figur'd with monstrous men and monstrous gods,
And in pure vesture enters their pure fanes,
A proud partaker of their festivals.
Captivity led captive, War o'erthrown,
They shall o'er Europe, shall o'er Earth extend
Empire that seas alone and skies confine,
And glory that shall strike the crystal stars.

END OF BOOK THE SIXTH

THE SEVENTH BOOK OF *GEBIR*

ARGUMENT

AGAINST colonization in peopled countries. All nature dissuades from whatever is hostile to equality. The day, according to expectation, of *Charoba's* marriage with *Gebir*. The games of the Tartessians, Gadites, Nebrissans, &c. Sensations of *Gebir*—of *Charoba*. Description of her bath. Preparations. Ardor of the people. She sets out. *Gebir* meets her. Observation by one of her handmaids. The procession. They mount their thrones. *Dalica* appears—throws perfumes over the head and feet of *Gebir*—draws over his shoulders the deadly garment. *Charoba*, who observes, but misinterprets the change in his countenance, with an emotion of tenderness and fear, expects the declaration of his love. He descends from his throne. Astonishment of the Iberians. Horror of *Charoba*—her grief—her love—repeats his name—embraces him in the agonies of despair—calls earth and heaven to attest her innocence—laments most passionately that wretchedness like her's must seem infinitely too great for any thing but guilt—implores instant death—appeals to *Dalica*—acquits *her* of any evil intentions—but accuses the *demons* of tainting the deadly robe—apostrophe to her parents, particularly to her mother—to *Gebir*. He recovers to perceive her sorrows, is consoled, and dies.

　　WHAT mortal first, by adverse fate assail'd,
Trampled by tyranny, or scoft by scorn,
Stung by remorse, or wrung by poverty,
Bade, with fond sigh, his native land farewel?
Wretched! but tenfold wretched, who resolv'd
Against the waves to plunge th' expatriate keel,
Deep with the richest harvest of his land!
　　Driven with that weak blast which Winter leaves,
Closing his palace-gates on Caucasus,
Oft hath a berry risen forth a shade:　　　　　　　10

From the same parent plant, another lies
Deaf to the daily call of weary hind—
Zephyrs pass by, and laugh at his distress.
By every lake's and every river's side
The Nymphs and Naiads teach Equality:
In voices gently querulous they ask
'Who would with aching head and toiling arms
Bear the full pitcher to the stream far off?
Who would, of power intent on high emprize,
Deem less the praise to fill the vacant gulph   20
Than raise Charybdis upon Etna's brow?'
Amidst her darkest caverns most retired,
Nature calls forth her filial Elements
To close around and crush that monster *Void*.—
Fire, springing fierce from his resplendent throne,
And Water, dashing the devoted wretch
Woundless and whole, with iron-colour'd mace,
Or whirling headlong in his war-belt's fold.
Mark well the lesson, man! and spare thy kind.
Go, from their midnight darkness wake the woods,   30
Woo the lone forest in her last retreat—
Many still bend their beauteous heads unblest
And sigh aloud for elemental man.
Thro' palaces and porches, evil eyes
Light upon ev'n the wretched, who have fled
The house of bondage, or the house of birth:
Suspicions, murmurs, treacheries, taunts, retorts,
Attend the brighter banners that invade;
And the first horn of hunter, pale with want,
Sounds to the chase; the second to the war.   40
    The long awaited day at last arrived,
When, linkt together by the seven-arm'd Nile,
Egypt with proud Iberia should unite.
Here the Tartessian, there the Gadite tents
Rang with impatient pleasure: here engaged
Woody Nebrissa's quiver-bearing crew,
Contending warm with amicable skill:
While they of Durius raced along the beach,
And scatter'd mud and jeers on those behind.
The strength of Bœtis, too, removed the helm,   50
And stript the corslet off, and staunched the foot
Against the mossy maple, while they tore
Their quivering lances from the hissing wound.
Others pushed forth the prows of their compeers;
And the wave, parted by the pouncing beak,
Swells up the sides, and closes far astern:
The silent oars now dip their level wings,
And weary with strong stroke the whitening wave.

Others, afraid of tardiness, return.
Now, entering the still harbour, every surge
Runs with a louder murmur up their keel,
And the slack cordage rattles round the mast.
Sleepless, with pleasure and expiring fears,
Had Gebir risen ere the break of dawn,
And o'er the plains appointed for the feast
Hurried with ardent step: the swains admired
What could so transversely sweep off the dew,
For never long one path had Gebir trod,
Nor long, unheeding man, one pace preserved.
Not thus Charoba. She despair'd the day.   70
The day was present: true: yet she despair'd.
In the too tender and once tortured heart
Doubts gather strength from habit, like disease;
Fears, like the needle verging to the pole,
Tremble and tremble into certainty.
How often, when her maids with merry voice
Call'd her, and told the sleepless queen 'twas morn,
How often would she feign some fresh delay,
And tell them (tho' they saw) that she arose.
Next to her chamber, closed by cedar doors,   80
A bath, of purest marble, purest wave,
On its fair surface bore its pavement high.
Arabian gold inclosed the crystal roof,
With fluttering boys adorn'd and girls unrobed,
These, when you touch the quiet water, start
From their aërial sunny arch, and pant
Entangled midst each other's flowery wreaths,
And each pursuing is in turn pursued.
   Here came at last, as ever wont at morn.
Charoba: long she linger'd at the brink,   90
Often she sighed, and, naked as she was,
Sat down, and leaning on the couch's edge,
On the soft inward pillow of her arm
Rested her burning cheek: she moved her eyes;
She blush'd; and blushing plung'd into the wave.
   Now brazen chariots thunder thro' each street,
And neighing steeds paw proudly from delay.
While o'er the palace breathes the dulcimer,
Lute, and aspiring harp, and lisping reed;
Loud rush the trumpets, bursting thro' the throng,   100
And urge the high-shoulder'd vulgar; now are heard
Curses and quarrels and constricted blows,
Threats and defiance and suburban war.
Hark! the reiterated clangor sounds!
Now murmurs, like the sea, or like the storm,
Or like the flames on forests, move and mount

From rank to rank, and loud and louder roll,
Till all the people is one vast applause.
Yes, 'tis herself—Charoba—now the strife!
To see again a form so often seen. 110
Feel they some partial pang, some secret void,
Some doubt of feasting those fond eyes again?
Panting imbibe they that refreshing sight
To reproduce in hour of bitterness?
She goes; the king awaits her from the camp.
Him she descried; and trembled ere he reached
Her car; but shudder'd paler at his voice.
So the pale silver at the festive board
Grows paler fill'd afresh and dew'd with wine;
So seems the tenderest herbage of the spring 120
To whiten, bending from a balmy gale.
The beauteous queen alighting he received,
And sighed to loose her from his arms; she hung
A little longer on them thro' her fears,
Her maidens followed her: and one that watch'd,
One that had call'd her in the morn, observ'd
How virgin passion with unfuel'd flame
Burns into whiteness; while the blushing cheek
Imagination heats and Shame imbues.
 Between both nations, drawn in ranks, they pass. 130
The priests, with linen ephods, linen robes,
Attend their steps, some follow, some precede,
Where, cloath'd with purple intertwined with gold,
Two lofty thrones commanded land and main.
Behind and near them, numerous were the tents
As freckled clouds o'erfloat our vernal skies,
Numerous as wander in warm moonlight nights,
Along Meander's or Cäyster's marsh,
Swans, pliant-neckt, and village storks, revered.
Throughout each nation moved the hum confused, 140
Like that from myriad wings, o'er Scythian cups
Of frothy milk, concreted soon with blood.
Throughout the fields the savory smoke ascends,
And boughs and branches shade the hides unbroached.
Some roll the flowery turf to form a seat,
And others press the helmet—now resounds
The signal!—queen and monarch mount the thrones.
The brazen clarion hoarsens: many leagues
Above them, many to the south, the hern
Rising with hurried croak and throat outstretched, 150
Plows up the silvering surface of her plain.
 Tottering, with age's zeal, and mischief's haste,
Now was discover'd Dalica: she reached
The throne: she lean'd against the pedestal;

And now ascending stood before the king.
Prayers for his health and safety she prefer'd,
And o'er his head and o'er his feet she threw
Myrrh, nard, and cassia, from three golden urns.
His robe of native woof she next removed,
And round his shoulders drew the garb accurst,   160
And bow'd her head, and parted: soon the queen
Saw the blood mantle in his manly cheeks,
And fear'd, and fault'ring sought her lost replies,
And blest the silence that she wished were broke.
Alas, unconscious maiden! night shall close,
And love, and sovereignty, and life dissolve,
And Egypt be one desart drench'd in blood.
    When thunder overhangs the fountain's head,
Losing their wonted freshness, every stream
Grows turbid, grows with sickly warmth suffused: 170
Thus were the brave Iberians, when they saw
The king of nations from his throne descend.
Scarcely, with pace uneven, knees unnerved,
Reach'd he the waters: in his troubled ear
They sounded murmuring drearily; they rose
Wild, in strange colours, to his parching eyes:
They seem'd to rush around him, seem'd to lift
From the receding earth his helpless feet.
He fell—Charoba shriek'd aloud—she ran—
Frantic with fears and fondness, wild with woe,   180
Nothing but Gebir dying she beheld.
The turban that detray'd its golden charge
Within, the veil that down her shoulders hung,
All fallen at her feet! the furthest wave
Creeping with silent progress up the sand,
Glided thro' all, and rais'd their hollow folds.
In vain they bore him to the sea, in vain
Rubb'd they his temples with the briny warmth.
He struggled from them, strong with agony,
He rose half up; he fell again; he cried   190
'*Charoba! O Charoba!*' She embraced
His neck, and raising on her knee one arm,
Sighed when it moved not, when it fell she shrieked,
And clasping loud both hands above her head,
She call'd on Gebir, call'd on earth, on heaven.
    'Who will believe me; what shall I protest;
How innocent, thus wretched? God of Gods,
Strike me—who most offend thee most defy—
Charoba most offends thee—strike me, hurl
From this accursed land, this faithless throne.   200
O Dalica! see here the royal feast!
See here the gorgeous robe! you little thought

How have the demons dyed that robe with death.
Where are ye, dear fond parents! when ye heard
My feet in childhood pat the palace floor,
Ye started forth, and kist away surprize—
Will ye now meet me! how, and where, and when?
And must I fill your bosom with my tears,
And, what I never have done, with your own!
Why have the Gods thus punish'd me? what harm 210
Have ever I done them? have I profaned
Their temples, ask'd too little, or too much?
Proud if they granted, griev'd if they withheld?
O mother! stand between your child and them!
Appease them, soothe them, soften their revenge,
Melt them to pity with maternal tears.
Alas, but if you cannot!—they themselves
Will then want pity rather than your child.
O Gebir! best of monarchs, best of men,
What realm hath ever thy firm even hand 220
Or lost by feebleness, or held by force!
Behold, thy cares and perils how repaid!
Behold the festive day, the nuptial hour!
Me miserable, desolate, undone!'
  Thus raved Charoba: horror, grief, amaze,
Pervaded all the host: all eyes were fixt:
All stricken motionless and mute—the feast
Was like the feast of Cepheus, when the sword
Of Phineus, white with wonder, shook restrain'd,
And the hilt rattled in his marble hand. 230
She heard not, saw not; every sense was gone;
One passion banish'd all; dominion, praise,
The world itself was nothing—Senseless man—
What would thy fancy figure now from worlds?
There is no world to those that grieve and love.
She hung upon his bosom, prest his lips,
Breath'd, and would feign it his that she resorbed.
She chafed the feathery softness of his veins,
That swell'd out black, like tendrils round their vase
After libation: lo! he moves! he groans! 240
He seems to struggle from the grasp of death.
Charoba shriek'd, and fell away; her hand
Still clasping his, a sudden blush o'erspread
Her pallid humid cheek, and disappear'd.
'Twas not the blush of shame—what shame has woe?—
'Twas not the genuine ray of hope; it flashed
With shuddering glimmer thro' unscatter'd clouds;
It flash'd from passions rapidly opposed.
  Never so eager, when the world was waves,
Stood the less daughter of the ark, and tried 250

(Innocent this temptation!) to recall
With folded vest, and casting arm, the dove:
Never so fearful, when amidst the vines
Rattled the hail, and when the light of heaven
Closed, since the wreck of Nature, first eclipsed—
As she was eager for his life's return,
As she was fearful how his groans might end.
They ended:—cold and languid calm succeeds.
His eyes have lost their lustre; but his voice
Is not unheard, tho' short: he spake these words.   260
    'And weepest thou, Charoba! shedding tears
More precious than the jewels that surround
The neck of kings entomb'd!—then weep, fair queen,
At once thy pity and my pangs assuage.
Ah! what is grandeur—glory—they are past!
When nothing else, nor life itself, remains,
Still the fond mourner may be call'd our own.
Should I complain of Fortune? how she errs,
Scattering her bounty upon barren ground,
Slow to allay the lingering thirst of Toil?   270
Fortune, 'tis true, may err, may hesitate;
Death follows close, nor hesitates nor errs.
I feel the stroke! I die!' He would extend
His dying arm; it fell upon his breast.
Cold sweat and shivering ran o'er every limb,
His eyes grew stiff; he struggled and expired.

THE END

[THE MORNING EAGLE]

From *Count Julian*, Act V, Scene 2

Tarik.   At last
He must be happy; for delicious calm
Follows the fierce enjoyment of revenge.
    Hernando. That calm was never his, no other will be!
Thou knowest not, and mayst thou never know,
How bitter is the tear that fiery shame
Scourges and tortures from the soldier's eye.
Whichever of these bad reports be true,
He hides it from all hearts, to wring his own,
And drags the heavy secret to the grave.
Not victory, that o'ershadows him, sees he!

No airy and light passion stirs abroad
To ruffle or to soothe him; all are quelled
Beneath a mightier, sterner, stress of mind:
Wakeful he sits, and lonely, and unmoved,
Beyond the arrows, views, or shouts of men;
As oftentimes an eagle, when the sun
Throws o'er the varying earth his early ray,
Stands solitary, stands immovable
Upon some highest cliff, and rolls his eye,
Clear, constant, unobservant, unabased,
In the cold light, above the dews of morn.
He now assumes that quietness of soul
Which never but in danger have I seen
On his staid breast.

[VERSES BY SPENSER — IMAGINARY]

How much is lost when neither heart nor eye
   Rosewinged Desire or fabling Hope deceives;
When boyhood with quick throb hath ceased to spy
   The dubious apple in the yellow leaves;

When, springing from the turf where youth reposed,
   We find but deserts in the far-sought shore;
When the huge book of Faery-land lies closed,
   And those strong brazen clasps will yield no more.

[MORE VERSES BY SPENSER]

Where forms the lotus, with its level leaves
   And solid blossoms, many floating isles,
What heavenly radiance swift descending cleaves
   The darksome wave! unwonted beauty smiles

On its pure bosom, on each bright-eyed flower,
   On every nymph, and twenty sate around . .
Lo! 'twas Diana . . from the sultry hour
   Hither she fled, nor fear'd she sight nor sound.

Unhappy youth, whom thirst and quiver-reeds
   Drew to these haunts, whom awe forbade to fly,
Three faithful dogs before him rais'd their heads,
   And watched and wonder'd at that fixed eye.

Forth sprang his favorite . . with her arrow-hand
   Too late the goddess hid what hand may hide,
Of every nymph and every reed complain'd,
   And dashed upon the bank the waters wide.

On the prone head and sandal'd feet they flew . .
   Lo! slender hoofs and branching horns appear!
The last marred voice not even the favorite knew,
   But bayed and fastened on the upbraiding deer.

Far be, chaste goddess, far from me and mine
   The stream that tempts thee in the summer noon!
Alas that vengeance dwells with charms divine . .

WRITTEN IN ENGLAND ON THE BATTLE OF ABOUKIR

LAND of all marvels in all ages past,
   Egypt, I hail thee from a far-off shore;
I hail thee, doom'd to rise again at last,
   And flourish, as in early youth, once more.

How long hast thou lain desolate! how long
   The voice of gladness in thy halls hath ceast!
Mute, e'en as Memnon's lyre, the poet's song,
   And half-supprest the chaunt of cloister'd priest.

Even he, loquacious as a vernal bird,
   Love, in thy plains and in thy groves is dumb,
Nor on thy thousand Nile-fed streams is heard
   The reed that whispers happier days to come.

O'er cities shadowing some dread name divine
   Palace and fane return the hyena's cry,
And hoofless camels in long single line
   Stalk slow, with foreheads level to the sky.

No errant outcast of a lawless isle,
   Mocker of heaven and earth, with vows and prayers,
Comes thy confiding offspring to beguile,
   And rivet to his wrist the chain he wears.

Britain speaks now . . her thunder thou hast heard . .
   Conqueror in every land, in every sea;
Valour and Truth proclaim the Almighty word,
   And all thou ever hast been, thou shalt be.

TO CORINTH

QUEEN of the double sea, beloved of him
Who shakes the world's foundations, thou hast seen
Glory in all her beauty, all her forms;
Seen her walk back with Theseus when he left
The bones of Sciron bleaching to the wind,
Above the ocean's roar and cormorant's flight,
So high that vastest billows from above
Shew but like herbage waving in the mead;
Seen generations throng thine Isthmian games,
And pass away . . . the beautiful, the brave,
And them who sang their praises.
                                        But, O Queen,
Audible still (and far beyond thy cliffs)
As when they first were uttered, are those words
Divine which praised the valiant and the just,
And tears have often stopt, upon that ridge
So perilous, him who brought before his eye
The Colchian babes.
                        'Stay! spare him! save the last!
Medea! . . . is that blood? again! it drops
From my imploring hand upon my feet . . .
I will invoke the Eumenides no more,
I will forgive thee, bless thee, bend to thee
In all thy wishes . . do but thou, Medea,
Tell me, one lives.'
                        'And shall I too deceive?'
Cries from the fiery car an angry voice;
And swifter than two falling stars descend
Two breathless bodies: warm, soft, motionless,
As flowers in stillest noon before the sun,
They lie three paces from him: such they lie
As when he left them sleeping side by side,
A mother's arm round each, a mother's cheeks
Between them, flushed with happiness and love.
He was more changed than they were . . . doomed to shew
Thee and the stranger, how defaced and scarred
Grief hunts us down the precipice of years,
And whom the faithless prey upon the last.
  To give the inertest masses of our Earth
Her loveliest forms was thine, to fix the Gods
Within thy walls, and hang their tripods round
With fruits and foliage knowing not decay.
A nobler work remains: thy citadel
Invites all Greece: o'er lands and floods remote
Many are the hearts that still beat high for thee:
Confide then in thy strength, and unappalled

Look down upon the plain, while yokemate kings
Run bellowing, where their herdsmen goad them on:
Instinct is sharp in them and terror true,
They smell the floor whereon their necks must lie.

REGENERATION

WE are what suns and winds and waters make us;
The mountains are our sponsors, and the rills
Fashion and win their nursling with their smiles.
But where the land is dim from tyranny,
There tiny pleasures occupy the place
Of glories and of duties; as the feet
Of fabled faeries when the sun goes down
Trip o'er the grass where wrestlers strove by day.
Then Justice, called the eternal one above,
Is more inconstant than the buoyant form
That bursts into existence from the froth
Of ever-varying ocean: what is best
Then becomes worst; what loveliest, most deformed.
The heart is hardest in the softest climes,
The passions flourish, the affections die.
O thou vast tablet of these awful truths,
That fillest all the space between the seas,
Spreading from Venice's deserted courts
To the Tarentine and Hydruntine mole,
What lifts thee up? what shakes thee? tis the breath
Of God! awake ye nations! spring to life!
Let the last work of his right hand appear
Fresh with his image . . . Man.
                              Thou recreant slave
That sittest afar off and helpest not,
O thou degenerate Albion! with what shame
Do I survey thee, pushing forth the spunge
At thy spear's length, in mockery at the thirst
Of holy Freedom in his agony,
And prompt and keen to pierce the wounded side!

Must Italy then wholly rot away
Amidst her slime, before she germinate
Into fresh vigour, into form again?
What thunder bursts upon mine ear! some isle
Hath surely risen from the gulphs profound,
Eager to suck the sunshine from the breast
Of beauteous Nature, and to catch the gale
From golden Hermus and Melæna's brow.
A greater thing than isle, than continent,

F

Than earth itself, than ocean circling earth,
Hath risen there; regenerate Man hath risen.
Generous old bard of Chios! not that Jove
Deprived thee in thy latter days of sight
Would I complain, but that no higher theme
Than a disdainful youth, a lawless King,
A pestilence, a pyre, awoke thy song,
When on the Chian coast, one javelin's throw
From where thy tombstone, where thy cradle stood,
Twice twenty self-devoted Greeks assailed
The naval host of Asia, at one blow
Scattered it into air . . . and Greece was free . . .
And ere these glories beamed, thy day had closed.

Let all that Elis ever saw give way,
All that Olympian Jove e'er smiled upon.
The Marathonian columns never told
A tale more glorious, never Salamis,
Nor, faithful in the centre of the false,
Platæa, nor Anthela, from whose mount
Benignant Ceres wards the blessed Laws,
And sees the Amphictyon dip his weary foot
In the warm streamlet of the strait below.[1]

Goddess! although thy brow was never reared
Among the Powers, that guarded or assailed
Perfidious Ilion, parricidal Thebes,
Or other walls whose war-belt e'er inclosed
Man's congregated crimes and vengeful Pain,
Yet hast thou touched the extremes of grief and joy . . .
Grief upon Enna's mead and Hell's ascent,
A solitary mother . . . joy beyond,
Far beyond, that thy woe, in this thy fane;
The tears were human, but the bliss divine.

I, in the land of strangers, and deprest
With sad and certain presage for my own,
Exult at hope's fresh dayspring, though afar,
There where my youth was not unexercised
By chiefs in willing war and faithful song:
Shades as they were, they were not empty shades,
Whose bodies haunt our world and blear our sun . . .
Obstruction worse than swamp and shapeless sands.
Peace, praise, eternal gladness, to the souls
That, rising from the seas into the heavens,
Have ransomed first their country with their blood!

[1] The Amphictyons met annually in the temple of Ceres near Anthela.

O thou immortal Spartan! at whose name
The marble table sounds beneath my palms,
Leonidas! even thou wilt not disdain
To mingle names august as these with thine;
Nor thou, twin star of glory, thou whose rays
Streamed over Corinth on the double sea,
Achaian and Saronic; whom the sons
Of Syracuse, when Death removed thy light,
Wept more than slavery ever made them weep,
But shed (if gratitude is sweet) sweet tears . . .
For the hand that then poured ashes o'er their heads
Was loosened from its desperate chain by thee.
What now can press mankind into one mass,
For Tyranny to tread the more secure?
From gold alone is drawn the guilty wire
That Adulation trills: she mocks the tone
Of Duty, Courage, Virtue, Piety,
And under her sits Hope! O how unlike
That graceful form in azure vest arrayed,
With brow serene, and eyes on heaven alone
In patience fixt, in fondness unobscured!
What monsters coil beneath the spreading tree
Of Despotism! what wastes extend around!
What poison floats upon the distant breeze!
But who are those that cull and deal its fruit?
Creatures that shun the light and fear the shade,
Bloated and fierce, Sleep's mien and Famine's cry . . .
Rise up again, rise in thy dignity,
Dejected Man, and scare this brood away.

[LISTEN, MAD GIRL!]

Listen, mad girl! for giving ear
    May save the eyes hard work:
Tender is he who holds you dear,
    But proud as pope or Turk.

Some have been seen, whom people thought
    Much prettier girls than you . .
Setting a lover's tears at nought,
    Like any other dew;

And some too have been heard to swear,
    While with wet lids they stood,
No man alive was worth a tear . .
    They never wept . . nor would.

[ON THE DEATH OF GEORGE HANGER, LORD COLERAINE, on April 1st, 1824]

DEATH! we don't halt then! march I must,
Mortally as I hate the dust.
I should have been in rare high glee
To make an April-fool of thee.

[KEATS]

FAIR and free of soul poesy, O Keats!
O how my temples throb, my heart-blood beats,
   At every image, every word of thine!
Thy bosom, pierced by Envy, drops to rest;
Nor hearest thou the friendlier voice, nor seest
   The sun of fancy climb along thy line.

But under it, altho a viperous brood
That stung an Orpheus (in a clime more rude
   Than Rhodope and Hæmus frown upon)
Still writhes and hisses, and peers out for more
Whose buoyant blood they leave concreted gore,
   Thy flowers root deep, and split the creviced stone.

Ill may I speculate on scenes to come,
Yet I would dream to meet thee at our home
   With Spenser's quiet, Chaucer's livelier ghost,
Cognate to thine . . not higher, and less fair . .
And Madalene and Isabella there
   Shall say, *without thee half our loves were lost.*

[BURNS]

HAD we two met, blythe-hearted Burns,
   Tho water is my daily drink,
   May God forgive me but I think
We should have roared out toasts by turns.

Inquisitive low-whispering cares
   Had found no room in either pate,
   Until I asked thee, rather late,
Is there a hand-rail to the stairs?

[TO IANTHE]

PAST ruin'd Ilion Helen lives,
  Alcestis rises from the shades;
Verse calls them forth; 'tis verse that gives
  Immortal youth to mortal maids.

Soon shall Oblivion's deepening veil
  Hide all the peopled hills you see,
The gay, the proud, while lovers hail
  In distant ages you and me.

The tear for fading beauty check,
  For passing glory cease to sigh;
One form shall rise above the wreck,
  One name, Ianthe, shall not die.

[A FAREWELL TO IANTHE]

O FOND, but fickle and untrue,
Ianthe take my last adieu.
Your heart one day will ask you why
You forced from me this farewell sigh.
Have you not feign'd that friends reprove
The mask of Friendship worn by Love?
Feign'd, that they whisper'd you should be
The same to others as to me?
Ah! little knew they what they said!
How would they blush to be obey'd!
  Too swiftly roll'd the wheels when last
These woods and airy downs we past.
Fain would we trace the winding path,
And hardly wisht for blissful Bath.
At every spring you caught my arm,
And every pebble roll'd alarm.
On me was turn'd that face divine,
The view was on the right so fine:
I smiled . . those conscious eyes withdrew . .
The left was now the finer view.
Each trembled for detected wiles,
And blushes tinged our fading smiles.
But Love turns Terror into jest . .
We laught, we kist, and we confest.
Laugh, kisses, confidence are past,
And Love goes too . . but goes the last.

[ACROSS THE SEA]

IANTHE! you are çall'd to cross the sea!
    A path forbidden *me!*
Remember, while the Sun his blessing sheds
    Upon the mountain-heads,
How often we have watcht him laying down
    His brow, and dropt our own
Against each other's, and how faint and short
    And sliding the support!
What will succede it now? Mine is unblest,
    Ianthe! nor will rest
But on the very thought that swells with pain.
    O bid me hope again!
O give me back what Earth, what (without you)
    Not Heaven itself can do—
One of the golden days that we have past,
    And let it be my last!
Or else the gift would be, however sweet,
    Fragile and incomplete.

[MILD IS THE PARTING YEAR]

MILD is the parting year, and sweet
    The odour of the falling spray;
Life passes on more rudely fleet,
    And balmless is its closing day.

I wait its close, I court its gloom,
    But mourn that never must there fall
Or on my breast or on my tomb
    The tear that would have soothed it all.

[FIESOLAN MUSINGS]

LET me sit here and muse by thee
Awhile, aerial Fiesole!
Thy shelter'd walks and cooler grots,
Villas and vines and olive-plots,
Catch me, entangle me, detain me,
And laugh to hear that aught can pain me.
'Twere just, if ever rose one sigh
To find the lighter mount more high,
Or any other natural thing
So trite that Fate would blush to sing,
Of Honour's sport or Fortune's frown,
Clung to my heart and kept it down.

But **shunn'd** have I on every side
The splash of newly-mounted Pride,
And never riskt my taking cold
In the damp chambers of the old.
   What has the zephyr brought so sweet!
'Tis the vine-blossom round my seat.
Ah! how much better here at ease
And quite alone to catch the breeze,
Than roughly wear life's waning day
On rotten forms with Castlereagh,
Mid public men for private ends,
A friend to foes, a foe to friends!
Long since with youthful chases warm,
And when ambition well might charm,
And when the choice before me lay,
I heard the din and turn'd away.
Hence oftentimes imperial Seine
Hath listen'd to my early strain,
And past the Rhine and past the Rhone
My Latian muse is heard and known,
Nor is the life of one recluse
An alien quite from public use.
Where alders mourn'd their fruitless beds
A thousand cedars raise their heads,
And from Segovia's hills remote,
My sheep enrich my neighbour's cote.
The wide and easy road I lead
Where never paced the harnest steed,
Where hardly dared the goat look down
Beneath her parent mountain's frown,
Suspended, while the torrent-spray
Springs o'er the crags that roll away.
Cares if I had, I turn'd those cares
Toward my partridges and hares,
At every dog and gun I heard
Ill-auguring for some **truant birds,**
Or whisker'd friend of jet-tipt ear,
Until the frighten'd eld limpt near.
These knew me . . and 'twas quite enough . .
I paid no *Morning Post* to puff,
Saw others fame and wealth increase,
Ate my own mutton-chop in peace,
Open'd my window, snacht my glass,
And, from the rills that chirp and pass,
A pure libation pour'd to thee,
Unsoil'd uncitied Liberty!
   Lanthony! an ungenial clime,
And the broad wing of restless Time,

Have rudely swept thy massy walls
And rockt thy abbots in their palls . .
I loved thee by thy streams of yore,
By distant streams I love thee more;
For never is the heart so true
As bidding what we love adieu.
Yet neither where we first drew breath,
Nor where our fathers sleep in death,
Nor where the mystic ring was given,
The link from earth that reaches heaven,
Nor London, Paris, Florence, Rome . .
In his own heart's the wise man's home . .
Stored with each keener, kinder, sense,
Too firm, too lofty, for offence,
Unlittered by the tools of state,
And greater than the great world's great.
If mine no glorious work may be,
Grant, Heaven! and 'tis enough for me,
(While many squally sails flit past,
And many break the ambitious mast)
From all that they pursue, exempt,
The stormless bay of deep contempt!

FÆSULAN IDYL

HERE, where precipitate Spring with one light bound
Into hot Summer's lusty arms expires;
And where go forth at morn, at eve, at night,
Soft airs, that want the lute to play with them,
And softer sighs, that know not what they want;
Under a wall, beneath an orange-tree
Whose tallest flowers could tell the lowlier ones
Of sights in Fiesole right up above,
While I was gazing a few paces off
At what they seemed to show me with their nods,
Their frequent whispers and their pointing shoots,
A gentle maid came down the garden-steps
And gathered the pure treasure in her lap.
I heard the branches rustle, and stept forth
To drive the ox away, or mule, or goat,
(Such I believed it must be); for sweet scents
Are the swift vehicles of stil sweeter thoughts,
And nurse and pillow the dull memory
That would let drop without them her best stores.
They bring me tales of youth and tones of love,
And 'tis and ever was my wish and way
To let all flowers live freely, and all die,
Whene'er their Genius bids their souls depart,

Among their kindred in their native place.
I never pluck the rose; the violet's head
Hath shaken with my breath upon its bank
And not reproacht me; the ever-sacred cup
Of the pure lily hath between my hands
Felt safe, unsoil'd, nor lost one grain of gold.
I saw the light that made the glossy leaves
More glossy; the fair arm, the fairer cheek
Warmed by the eye intent on its pursuit;
I saw the foot, that, altho half-erect
From its grey slipper, could not lift her up
To what she wanted: I held down a branch
And gather'd her some blossoms, since their hour
Was come, and bees had wounded them, and flies
Of harder wing were working their way thro
And scattering them in fragments under foot.
So crisp were some, they rattled unevolved,
Others, ere broken off, fell into shells,
For such appear the petals when detacht,
Unbending, brittle, lucid, white like snow,
And like snow not seen thro, by eye or sun:
Yet every one her gown received from me
Was fairer than the first . . I thought not so,
But so she praised them to reward my care.
I said: *you find the largest.*   *This indeed,*
Cried she, *is large and sweet.*
                              She held one forth,
Whether for me to look at or to take
She knew not, nor did I; but taking it
Would best have solved (and this she felt) her doubts.
I dared not touch it; for it seemed a part
Of her own self; fresh, full, the most mature
Of blossoms, yet a blossom; with a touch
To fall, and yet unfallen.
                              She drew back
The boon she tendered, and then, finding not
The ribbon at her waist to fix it in,
Dropt it, as loth to drop it, on the rest.

EPITHALAMIUM [FOR BYRON]

WEEP Venus, and ye
Adorable Three
Who Venus for ever environ!
Pounds shillings and pence
And shrewd sober sense
Have clapt the strait waistcoat on * * *

Off, Mainot and Turk,
With pistol and dirk,
Nor palace nor pinnace set fire on:
The cord's fatal jerk
Has done its last work,
And the noose is now slipt upon * * *.

[ON VISCOUNT MELVILLE, IMPEACHED 1806]

GOD's laws declare,
Thou shalt not swear
By aught in heaven above or earth below.
Upon my honour! Melville cries . .
He swears, and lies . .
Does Melville then break God's commandment? No.

[ANNE]

EXHAUSTED now her sighs, and dry her tears,
For twenty youths these more than twenty years,
Anne, turning nun, swears God alone shall have her . .
God ought to bow profoundly for the favour.

[WILLIAM GIFFORD]

CLAP, clap the double nightcap on!
Gifford will read you his amours . .
Lazy as Scheld and cold as Don . .
Kneel, and thank Heaven they are not yours.

DIRCE

STAND close around, ye Stygian set,
With Dirce in one boat conveyed!
Or Charon, seeing, may forget
That he is old and she a shade.

EPISTLE TO A BARRISTER [WILLIAM ELIAS TAUNTON]

HAIL, paragon of T * * ons! hail
Thou glory of the triple tail!
Which, to denote thy rank, descends
Like three avenging halter-ends.
O with what art thou mixest up
The hemlock of thy attic cup!
O with what ready hearty will
To all God's creatures, good and ill,

To wise and simple, friend and foe,
Its tranquilizing juices flow!   10
Sly Taffey calls thee merry prig,
And taps thy cheek and twirls thy wig:
The faithful Ketch partakes thy glee
And lights his hempspun joke from thee.
Two badger-eyes has Themis; one
Is always leering toward the throne;
The other wanders, this way, that way,
But sees the gap and leaves the gateway.
The scowl of those who snore she wears,
With the hard hand that clips and sheers;   20
Yet she benignly strokes thy head,
And wakes the judge to hear thee plead.
    Let him extoll, extoll who can,
So modest, so admired a man:
I stand afar, lest thou espy
My raptures with a downcast eye.
But sometime (may the day be near!)
My votive garland shalt thou wear.
Not what the Graces weave for sport
Round Cupids in the Paphian court,   30
Or Bacchus ever twined about
The temples of a Thracian rout,
But what upon thy natal day
Fate, while her sisters shared the lay,
Gave Nemesis to keep in store,
And chaunted .. *this his gransire wore,*
And, when the father's race is run,
Shall be the guerdon of the son.
    T .. onian necks no wreath becomes
That faintly breathes or briefly blooms;   40
But such as raise mankind on high,
Nor leave the exalted when they die ..
No common hedge such wreathes affords,
But proud pelissed Sarmatian lords
Survey them from their castle-towers;
And cloistered virgins press their flowers,
Subdue their stems with agile hand,
And follow them afar from land:
Some for warm Lybia wing their way,
And others into Flora's bay.   50
Averse to forms, averse to dress,
Lover of Nature's nakedness,
To thee all wisdom and all wit,
All Pindus, is not worth the pit ..
Mortals warm-hearted and warm-pated,
Fun-fanciers unsophisticated,

Who hold it first and last of rules
That learning is the staff of fools,
Swear hearts are false where lips are dry,
And in the cup lies Honesty;   60
Clap who laughs hearty and talks loud,
And curse your grave and damn your proud,
And *split 'em but he's heart of oak*
Who flings it at your gentle-folk,
And shews 'em they are flesh and blood,
Like us, no better, if so good.
   When thou wert on thy nurse's breast,
And fears thy father's heart opprest,
Sedately wise Cecropian maid!
Here pour thy precious gifts! he said: 70
The Goddess heard the dubious vow,
And smear'd her olive o'er thy brow,
Sent resolute and dashing Pun,
That takes repulse and shame from none,
In readiness to scour the streets
And lift a leg at all he meets.
Thus, seated o'er the Sunian seas,
Generous ungirt Diogenes
Gave every passager his rub
From the salt-crusted cynic tub;   80
Thus, where some horse hath sown his oats,
The sparrows raise their cheery throats,
And, loving best the dirtiest ground,
Roll their dull feathers round and round.
   Alas I fall! O cease to frown!
The weighty subject draws me down.
Too true; I feel the feeble line
Unworthy of thy name and mine.
Yet its loose threads shall men explore,
As children shells upon the shore: 90
And thou shalt flourish fresh in song
When Nature's verdict stops my tongue;
When Kenyon's pattering pasteboard storm,
And Latin from the second form,
Like hail upon a summer's day,
Falls, bounces, glimmers, melts away;
When all the riches of each Scott
Go, where they ne'er went yet, to pot;
When heedless whistlers speed the plough
Across old Thurlow's whiten'd brow;   100
When all the costliest fur in Britain
Lies level with the wayside kitten,
And the last worm has left the jaws
That blew out life from under laws;

When gibbet-irons with rust are dumb,
Nor wave without their pendulum;
When into dust the winds have blown
What once was sinew, blood, and bone,
What, even while they fill'd with glee
Afar the house of revelry,   110
Breath'd murder into every breath
On Kennington and Hounslow heath,
Lent the faint lightning fresh affright
And hung with deeper gloom the night.
    These are thy works, almighty maker
Of county jobs for undertaker!
When cash and kindred clients fail,
And few will swear and none will bail,
Then the deep mist of error clears,
And Vice's odious form appears.   120
'Had I discover'd it before,
Not all Peru's persuasive ore
Should have induced me to defend
A life no warnings can amend.'
At these thy words the wife declares
A something met her on the stairs:
In the church-yard a light was seen,
And a strange circle markt the green;
Then the poor husband from her chest
Rakes his worst cloaths, and wills his best.   130
    To thee our daily thanks are due,
Who live with no such downcast crew.
Had Cacus school'd them in his den,
Thou wouldst have proved them honest men.
    My sheep are flayed; the flayer bears
The best of names . . our vicar swears . .
And why reproach the mild divine?
He loves his flock . . his flock loves mine.
My timber stolen . . could I know
The mark I made a month ago?   140
My barns cleared out . . my house burnt down . .
Could the whole loss excede a crown?
Shame! are such trifles worth my cares?
I'm freed from rats and from repairs.
    A half-starved staring seagull brood
Flies every honest livelihood,
Quits fierce Malay and shrewd Chinese
And ransackt India's pearl-paved seas.
Hears, sped by thee, how talents fare,
And rises into mountain air.   150
Seamen are bold, but none are bolder
Than those with *cat-claws* on the shoulder,

Whose captain, for his gaping desk,
Has given it the picturesque,
The love of which is gone so deep
They cannot eat, they cannot sleep,
But must indulge in cooling vales,
And hang their pensive heads in Wales.
One, as the wildgoose of a nest,
Stretches his neck to guide the rest,   160
Picks up five hundreds with a bride
And shews her London and sea-side;
Snatches her, ere it runs too late
To pay so many a turnpike-gate,
Settles at once upon my farm,
And spreads a press-gang's dread alarm.
Box-coat and trowser dash together,
The dog-cart and the ostrich-feather,
And brass-loopt hat and broad-frog'd habit,
Most richly ermin'd o'er . . with rabbit.   170
The Welsh look up with wondering eyes,
And ruminate on prophecies;
The tripod and the pot-link turn,
And watch the faggots, how they burn,
Nail a worn horse-shoe on the door
Where never one was nail'd before,
Wash the white threshold-stone anew,
And rub the sleepless bed with rue,
And weary heaven with charms and vows
To guard their children and their cows.   180
Could not the cloth this pest foretell?
Nor the wise woman at the well?
Nor deeper seer who knew what mare
Must disappear by Radnor fair?
The thumping jumping gospel-preacher
Could not he, here too, be their teacher?
The lamb, he cries, *unless ye sin,*
Extends no crook to shank you in.
Graceless as well may be the strangers,
They beard you at your very mangers.   190
For speeding evangelic flights
Requires some boisterous roaring nights;
Pitch on a vantage-ground like swallows,
And soar to heaven from the gallows.
With such faint hearts and such lank jowls
You cannot sin to save your souls,
While they are ready for the crisis . .
Go, do ye likewise, my advice is.
  The daring ambidexterous wench,
Whose fist no collier can unclench,   200

Bites what is needless off her lambs,
Pries for the riddle on the rams,
Curses and kicks them who omit
The duties that their state befit,
Pares from their feet the cankery rot,
And skims, while pit there is, the pot;
Bestows herself the savoury largess,
Mixt with cow-cabbage and crab-verjuice:
And 'dont 'e, Thomas, I desire,
Care a crackt farding for the squire.   210
His lady . . I know who's her betters . .
Before she squall'd I told my letters,
For twenty loaves could knead the dough,
And lift brim-full our biggest trough.
A lady! that will never do . .
Why! she is only five feet two.'
   Now raises she her swelling chine
And prances passing five feet nine,
Jerks a cock's feather from the bag,
And freshens it with oily rag.   220
Now strides she to the full fireside,
With silent step and dignified,
And now relaxes into grace
And asks them how it suits her face;
Then carts it to the neighbouring town,
And trips it till the floors come down,
In many-coloured ribbons drest
And beet-dyed shoes and brimstone vest.
   But morning comes, and sundry fears
For the fee-simple of two ears,   230
That upon frailest tenure hung,
Dependent from a perjured tongue.
'Thomas, she cries, I love thy mettle!
Give us a lift, lad, at the kettle.
There!' . . and such spirit to encourage,
Souces a lardpot in his porrage.
Up darts the buoyant brightening grease
Like the fresh sun upon the seas,
And quiets with its rising glories
Those estuaries and promontories,   240
That never own'd another prince
Within their world's circumference;
And the proud foam and clamorous wind
To its mild empire are resign'd.
Who could imagine that beheld
How this vast region once rebel'd,
Threw up the humble, down the high,
Like turbulent democracy,

Amidst its plenty would not smile,
But hissed and grumbled all the while.   250
   The dame her hearty work pursues,
And hurries round the mingling juice.
'Grub the plantation up, set fire on't,
And, if he douts it, dout the tyrant.
Hard swearing never was hard work,
And if you kill, you kill a Turk.
What! hang a fellow-creature! *shall us*,
When *whiff* will blow him from the gallows!
Our Fred's, I warrant, is the nape
That never flincht from Tyburn tape,   260
Nor ever will the lucky hound
Turn tail till he is off the ground.'
   A year is past: I beg my rent:
I must mistake . . that was not meant.
I tarry on: two years elapse:
The balance may be theirs perhaps.
For insolent requests like these
Their gentle hands uproot my trees,
While those they told me hurt their grain,
I fell, their gentle hands detain;   270
My woods, my groves, my walks beset
With pistol, dirk, and bayonet,
Force my grey labourers to yield,
And stab the women in the field.
Of late a sort of suitor there is
Who courts a horsewhip like an heiress.
Kick him; not Midas would enrich
With surer stroke the flaccid breech;
The blow above reiterate . .
A broken head's a good estate;   280
Add *swindler* . . and behold! next minute
He's out of jail and you are in it.
The land that rears sure-footed ponies
Rears surer-footed testimonies,
And every neighbour, staunch and true,
Swears, and *Got pless her*, what will do.
My gentry tell unpilloried lies,
But prompt and push to perjuries;
Yet tho' you flusht them as they blundered
Thro' the rank stubble of three hundred,   290
Exclaim *a perjury!* and you libel . .
Each his own way may use his bible;
Else how is ours a freeborn nation,
Or wherefore was the Reformation?
If you demand your debts, beware,
But rob'd, cry *robbers!* if you dare:

You only lost a farm of late,
Stir, and you pay your whole estate:
Expose their villainies; Dick Loose
Will shudder at the gross abuse,   300
Free them from prison on their bail,
And pledge them in his mellowest ale.
The lathy lantern-visaged Crawle
His queries and his doubts will drawl.
He the rich blacksmith's daughter won,
And wiled him to exclude the son.
Behold him at a lady's side!
And look, how he has learnt to ride,
Who pigged with choristers and scouts,
And rode but upon *roundabouts*.   310
Unenvied for too fair report
His father sweeps the bishop's court,
And legibly enough records
Two anti-paracletic words:
The one should only be applied
To Priam's and to * * 's bride,
And those few more who growl and bite,
Or are too watchful in the night.
The other is so rude a name
It well deserves the sheet of shame,   320
Which his old honest rib repairs,
And scours from ironmoulds, and airs.
With brain of lead and brow of brass
Stands ready prowling Barnabas,
To whisper him of timorous look
You kiss the cover, not the book.
That Barnabas who, when he stood
Within the close o'erarching wood,
(A wood which on no forest frowns,
But tapers up in market-towns)   330
And stretcht his vast extent of chin
To all without, to none within,
In many breasts rais'd fierce desire
To stick it near the kitchen-fire,
In the dutch oven glittering bright
With its clear rashers red and white.
'Ah what a burning shame, they say,
So many eggs are thrown away!'
'Tis death to puddings, cries a wench,
Between the judges and the French.   340
Look only there! how living rises
From war and popery and assizes!'
   The honest open-hearted Jack
Stands, fit successor, at his back.

Him pockets turn'd and watches twitcht
From jovial snoring friends enricht;
Him the shared tax from many a town,
A true copartner of the crown,
And, eased of his ill-gotten wealth,
An uncle sent to heaven by stealth.   350
    Attended with each bright compeer,
O T * * on, I must leave thee here,
Where, thanks and thanks again to thee!
The poor lost outcasts still are free.
Who wants a character or home,
A shirt or shilling, let him come:
Who flies his dun, or dupes his friend,
Lo! England's furthest safest end:
Who lurks from sea to thieve on shore,
Club the clipt dollar, one mate more!   360
No scruple checks, no conscience shocks,
Hope's at the bottom of the box.
Here all but Innocence may trust,
And all find Justice but the just.

[NEEDWOOD FOREST]

UNDER the hollies of thy breezy glade,
    Needwood, in youth with idle pace I rode,
Where pebbly rills their varied chirrup made,
    Rills which the fawn with tottering knee bestrode.

Twilight was waning, yet I checkt my pace,
    Slow as it was, and longer would remain;
Here first, here only, had I seen the face
    Of Nature free from change and pure from stain.

Here in the glory of her power she lay,
    Here she rejoiced in all the bloom of health;
Soon must I meet her faint and led astray,
    Freckled with feverish whims and wasted wealth.

[LUCILLA ASKS ME]

IN Clementina's artless mien
    Lucilla asks me what I see,
And are the roses of sixteen
    Enough for me?

Lucilla asks, if that be all,
  Have I not cull'd as sweet before . .
Ah yes, Lucilla! and their fall
    I still deplore.

I now behold another scene,
  Where Pleasure beams with heaven's own light,
More pure, more constant, more serene,
    And not less bright . .

Faith, on whose breast the Loves repose,
  Whose chain of flowers no force can sever,
And Modesty who, when she goes,
    Is gone for ever.

[FRIENDSHIP]

Friendship! I place no trust in thee,
  Tho' flourishing so fair in fable,
Or seated with Mythology,
  Or with a bumper-glass at table.

Since first my razor ranged for beard,
  Friendship! in many another place
Thy voice (and loud enough) I've heard,
  But never have beheld thy face.

[TO FORTUNE]

Wert thou but blind, O Fortune, then perhaps
Thou mightest always have avoided me:
For never voice of mine (young, middle-aged,
Or going down on tottering knee the shelf
That crumbles with us to the vale of years)
Called thee aside, whether thou rannest on
To others who expected, or didst throw
Into the sleeper's lap the unsought prize.
But blind thou art not; the refreshing cup
For which my hot heart thirsted, thou hast ever
(When it was full and at the lip) struck down.

ON A POET IN A WELSH CHURCH-YARD

KIND souls! who strive what pious hand shall bring
The first-found crocus from reluctant Spring,
Or blow your wintry fingers while they strew
This sunless turf with rosemary and rue,
Bend o'er your lovers first, but mind to save
One sprig of each to trim a poet's grave.

FOR AN EPITAPH AT FIESOLE

Lo! where the four mimosas blend their shade,
In calm repose at last is Landor laid;
For ere he slept he saw them planted here
By her his soul had ever held most dear,
And he had lived enough when he had dried her tear.

TO WORDSWORTH

THOSE who have laid the harp aside
    And turn'd to idler things,
From very restlessness have tried
    The loose and dusty strings;
And, catching back some favourite strain,
Run with it o'er the chords again.

But Memory is not a Muse,
    O Wordsworth!—though 'tis said
They all descend from her, and use
    To haunt her fountain-head:
That other men should work for me
In the rich mines of Poesie,

Pleases me better than the toil,
    Of smoothing under hardened hand,
With attic emery and oil,
    The shining point for Wisdom's wand;
Like those thou temperest 'mid the rills
Descending from thy native hills.

Without his governance, in vain
    Manhood is strong, and youth is bold.
If oftentimes the o'er-piled strain
    Clogs in the furnace, and grows cold,
Beneath his pinions deep and frore,
And swells, and melts, and flows no more,

That is because the heat beneath,
   Pants in its cavern poorly fed.
Life springs not from the couch of Death,
   Nor Muse nor Grace can raise the dead;
Unturn'd then let the mass remain,
Intractable to sun or rain.

A marsh, where only flat leaves lie,
And showing but the broken sky,
Too surely is the sweetest lay
That wins the ear and wastes the day;
Where youthful Francy pouts alone,
And lets not Wisdom touch her zone.
He who would build his fame up high,
The rule and plummet must apply,
Nor say—I'll do what I have plann'd,
Before he try if loam or sand
Be still remaining in the place
Delved for each polish'd pillar's base.
With skilful eye and fit device,
Thou raisest every edifice:
Whether in sheltered vale it stand
Or overlook the Dardan strand,
Amid those cypresses that mourn
Laodamia's love forlorn.

We both have run o'er half the space
Bounded for mortals' earthly race;
We both have crossed life's fervid line,
And other stars before us shine.
May they be bright and prosperous
As those that have been stars for us!
Our course by Milton's light was sped,
And Shakespeare shining overhead:
Chatting on deck was Dryden too,
The Bacon of the rhyming crew;
None ever crost our mystic sea,
More richly stored with thought than he;
Tho' never tender nor sublime,
He struggles with and conquers Time.
To learn my lore on Chaucer's knee,
I've left much prouder company.
Thee, gentle Spenser fondly led;
But me he mostly sent to bed.

I wish them every joy above
That highly blessed spirits prove,
Save one—and that too shall be theirs,
But after many rolling years,
When 'mid their light, thy light appears.

[TO THE POET T. J. MATHIAS]

THE Piper's music fills the street,
The Piper's music makes the heat
   Hotter by ten degrees:
Hand us a Sonnet, dear Mathias,
Hand us a Sonnet cool and dry as
   Your very best, and we shall freeze.

[THE MERMAID]

THE mermaid sat upon the rocks
   All day long,
Admiring her beauty and combing her locks,
   And singing a mermaid song.

And hear the mermaid's song you may,
   As sure as sure can be,
If you will but follow the sun all day,
   And souse with him into the sea.

[LEAVES AND GIRLS]

NATURALLY, as fall upon the ground
The leaves in winter and the girls in spring.

[TO CHLOE]

CHLOE! mean men must ever make mean loves,
They deal in dog-roses, but I in cloves.
They are just scorch'd enough to blow their fingers,
I am a phoenix downright burnt to cinders.

[LINES BY MIMNERMUS—IMAGINARY]

I WISH not Thasos rich in mines,
Nor Naxos girt around with vines,
Nor Crete nor Samos, the abodes
Of those who govern men and Gods,
Nor wider Lydia, where the sound

Of tymbrels shakes the thymy ground,
And with white feet and with hoofs cloven
The dedal dance is spun and woven:
Meanwhile each prying younger thing
Is sent for water to the spring,
Under where red Priapus rears
His club amid the junipers;
In this whole world enough for me
Is any spot the Gods decree;
Albeit the pious and the wise
Would tarry where, like mulberries,
In the first hour of ripeness fall
The tender creatures, one and all.
To take what falls with even mind
Jove wills, and we must be resign'd.

HEGEMON TO PRAXINOE

Is there any season, O my soul,
When the sources of bitter tears dry up,
And the uprooted flowers take their places again
    Along the torrent-bed?

Could I wish to live, it would be for that season,
To repose my limbs and press my temples there.
But should I not speedily start away
    In the hope to trace and follow thy steps!

Thou art gone, thou art gone, Praxinoe!
And hast taken far from me thy lovely youth,
Leaving me naught that was desirable in mine.
    Alas! alas! what hast thou left me?

The helplessness of childhood, the solitude of age,
The laughter of the happy, the pity of the scorner,
A colourless and broken shadow am I,
    Seen glancing in troubled waters.

My thoughts too are scattered; thou hast cast them off;
They beat against thee, they would cling to thee,
But they are viler than the loose dark weeds,
    Without a place to root or rest in.

I would throw them across my lyre; they drop from it;
My lyre will sound only two measures;
That Pity will never, never come,
    Or come to the sleep that awakeneth not unto her.

[EPITAPH ON A TYRANT]

THE pigmy despot Mutinas lies here!
He was not godless; no: his God was Fear.

[THE SHORTEST DAY]

HAPPY to me has been the day,
  The shortest of the year,
Though some, alas! are far away
Who made the longest yet more brief appear.

[BY ALCÆUS—IMAGINARY]

1

WORMWOOD and rue be on his tongue
  And ashes on his head,
Who chills the feast and checks the song
  With emblems of the dead!

2

By young and jovial, wise and brave,
  Such mummers are derided.
His sacred rites shall Bacchus have,
  Unspared and undivided.

3

Coucht by my friends, I fear no mask
  Impending from above,
I only fear the later flask
  That holds me from my love.

A MORAL

PLEASURES! away; they please no more.
Friends! are they what they were before?
Loves! they are very idle things,
The best about them are their wings.
The dance! 'tis what the bear can do;
Musick! I hate your musick too.

  Whene'er these witnesses that Time
Hath snatcht the chaplet from our prime,
Are call'd by Nature, as we go
With eye more wary, step more slow,
And will be heard and noted down,
However we may fret or frown,
Shall we desire to leave the scene

Where all our former joys have been?
No, 'twere ungrateful and unwise . .
But when die down our charities
For human weal and human woes,
Then is the time our eyes should close.

ODE TO MILETUS

1

MAIDEN there was whom Jove
Illuded into love,
   Happy and pure was she;
Glorious from her the shore became,
And Helle lifted up her name
To shine eternal o'er the river-sea.

2

And many tears are shed
Upon thy bridal-bed,
Star of the swimmer in the lonely night!
   Who with unbraided hair
   Wipedst a breast so fair,
Bounding with toil, more bounding with delight.

3

But they whose prow hath past thy straits
And, ranged before Byzantion's gates,
Bring to the Gods of sea the victim due,
   Even from the altar raise their eyes,
   And drop the chalice with surprise,
And at such grandeur have forgotten you.

4

At last there swells the hymn of praise . .
And who inspires those sacred lays?
   'The founder of the walls ye see.'
What human power could elevate
Those walls, that citadel, that gate?
   'Miletus, O my sons! was he.'

5

Hail then, Miletus! hail beloved town
   Parent of me and mine!
But let not power alone be thy renown,
   Nor chiefs of ancient line,

6

Nor visits of the Gods, unless
   They leave their thoughts below,
And teach us that we most should bless
   Those to whom most we owe.

7

Restless is Wealth; the nerves of Power
   Sink, as a lute's in rain:
The Gods lend only for an hour
   And then call back again

8

All else than Wisdom; she alone,
   In Truth's or Virtue's form,
Descending from the starry throne
   Thro' radiance and thro' storm,

9

Remains as long as godlike men
   Afford her audience meet,
Nor Time nor War tread down agen
   The traces of her feet.

10

Always hast thou, Miletus, been the friend,
   Protector, guardian, father, of the wise;
Therefore shall thy dominion never end
   Til Fame, despoil'd of voice and pinion, dies.

11

With favoring shouts and flowers thrown fast behind,
   Arctinus ran his race
No wanderer he, alone and blind . .
   And Melesander was untorn by Thrace.

12

There have been, but not here,
Rich men who swept aside the royal feast
   On child's or bondman's breast,
Bidding the wise and aged disappear.

13

   Revere the aged and the wise,
Aspasia . . but thy sandal is not worn
   To trample on these things of scorn . .
By his own sting the fire-bound scorpion dies.

ERINNA TO LOVE

1

WHO breathes to thee the holiest prayer,
O Love! is ever least thy care.
Alas! I may not ask thee why 'tis so . .
    Because a fiery scroll I see
    Hung at the throne of Destiny,
Reason with Love and register with Woe.

2

    Few question thee, for thou art strong
    And, laughing loud at right and wrong,
Seizest, and dashest down, the rich, the poor;
    Thy scepter's iron studs alike
    The meaner and the prouder strike,
And wise and simple fear thee and adore.

[LINES BY SAPPHO—IMAGINARY]

SWEET girls! upon whose breast that God descends
    Whom first ye pray to come, and next to spare,
O tell me whither now his course he bends,
    Tell my what hymn shall thither waft my prayer!
Alas! my voice and lyre alike he flies,
And only in my dreams, nor kindly then, replies.

TO LYSIS

    A CURSE upon the kind of old
        Who would have kidnapt all the Muses!
    Whether to barter them for gold
        Or keep them for his proper uses.
    Lysis! aware he meant them ill,
        Birds they became, and flew away . .
    Thy Muse alone continues still
        A titmouse to this very day.

[BEAUTY]

1

BEAUTY! thou art a wanderer on the earth,
    And hast no temple in the fairest ile
Or city over-sea, where Wealth and Mirth
    And all the Graces, all the Muses, smile.

2

Yet these have always nurst thee, with such fond,
　Such lasting love, that they have followed up
Thy steps thro' every land, and placed beyond
　The reach of thirsty Time thy nectar-cup.

3

Thou art a wanderer, Beauty! like the rays
　That now upon the platan, now upon
The sleepy lake, glance quick or idly gaze,
　And now are manifold and now are none.

4

I have call'd, panting, after thee, and thou
　Hast turn'd and lookt and said some pretty word,
Parting the hair, perhaps, upon my brow,
　And telling me none ever was prefer'd.

5

In more than one bright form hast thou appear'd,
　In more than one sweet dialect hast thou spoken:
Beauty! thy spells the heart within me heard,
　Griev'd that they bound it, grieves that they are broken.

[YOUNG TO OLD]

I HAVE some merit too, old man!
And show me greater if you can.
I always took what Beauty gave,
Nor, when she snatcht it back, lookt grave.
Us modest youths it most beseems
To drink from out the running streams:
Love on their banks delights to dwell . . .
The bucket of the household well
He never tugs at, thinking fit
Only to quench his torch in it.
Shameless old fellow! do you boast
Of conquests upon every coast?
I, O ye Gods! should be content
(Yea, after all the sighs I've spent,
The sighs, and, what is yet more hard,
The minas, talents, gone in nard!)
With only one: I would confine
Meekly this homesick heart of mine
'Twixt Lampsacus and Hammon's shrine.

[PYRRHA]

1

PYRRHA! your smiles are gleams of sun
That after one another run
Incessantly, and think it fun.

2

Pyrrha! your tears are short sweet rain
That glimmering on the flower-lit plain
Zephyrs kiss back to heaven again.

3

Pyrrha! both anguish me: do please
To shed but (if you wish me ease)
Twenty of those, and two of these.

[THE LIGHTER HOURS]

WHERE are the blooms of many dyes
That used in every path to rise?
   Whither are gone the lighter hours?
What leave they? . . I can only send
My wisest, loveliest, latest friend
   These weather-worn and formless flowers.

SAPPHO TO HESPERUS

1

I HAVE beheld thee in the morning hour
   A solitary star, with thankless eyes,
   Ungrateful as I am! who bade thee rise
When sleep all night had wandered from my bower.

2

   Can it be true that thou art he
   Who shinest now above the sea
Amidst a thousand, but more bright?
   Ah yes, the very same art thou
   That heard me then, and hearest now . .
Thou seemest, star of love, to throb with light.

THE DEATH OF ARTEMIDORA

'ARTEMIDORA! Gods invisible,
While thou art lying faint along the couch,
Have tied the sandal to thy veined feet,
And stand beside thee, ready to convey
Thy weary steps where other rivers flow.

Refreshing shades will waft thy weariness
Away, and voices like thine own come nigh,
Soliciting, nor vainly, thy embrace.'
　Artemidora sigh'd, and would have press'd
The hand now pressing hers, but was too weak.
Fate's shears were over her dark hair unseen
While thus Elpenor spake: he look'd into
Eyes that had given light and life erewhile
To those above them, those now dim with tears
And watchfulness. Again he spake of joy
Eternal. At that word, that sad word, *joy,*
Faithful and fond her bosom heav'd once more,
Her head fell back: one sob, one loud deep sob
Swell'd through the darkened chamber; 'twas not hers:
With her that old boat incorruptible,
Unwearied, undiverted in its course,
Had plash'd the water up the farther strand.

[IN THE DECLINE OF LIFE]

Love ran with me, then walk'd, then sate,
Then said *'Come, come! it grows too late:'*
And then he would have gone . . but . . no . .
You caught his eye; he could not go.

[NICONÖE AND PRIAPOS]

Niconöe is inclined to deck
Thy ruddy shoulder and thick neck
　With her own fawn-skin, Lampsacene!
Beside, she brings a golden ewer
To cool thy hands in, very sure
　Among what herbage they have been.

Ah! thou hast wicked leering eyes,
And any maiden were unwise
　Who should invest thee face to face;
Therefore she does it from behind,
And blesses thee, so just and kind
　In giving her the prize for grace.

[ON LOVE, ON GRIEF]

On love, on grief, on every human thing,
Time sprinkles Lethe's water with his wing.

THE DEATH OF CLYTEMNESTRA

ORESTES AND ELECTRA

Electra. Pass on, my brother! she awaits the wretch,
Dishonorer, despoiler, murderer . . . .
None other name shall name him . . . . she awaits
As would a lover . .
      Heavenly Gods! what poison
O'erflows my lips!
     Adultress! husband-slayer!
Strike her, the tigress!
      Think upon our father . .
Give the sword scope . . think what a man was he,
How fond of her! how kind to all about,
That he might gladden and teach *us* . . how proud
Of thee, Orestes! tossing thee above
His joyous head and calling thee his crown.
Ah! boys remember not what melts our hearts
And marks them evermore!
       Bite not thy lip,
Nor tramp as an unsteddy colt the ground,
Nor stare against the wall, but think again
How better than all fathers was our father.
Go . .
  Orestes. Loose me, then! for this white hand, Electra,
Hath fastened upon mine with fiercer grasp
Than mine can grasp the sword.
  Electra.   Go, sweet Orestes!
I knew not I was holding thee . . Avenge him!
(*Alone.*) How he sprang from me!
      . . Sure, he now has reacht
The room before the bath . .
      The bath-door creaks!
. . It hath creakt thus since he . . since thou, O father!
Ever since thou didst loosen its strong valves,
Either with all thy dying weight, or strength
Agonized with her stabs . .
      What plunge was that?
Ah me!
  . . What groans are those?
  Orestes (*returning*).   They sound through hell
Rejoicing the Eumenides.
       She slew
Our father; she made thee the scorn of slaves;
Me (son of him who ruled this land and more)
She made an outcast . . .
      Would I had been so
For ever! ere such vengeance . . . .

Electra.   O that Zeus
Had let thy arm fall sooner at thy side
Without those drops! list! they are audible . .
For they are many . . from the sword's point falling,
And down from the mid blade!
                              Too rash Orestes!
Couldst thou not then have spared our wretched mother?
   Orestes. The Gods could not.
   Electra.   She was not theirs, Orestes!
   Orestes. And didst not thou . . .
   Electra.   'Twas I, 'twas I, who did it;
Of our unhappiest house the most unhappy!
Under this roof, by every God accurst,
There is no grief, there is no guilt, but mine.
   Orestes. Electra! no!
                              'Tis now my time to suffer. .
Mine be, with all its pangs, the righteous deed.

THE MADNESS OF ORESTES

ORESTES AND ELECTRA.

   Orestes. Heavy and murderous dreams, O my Electra,
Have dragged me from myself.
                              Is this Mycenai?
Are we . . . . . . are all who should be . . . . . . in our house?
Living? unhurt? our father here? our mother?
Why that deep gasp? for 'twas not sigh nor groan.
She then . . . . . . 'twas she who fell! when? how? beware!
No, no, speak out at once, that my full heart
May meet it, and may share with thee in all . .
 In all . . . but that one thing.
                              It was a dream.
We may share all.
                    They live: both live:
                                   O say it!
   Electra. The Gods have placed them from us, and there rolls
Between us that dark river . . . . .
   Orestes.   Blood! blood! blood!
I see it roll; I see the hand above it,
Imploring; I see *her.*
                    Hiss me not back
Ye snake-hair'd maids! I will look on; I will
Hear the words gurgle thro' that cursed stream,
And catch that hand . . that hand . . which slew my father!
It cannot be . . . . how could it slay my father?
Death to the slave who spoke it! . . . . slay my father!
It tost me up to him to earn a smile,

And was a smile then such a precious boon,
And royal state and proud affection nothing?
Ay, and thee too, Electra, she once taught
To take the sceptre from him at the door . .
Not the bath-door, not the bath-door, mind that! . .
And place it in the vestibule, against
The spear of Pallas, where it used to stand.
Where is it now? methinks I missed it there.
How we have trembled to be seen to move it!
Both looking up, lest that stern face should frown,
Which always gazed on Zeus right opposite.
Oh! could but one tear more fall from my eyes,
It would shake off those horrid visages,
And melt them into air.
                              I am not your's,
Fell Goddesses! A just and generous Power,
A bright-hair'd God, directed me.
                                          And thus
Abased is he whom such a God inspired!
                              (*After a pause.*)
Into whose kingdom went they? did they go
Together?
   Electra.   Oh! they were not long apart.
   Orestes. I know why thou art pale; I know whose head
Thy flowerlike hands have garlanded; I know
For whom thou hast unbraided all thy love.
He well deserves it . . . . . . he shall have it all.
Glory and love shall crown thee, my brave sister!
   Electra. I am not she of Sparta. Let me live
(If live I must, Orestes!) not unnamed
Nor named too often. Speak no more of love,
Ill-omen'd and opprobrious in this house . .
A mother should have had, a father had it,
O may a brother let it dwell with him,
Unchangeable, unquestioned, solitary,
Strengthened and hallowed in the depths of grief!
Gaze not so angrily . . I dare not see thee,
I dare not look where comfort should be found.
   Orestes. I dare and do behold them all day long,
And, were that face away so like my mother's,
I would advance and question and compell them . .
They hear me, and they know it.
   Electra.   Hear me too,
Ye mighty ones! to me invisible!
And spare him! spare him! for without the Gods
He wrought not what he wrought: And are not ye
Partakers of their counsels and their power?
O spare the son of him whom ye and they

Sent against Ilion, to perform your will
And bid the rulers of the earth be just.
   Orestes. And dare they frighten thee too? frighten thee!
And bend thee into prayer?
                         Off, hateful eyes!
Look upon me, not her.
                      Ay, thus, 'tis well.
Cheer, cheer thee, my Electra!
                    I am strong,
Stronger than ever . . steel, fire, adamant . .
But cannot bear thy brow upon my neck,
Cannot bear these wild writhings, these loud sobs,
By all the Gods! I think thou art half-mad . . . . . .
I must away . . . . . . follow me not . . . . . . stand there!

A SATIRE ON SATIRISTS, AND ADMONITION
TO DETRACTORS

PREFACE

IT is only our intimate friends who like us best when we write
well: the greater part of readers are complacent at imagining their
superiority as they discover our aberrations. Every ball we send
rolling before us is a stumble and strain to those who are impatient
of standing to catch us out at the wicket. Such as cannot find
employment in mischievous actions, look for consolation in mis-
chievous thoughts, and solicit, and seldom fail in obtaining, a fit
audience, and not few, to applaud them.

The Preface is growing too long for the Work, but the reader
will find that it is not inappropriate.

> FOR eaters of goose-liver there is drest
> This part alone; the cats divide the rest;
> The fire that plumps it, leaves the creature dry,
> So too with poets does the poetry;
> This is their liver, trufled, tender, sweet,
> And all beside is sad unchristian meat.[1]
>
> Let thou the Muse's spangled tissue play
> About thy head and bosom, night and day,
> But throw the bone 'twas workt upon, away.
>
> Thinly by Nature is our honey spread   10
> On very coarse and very bitter bread.

---

[1] *And all beside is sad unchristian meat.*—He who could partake of such an abomin-
able luxury, knowing its process, ought not even to be buried where men are
buried, but (in strict retributive justice) given to the kites and crows.

And from our corners we descry asquint
A prettier book than ours, a sharper print;
And in this school-room call the cleverest lad
If sober, stupid, and if fiery, mad.

   Who in hard stems and clotted leaves would rout,
When the whole essence he may have without?
Who to the husks of poets would sit down,
When Murray sells the kernels for a crown?
Grant me, propitious Fate! to meet our best   20
Only on Pindus, and in heaven the rest;
Leaving, to walk beside me while I stay,
The kind companion of an earlier day,
Whom genius, virtue, manly grief, endear,
And bonds draw closer every circling year.

   In fashionable squares and new-built streets
Suburban Muses take their several beats;
And whoso passes their select purlieus
Is thief or strumpet, anything but Muse.
Sooner shall Tuscan Vallombrosa lack wood   30
Than Britain Grub-street, Billingsgate, and Blackwood.
Slave-merchants, scalpers, cannibals, agree . . .
In *Letter-land* no brotherhood must be.
If there were living upon earth but twain,
One would be Abel and the other Cain.
Here, be our cause the wrong one or the right,
Better to pay than play, to run than fight.
Foul are the boxers, seconds, ring, and green . . .
And we wear gloves, and much prefer the clean.
The strife of letters will allow no peace,   40
No *Truce of God*, no sabbath's armistice.
'Down with your money! down with it, newcomer!
'And rise Sir Sotheby,[1] and stand by Homer.
'O'er Pope, o'er Cowper, lift thy licensed head,
'Beat all the living, challenge all the dead.
'He who refuses us our fare, forgets
'Our junction-magazines and branch-gazettes;
'Our rail-ways running into every town,
'And our facilities for *setting down*.
'Precaution taken, each may find his friend,   50
'Who makes the limberest thread-case stand on end.
'Few are the authors here with lives uncharm'd,
'And thinnest ghosts march through their moonlight, arm'd.'

---

[1] Who can account for the eulogies of Blackwood on Sotheby's Homer, as compared with Pope's and Cowper's? Eulogy is not reported to be the side he lies upon, in general.

There never squatted a more sordid brood
Beneath the battlements of Holyrood,
Than that which now across the clotted perch
Crookens the claw and screams for court and church.
What is the church to them? or what the court?
Think ye they care one grain of millet for't?
But they have ken'd the swell of looser crop,   60
And round about the midden hop and hop.
The field they would have flown into, is clear,
Pickt every horse-fall, empty every ear.

To such the trembling verse-boy brings his task,
Of such the one-spurr'd critick begs to ask,
Hath Sheffield's glorious son[1] the genuine vein?
Did *Paracelsus*[2] spring from poet's brain?
When all expect it, *yes* will never do,
The cautious and the business-like say *no*.
Criticks and maidens should not smile too fast;   70
A *yes*, though drawl'd out faintly, comes at last.

Well; you have seen our Prosperos, at whose beck
Our ship, with all her royalty, is wreck.
From sire to son descends the wizard book
That works such marvels.
      Look behind you! look!
There issue from the Treasury, dull and dry as
The leaves in winter, Gifford and Matthias.
Brighter and braver Peter Pindar started,
And ranged around him all the lighter-hearted.
When Peter Pindar sank into decline,   80
Him W . . son followed, of congenial quill,
As near the dirt,[3] and no less prone to ill.

[1] The *Corn-law Rhymer*, as he condescends to style himself, has written sonnets, which may be ranked among the noblest in our language.

[2] *Paracelsus* has found a critick capable of appreciating him. It is not often that the generous are so judicious, nor always that the judicious are so generous.

[3] '*As near the dirt*,' &c.—The professor, if not Horatian in his art, is perfectly so in his opinion, exprest by the poet in the verse—'Nec latuit malè qui vivens moriensque fefellit.'
> He surely is as wise as any
> Who cheats the world and turns the penny;
> And if he does it all life thro
> 'Tis more than most wise men can do.

It must be acknowledged that some commentators have given the passage a different interpretation.

The learned professor is an important contributor to Blackwood, especially in those graces of delicate wit so attractive to his subscribers. Nevertheless, Lord Byron, who was not quite susceptible of it, declared that 'a gentleman could not write in Blackwood'. Has this assertion been ever disproved by experiment? If a gentleman could not write in it, why should a gentleman be accused of reading it? Could anything be more unjust or affronting?

Walcot, of English heart, had English pen,
Buffoon he might be, but for hire was none;
Nor, plumed and mounted on Professor's chair,
Offer'd to grin for wagers at a fair.
Who would not join the joke when hands like these
Lead proudly forward Alcibiades,
Train'd up to fashion by the Nymphs of Leith,   90
And whiffing his cigar through cheesy teeth.

Honester men and wiser, you will say,
Were satirists,
            Unhurt? for spite? for pay?
Their courteous soldiership, outshining ours,
Mounted the engine, and took aim from tow'rs.
From putrid ditches we more safely fight,
And push our zig-zag parallels by night.
Dryden's rich numbers rattle terse and round,
Profuse, and nothing *plattery* in the sound.
And, here almost his equal, if but here,   100
Pope pleas'd alike the playful and severe.
The slimmer cur at growler Johnson snarls,
But cowers beneath his bugle-blast for Charles.[1]
From *Vanity* and *London* far removed,[2]
With that pure Spirit his pure spirit loved,
In thorny paths the pensive Cowper trod,
But angels prompted, and the word was God.

Churchmen have chaunted satire, and the pews
Heard good sound doctrine from the sable Muse.
Frost-bitten, and lumbaginous, when Donne,   110
With verses gnarl'd and knotted, hobbled on,
Thro listening palaces did rhymeless South
Pour sparkling waters from his golden mouth.
Prim, in spruce party-colours Mason shone,
His Muse lookt well in gall-dyed crape alone.

[1] Many have ridiculed, and with no little justice, the pompous diction of Johnson on ordinary occasions; and some have attempted to depreciate his imitations of Juvenal. But among our clippers and sweaters of sterling coin, not one will ever write such vigorous verses as those on Charles the Twelfth, or such vigorous prose as the Lives of Savage and Dryden.

[2] Wide indeed is the difference between the manner of Cowper and Johnson. Cowper is often witty, light, and playful; Johnson never. Neither he nor Juvenal are to be called satirists, but acute rhetoricians and animated declaimers. Although it cannot be said of Satire,
            'Renidet usquequaque,'
yet the smile is habitual to her countenance. If her laces are now and then loosened, it is not that she may give vent to her anger, energy to her action, or display and grandiloquence to her moral sentences. She has little to do with Philosophy, less with Rhetorick, and nothing with the Furies.

Beneath the starry sky, mid garden glooms,
In meditation deep, and dense perfumes,
Young's cassock was flounced round with plaintive pun . . .
And pithier Churchill swore he would have none.
He bared his own broad vices, but the knots   120
Of the loud scourge fell sorest upon Scots.
Yet, when the cassock he had thrown aside,
No better man his godless lips belied:
He pelted no shy poet thro' the streets,
No Lamb he vilified, he stabb'd no Keats:[1]
His cleanlier fingers in no combat close
To scratch the pimples[2] upon Hazlit's nose:
Hunt's Cold-bath-field may bloom with bowers, for him,
And Coleridge[3] may be sound in wind and limb.
On bell-hung drays all coarser parcels find   130
The way to Blackwood; rings, and records kind,
A thoughtless book-keeper detains behind.

---

[1] Lamb, Keats, Hazlit, Coleridge, all in short who, recently dead, are now dividing amongst them the admiration of their country, were turned into ridicule by the worthy men employed by Mr. Blackwood. Whatever could lessen their estimation, whatever could injure their fortune, whatever could make their poverty more bitter, whatever could cast them down from their aspirations after fame, and whatever had a tendency to drive them into the grave, which now has opened to them, was incessantly brought into action against them by these zealots for our religion and laws. A more deliberate, a more torturing murder never was committed, than the murder of Keats; a young man adorned, it is said by those who knew him intimately, with everything graceful, generous, and manly. I have seen those thoughtful and melancholy at the mention of him, whom I never have seen so on any other occasion; and it was many years after his decease. The chief perpetrator of his murder knew beforehand he could not be hanged for it, and was occupying a station whence he might be called by his faction to hang others far less guilty. While he was rising to the highest rank in the profession and in the state, his victim sank under him, in long agonies, to an untimely grave. When men strike at genius, they strike at the face of God in the only way wherein he ever manifests it to them.

[2] '*To scratch the pimples upon Hazlit's nose*, &c.'—Ridicule of these, together with a compendious list of similar vulgarities, is now lying before me. The author to whom I am indebted for the extracts, and for nearly all I ever knew or heard of the writers, is about to publish as much as suits his undertaking, in a *Life of Keats*. Such an exposure of impudence and falsehood is not likely to injure the character of the Magazine, or diminish the number of its subscribers. To those who are habituated to the ginshop the dram is sustenance, and they feel themselves both uncomfortable and empty without the hot excitement. Blackwood's is really a gin-palace.

[3] The worst that can be said against Coleridge in his literary character, with which alone we have anything to do, is that he spoke as the poet says the lover loved,

     'Not wisely, but too well,'
spouting forth whatever was shining, fit or unfit.

He was fond of beating his breast against the close-wired cage of Metaphysics, where he could only show how delicately his wings were formed, and how beautiful were the feathers he shedd at every effort.

The *Gentleman's*, the *Lady's*, we have seen,
Now blusters forth the *Blackguard's Magazine*:
And (Heaven from joint-stock companies protect us!)
Dustman and nightman issue their *Prospectus*.
If, as we pass, a splash is all we feel,
Thanks to the blue brigade enroll'd by Peel.
While from the south such knaves are carted forth,
Gildons and Curls stil flourish in the north;   140
And others, baser in degree and mind,
Tenant the outhouse Burke with life resign'd.
See the shrewd curriers, knife in mouth, deride
Now the flay'd victim, now the price divide . .
No; rather see, while Satyrs dance around,
Yon little man with vine and ivy crown'd,
Raising his easy arm, secure to hit
¹The scope of pleasure with the shafts of wit.

Satire! I never call'd thee very fair,
But if thou art inclined to hear my pray'r,   150
Grant the bright surface that our form reflects,
The healthy font that braces our defects:
But O! to fulminate with forked line
Another's fame or fortune, ne'er be mine!
Against the wretch who dares it, high or low,
Against him only, I direct my blow.

When Byron by the borderers was assail'd,
Tho Byron then was only silken-mail'd,
The squad of Brougham and Jeffrey fared but ill,
And on the lordling's split the lawyer's quill.   160
This chief came smirking onward, that lookt arch,
But both retreated to the old *Rogue's March*:
And if, with broken head and bagpipe lost,
It should be stil the tune they like the most,
There is a reason, were it safe to tell . . .
Some who fight poorly, plunder pretty well.
Byron was not *all* Byron; one small part
Bore the impression of a human heart.
Guided by no clear love-star's panting light

¹ Nothing can be lighter or pleasanter or more brilliant. Pope, before he composed his verses to Lady M. W. Montague, forgot his sacrifice to the Graces. Dryden often neglected them; in our others we rarely find those exquisite touches which characterise the poet of Ireland. Prior is among the best, where he ridicules the platitudes of Boileau; the worst lyrick poet upon record, not excepting Pope, not excepting Addison. One would have imagined that Johnson had at his disposal the means of rendering justice to Prior, tho he never had enough about him to satisfy the demands of Milton, or even of Thompson and Collins.

Thro the sharp surges of a northern night,　　　　　　170
In Satire's narrow strait he swam the best,
Scattering the foam that hist about his breast.
He, who might else have been more tender, first
From Scottish saltness caught his rabid thirst.
Praise Keats . .
　　　　　'I think I've heard of him.'
　　　　　　　　　　　'With you
Shelley stands foremost.'
　　　　　　　. . And his lip was blue.
'I hear with pleasure any one commend
So good a soul; for Shelley is my friend.'
One leaf from Southey's laurel made explode
All his combustibles . .
　　　　　　　　'An ass! by God!'　　　　　　180
Who yet surmounted in romantick Spain
Highths our brisk courser never could attain.

　　I lagged; he call'd me; urgent to prolong
My matin chirpings into mellower song.
Mournfuller tones came then . . O ne'er be they
Drown'd in night howlings from the Forth and Spey!

　　Twice is almighty Homer far above
Troy and her towers, Olympus and his Jove.
First, when the God-led Priam bends before
Him sprung from Thetis, dark with Hector's gore:　　190
A second time, when both alike have bled,
And Agamemnon speaks among the dead.
Call'd up by Genius in an after-age,
That awful spectre shook the Athenian stage.
From eve to morn, from morn to parting night,
Father and daughter stood before my sight.
I felt the looks they gave, the words they said,
And reconducted each serener shade.
Ever shall these to me be well-spent days,
Sweet fell the tears upon them, sweet the praise.　　200
Far from the footstool of the tragick throne,
I am tragedian in this scene alone.
Station the Greek and Briton side by side,[1]
And, if derision is deserv'd, deride.

[1] *'Station the Greek and Briton side by side.'* Surely there can be no fairer method of overturning an offensive reputation, from which the scaffolding is not yet taken down, than by placing against it the best passages, and most nearly parallel in the subject, from Eschylus and Sophocles. To this labour the whole body of Scotch critics and poets are hereby invited, and moreover to add the ornaments of translation.

Shew me a genuine poet[1] of our times
Unwrung with strictures or ungall'd with rhymes.
The strong are rowell'd, while the dull stand still,
And those who feed on thistles feed their fill.

On our wide downs there have been, and there are,
Such as indignant Justice should not spare.   210
Under my wrist ne'er shall her whip be crackt
Where poet leaves a poet's fame intact.
When from their rocks and mountains they descend
To tear the stranger or to pluck the friend,
I spring between them and their hoped-for-prey
And whoop them from the fiendish feast away.
Come, if you hate tame vultures, if you shun
The hencoop daws that never see the sun,
Come into purer air, where lake and hill
With wholesome breath the heaving bosom fill.   220
Whom seek we there? alas! we seek in vain
The gentle breast amid the gentle strain.

Ion may knock where Self hath most to do,
Knock at the freshman's in his first Review,
At under-secretary Stanley's too . .
Ion came forth, the generous, brave, and wise,
And tears stood tingling in unwonted eyes.
The proud policeman strain'd each harden'd ball
Round as a fishes, lest a drop should fall.
The exciseman from Gravesend, the steamer's clerk,   230
The usurer, the bencher, cried out '*Hark!*'
Dundas had fear'd his brazen brow might melt,
Pitt almost fainted, Melbourne almost felt . .
Amid the mighty storm that swell'd around,
Wordsworth was calm, and bravely stood his ground.
No more on daisies and on pilewort fed,
By weary Duddon's ever tumbled bed,
The Grasmere cuckoo leaves those sylvan scenes,
And, percht on shovel hats and dandy deans,
And prickt with spicy cheer, at Philpot's nod   240
Devoutly fathers Slaughter upon God.
Might we not wish some wiser seer had said
Where lurks the mother of that hopeful maid?

Now Wordsworth! lest we never meet again,
Write, on the prose-side tablet of thy brain,
A worldly counsel to a worldly mind,
And grow less captious if thou grow less kind.

[1] It appears to be at Edinburgh as I remember it was at Oxford. The bargemen usually made choice of some well-drest gownsman for their attacks: scouts and servitors went *scot-free*: to quarrel with them did not answer.

94

Leave Moore, sad torturer of the virgin breast,
One lyre for beauty, one for the opprest:
Leave Campbell Wyoming's deserted farms   250
And Hohenlinden's trumpet-tongued alarms.
Permit us to be pleas'd, or even to please,
And try at other strains than such as these . . .

   'I do assert it boldly, 'tis a shame
'To honor Dryden with a poet's name.
'What in the name of goodness can we hope
'When criticks praise the tinkling tin of Pope?
'They are, no doubt, exceedingly good men,
'Pity, they flirt so flippant with the pen!
'In Scott there is, we must admit, one line   260
'Far better than the rest, and almost fine.
'Hear what I wrote upon the subject! now!
'This is the way to write, you will allow.
'As for your Germans, petty pismire hosts,
'Nathans, Iphigeneias, Meisters, Fausts,
'Any two stanzas here are worth 'em all . .
'So let your Privy Council give the wall.
'Göethe may be a baron or a graf,
'Call him a poet, and you make me laugh:
'Either my judgement is entirely lost or   270
'Never was there so cursed an impostor.'[1]
Peace to the soother of Orestes! peace
To the first Spirit that awoke on Greece!
Spare even Byron, who spared none himself,
And lay him gently on the lady's shelf.
Ah surely 'tis enough if Lamartine
Sticks his crisp winter-cabbage ever-green
To those gilt bays! and Chateaubriant's sand,[2]
Hot, sterile, gusty, sweeps that slimy land;
The land of squashy fruits, in puddles set,   280
The land of poppies and of minionette,
But massier things and loftier here and there
Surprise us . . losing base and point in air.

[1] *'Impostor'* was the expression.
  Two thousand years and more had elapsed, and nothing like the pure Grecian had appeared in the world until the *Iphigeneia* of Goethe, excepting a few verses of Catullus and Horace. We English had indeed somewhat more than an equivalent in Shakespeare and Milton; the Italians in Dante, but the *Iphigeneia* is fairly worth all the poetry of the Continent since the *Divina Commedia*.

  [2] *'Chateaubriant's sand.'*—Whenever we enter into another treaty with France, let a clause be inserted against the reduction of English poetry to French. Our occasional laugh, however hearty, is a poor compensation to the unhappy poets in *hot water*.
  The most racy of the French is now living in the midst of them, Beranger: otherwise, for purity, simplicity, and pathos, they must turn over two whole centuries, full of mummies in periwigs, distortions, and distillations.

Tho' Southey's poetry to thee should seem
Not worth five shillings (such thy phrase) the ream,
Courage! good wary Wordsworth! and disburse
The whole amount from that prudential purse.
Here, take my word, 'tis neither shame nor sin
To venture boldly, all thy own thrown in,
With purest incense to the Eternal Mind   290
That spacious urn, his heart, lights half mankind.
Batter it, bruize it, blacken it at will,
It hath its weight and precious substance still.
We, who love order, yield our betters place
With duteous zeal, and, if we can, with grace.
Roderick, Kehama, Thalaba, belong
To mightier movers of majestick song.
To such as these we give, by just controul,
Not our five shillings, but our heart and soul.
Try what it is to pierce the mails of men   300
In their proud moods . . kings, patriots, heroes . . then
Back wilt thou run as if on Kalgarth-flat
A shower had caught thee in thy Sunday hat.
Are there no duodecimos of mind
Stitcht to tear up? wherein 'tis hard to find
One happy fancy, one affection kind.
Why every author on thy hearthstone burn?
Why every neighbour twitcht and shov'd in turn?
Rather than thus eternally cry *hang 'em*,
I'd almost praise the workmanship of Wrangham.   310
But, O true poet of the country! why
With goatskin glove an ancient friend defy?
Should Gifford lead thee? should Matthias? they
Were only fit to flap the flies away,
Leave 'em their night, for they have had their day.
What would they give to drive a Collins wild,
Or taunt a Spenser on his burning child!
What would they give to drag a Milton back
From heaven, or cord a Shakspeare to the rack.
These, and their corporal Canning, are forgotten,   320
Since fruits soon perish when the core is rotten.
Throw, throw the marching-guinea back, 'tis solely
For poets under standard highth, like Croly.
Alas! to strike with little chance to hit
Proves how much longer-winded wrath than wit.
The frequent stroke, the plunge, the puffing, show
A hapless swimmer going fast below.
Verses (and thine are such) undoom'd to die,
From gentle thoughts should raise the willing sigh.
If youth had starts of jealousy, let age   330
Rest with composure on another's page.

Take by the hand the timid, rear the young,
Shun the malignant, and respect the strong.
Censure's coarse bar, corroded, crusts away,
And the unwasted captive starts on day.
Another date hath Praise's golden key.
With that alone men reach Eternity.
He who hath lent it, tho' awhile he wait,
Yet Genius shall restore it at the gate.
Think timely, for our coming years are few,   340
Their worst diseases mortals may subdue;
Which, if they grow around the loftier mind,
Death, when ourselves are gathered, leaves behind.
Our frowardness, our malice, our distrust,
Cling to our name and sink not with our dust.
Like prince and pauper in our flesh and blood,
Perish like them we cannot, if we wou'd.
Is not our sofa softer when one end
Sinks to the welcome pressure of a friend?
If he hath rais'd us in our low estate,   350
Are we not happier when they call him great?
Some who sate round us while the grass was green
Fear the chill air and quit the duller scene:
Some, unreturning, thro' our doors have past,
And haply we may live to see the last.

END

ESPOUSALS OF H.M. OF PORTUGAL

YOUNGSTER of Coburg! thou hast found a throne
Easy to mount, and easier to slip down:
But, in the name of wonder! who beside
Of mortal men could mount thy royal bride?
So vast an enterprize requires the force
And ladder too that scaled the Trojan horse,
In whose rank orifice some hundreds hid
Themselves and arms, and down the rampire slid.
Thou hast achieved a mightier deed and bolder,
And hast not dislocated hip or shoulder.

FAREWELL TO ITALY

I LEAVE thee, beauteous Italy! no more
From the high terraces, at even-tide,
To look supine into thy depths of sky,
Thy golden moon between the cliff and me,
Or thy dark spires of fretted cypresses

Bordering the channel of the milky-way.
Fiesole and Valdarno must be dreams
Hereafter, and my own lost Affrico
Murmur to me but in the poet's song.
I did believe, (what have I not believed?)
Weary with age, but unopprest by pain,
To close in thy soft clime my quiet day,
And rest my bones in the Mimosa's shade.
Hope! Hope! few ever cherisht thee so little;
Few are the heads thou hast so rarely raised;
But thou didst promise this, and all was well.
For we are fond of thinking where to lie
When every pulse hath ceast, when the lone heart
Can lift no aspiration . . . reasoning
As if the sight were unimpaired by death,—
Were unobstructed by the coffin-lid,
And the sun cheered corruption!
                                        Over all
The smiles of Nature shed a potent charm,
And light us to our chamber at the grave.

[HIS BIRTHDAY]

THE day returns, my natal day,
    Borne on the storm and pale with snow,
And seems to ask me why I stay,
    Stricken by Time and bowed by Woe.

Many were once the friends who came
    To wish me joy; and there are some
Who wish it now; but not the same;
    They are whence friend can never come;

Nor are they you my love watcht o'er
    Cradled in innocence and sleep;
You smile into my eyes no more,
    Nor see the bitter tears they weep.

EPITAPH [ON FRANCIS I, EMPEROR OF AUSTRIA]

So then at last the emperor Franz,
On spindle shanks hath joined Death's dance.
Prythee, good Saint Nepomucene,
Push the pale wretch behind the screen;—
For if your Master's Son should know,

He'd kick him to the gulph below:
Then would the Devil rave and rant,
That Hell has more than Hell can want
Of such exceedingly good men,
And fork him to you back agen.

TRELAWNY

It is not every traveler
Who like Trelawny can aver
In every State he left behind
An image the Nine Months may find.

Considerate, he perceived the need
Of some improvement in the breed,
And set as heartily to work
As when he fought against the Turk.

THE PILGRIM'S SHELL

Under a tuft of eglantine, at noon,
I saw a pilgrim loosen his broad shell
To catch the water off a stony tongue;
Medusa's it might be, or Pan's, erewhile,
For the huge head was shapeless, eaten out
By time and tempest here, and here embost
With clasping tangles of dark maidenhair.

'How happy is thy thirst! how soon assuaged!
How sweet that coldest water this hot day!'
Whispered my thoughts; not having yet observ'd
His shell so shallow and so chipt around.
Tall though he was, he held it higher, to meet
The sparkler at its outset: with fresh leap,
Vigorous as one just free upon the world,
Impetuous too as one first checkt, with stamp
Heavy as ten such sparklers might be deemed,
Rusht it amain, from cavity and rim
And rim's divergent channels, and dropt thick
(Issuing at wrist and elbow) on the grass.
The pilgrim shook his head, and fixing up
His scallop,
            'There is something yet,' said he,
'Too scanty in this world for my desires!'

TO MY CHILD CARLINO

CARLINO! what art thou about, my boy?
Often I ask that question, though in vain;
For we are far apart: ah! therefore 'tis
I often ask it; not in such a tone
As wiser fathers do, who know too well.
Were we not children, you and I together?
Stole we not glances from each other's eyes?
Swore we not secrecy in such misdeeds?
Well could we trust each other. Tell me, then,
What thou art doing. Carving out thy name,
Or haply mine, upon my favourite seat,
With the new knife I sent thee over-sea?
Or hast thou broken it, and hid the hilt
Among the myrtles, starr'd with flowers, behind?
Or under that high throne whence fifty lilies
(With sworded tuberoses dense around)
Lift up their heads at once . . . not without fear
That they were looking at thee all the while?
    Does Cincirillo follow thee about?
Inverting one swart foot suspensively,
And wagging his dread jaw, at every chirp
Of bird above him on the olive-branch?
Frighten him then away! 'twas he who slew
Our pigeons, our white pigeons, peacock-tailed,
That fear'd not you and me . . . alas, nor him!
I flattened his striped sides along my knee,
And reasoned with him on his bloody mind,
Till he looked blandly, and half-closed his eyes
To ponder on my lecture in the shade.
I doubt his memory much, his heart a little,
And in some minor matters (may I say it?)
Could wish him rather sager. But from thee
God hold back wisdom yet for many years!
Whether in early season or in late
It always comes high priced. For thy pure breast
I have no lesson; it for me has many.
Come, throw it open then! What sports, what cares
(Since there are none too young for these) engage
Thy busy thoughts? Are you again at work,
Walter and you, with those sly labourers,
Geppo, Giovanni, Cecco, and Poeta,
To build more solidly your broken dam
Among the poplars, whence the nightingale
Inquisitively watched you all day long?
I was not of your council in the scheme,
Or might have saved you silver without end,

And sighs too without number. Art thou gone
Below the mulberry, where that cold pool
Urged to devise a warmer, and more fit
For mighty swimmers, swimming three abreast?
Or art thou panting in this summer noon
Upon the lowest step before the hall,
Drawing a slice of watermelon, long
As Cupid's bow, athwart thy wetted lips
(Like one who plays Pan's pipe) and letting drop
The sable seeds from all their separate cells,
And leaving bays profound and rocks abrupt,
Redder than coral round Calypso's cave?

ESSEX AND BACON

[Robert Devereux, Earl of Essex, beheaded February 25, 1601.
Francis Bacon.]

Essex. I did believe, sir, I had helpt to raise
Many to wealth and station, some to fame,
And one to friendship.
    Bacon.   You, my noble earl,
Have done it; and much more. We must lament
A power thus past (or rather thrown) away.
    Essex. Thou? thou lament it, Bacon?
    Bacon.   To my soul.
    Essex. Why then, with energy beyond the pitch
Of brawling law, cry vengeance? when my fortune
Was pierced with every bolt from every hand,
Soon as the golden links were snapt asunder
Which those who rule the earth held round that bird
Who bore their lightnings and struck down their foes.
    Bacon. My gracious lord! were always their commands
Well waited for?
    Essex.   Nay, by my troth, my zeal
Outflew them.
    Bacon.   Your return was unadvised.
    Essex. Unwelcome: that is worse.
    Bacon.   The worst of all
Was summoning to arms a loyal land,
Basking in peace and plenteousness.
    Essex.   How far
Extended this your basking? court indeed
And inns of law were warm enough; on those
The sun beats all the day, through all the year;
Everything there so still and orderly,
That he who sneezes in them is caught up
And cudgell'd for his pains.

Bacon.   Should he awake
Trumpets by sneezing, should he blow up banners,
'Twere well if only cudgels fell on him:
Our laws have sharper instruments, my lord!
　Essex. I know it; and I knew it ere I rose.
　Bacon. O! had this never happened!
　Essex.   Then wouldst thou
Have lost some smiles, some parlyings, some tags
Of ermine, and, what more thou valuest
(As any wise man would) some little gold.
　Bacon. Dross!
　Essex (smiling). Very true! . . as men are dust and ashes.
　Bacon. Such thoughts become all mortals; most of all
Those who have fallen under high displeasure,
Who have their God and Prince to reconcile,
And are about to change this brief vile life . . .
Nay, nay, my lord! your life may rest unchanged
For years to come, if you, upon your knees,
Humbly ask pardon . .
　Essex (fiercely).   Pardon!
　　　　　(*After hesitation.*) I will ask it . .
　Bacon. . . Before the privy council, and the court
Especially assembled.
　Essex (indignantly).   Not before
The best among them, were he quite alone,
No, by the soul of Essex! were he Raleigh . .
The only great man there.
　Bacon.   Are we so scorned?
　Essex. Bacon! I did not say the only wise one:
So, do not break thy ring, or loose the stone.
　Bacon. My lord! my finger might have been uneasy
Without such notice from that once high peer
Erewhile the Earl of Essex . . until treason
Leveled him lower than burgess or than churl.
　Essex. I will not say thou liest; for thy tongue
Lags far behind thy heart; thy strongest wit
May stretch and strain, but never make them yoke-mates.
　Bacon. This cork appliance, this hard breathing, served
While there was water under for support,
But cut a dismal figure in the mud.
　Essex. To servile souls how abject seem the fallen!
Benchers and message-bearers stride o'er Essex!
　Bacon. Unmasted pinnace may row safely under
No high colossus, without pricking it.
But, sure, the valiant Earl is somewhat chafed . .
Who could have thought it! . . by a worm like me!
　Essex. Begone! I have fairly weighed thee.
　Bacon (alone.)   He weigh me!

No man is stout enough[1] to trim the balance,
Much less to throw the weight in . .
                                        He weigh me!
Flaunting and brittle as a honeysuckle,
Sweet in the chamber, in the field blown down,
Ramping in vain to reach again its prop,
And crusht by the first footfall.
                                        Arrogance
Stares, but sees badly . . snatches with quick gripe
What seems within the reach, and, being infirm
Of stand, is overbalanced.
                                        Shall I bear
Foul words upon me?
                                I have thrown them back
Manfully to the beard that wagged with them . .
My courage is now safe beyond suspicion . .
Myself can hardly doubt it after this . .
Yet that audacious criminal dared spit
Reproaches! seldom are they bearable,
But, springing up from reason, sting like asps . .
Not that the man has reason . . he has none . .
For, what had I to do with it? I spoke . .
And, when we are commanded, we must speak.
It was her Grace . . and surely she knows best.
I may now wash my hands of him at last,
I have but done my duty . . fall who may.

WALTER TYRREL AND WILLIAM RUFUS

[Scene: The New Forest, August 2, 1100.]

Rufus. Tyrrel, spur onward! we must not await
The laggard lords: when they have heard the dogs
I warrant they will follow fast enough,
Each for his haunch. Thy roan is mettlesome;
How the rogue sidles up to me, and claims
Acquaintance with young Yorkshire! not afraid
Of wrinkling lip, nor ear laid down like grass
By summer thunder shower on Windsor mead.

---

[1] Bacon little knew or suspected that there was then existing (the only one that ever did exist) his superior in intellectual power. Position gives magnitude. While the world was rolling above Shakespeare, he was seen imperfectly: when he rose above the world, it was discovered that he was greater than the world. The most honest of his contemporaries would scarcely have admitted this, even had they known it. But vast objects of remote altitude must be looked at a long while before they are ascertained. Ages are the telescope-tubes that must be lengthened out for Shakspeare; and generations of men serve but as single witnesses to his claims.

Tyrrel. Behold, my liege! hither they troop amain,
Over yon gap.
    Rufus.   Over my pales! the dolts
Have broken down my pales!
    Tyrrel.   Please you, my liege,
Unless they had, they must have ridden round
Eleven miles.
    Rufus.   Why not have ridden round
Eleven miles? or twenty, were there need.
By our Lady! they shall be our carpenters
And mend what they have marred. At any time
I can make fifty lords; but who can make
As many head of deer, if mine escape?
And sure they will, unless they too are mad.
Call me that bishop .. him with hunting-cap
Surcharged with cross, and scarlet above knee.
      Tyrrel (galloping forward). Ho! my lord bishop!
    Bishop.   Who calls me?
    Tyrrel.   Your slave.
    Bishop. Well said, if toned as well and timed as well.
Who art thou? citizen or hind? what wantest?
    Tyrrel. My lord! your presence; but before the king;
Where it may grow more placid at its leisure.
The morn is only streakt with red, my lord!
You beat her out and out: how prettily
You wear your stocking over head and ears!
Keep off the gorse and broom! they soon catch fire!
    Bishop. The king shall hear of this! I recognise
Sir Walter Tyrrel.
    Tyrrel.   And Sir Walter Tyrrel
By the same token duly recognises
The Church's well-begotten son, well-fed,
Well-mounted, and all well, except well-spoken,
The spiritual lord of Winchester.
    Bishop. Ay, by God's grace! pert losel!
    Tyrrel.   Prick along
Lord bishop! quicker! catch fresh air! we want it;
We have had foul enough till dinner-time.
    Bishop. Varlet! I may chastise this insolence.
    Tyrrel. I like those feathers: but there crows no cock
Without an answer. Though the noisiest throat
Sings from the bellfrey of snug Winchester,
Yet he from Westminster hath stouter spurs.
    Bishop. God's blood! were I no bishop. . .
    Tyrrel.   Then thy own
Were cooler.
    Bishop. Whip that hound aside! O Christ!

The beast has paw'd my housings! What a day
For dirt!
 Tyrrel. The scent lies well; pity no more
The housings; look, my lord! here trots the king!
 Rufus. Which of you broke my palings down?
 Bishop.   God knows,
Most gracious sir.
 Rufus.   No doubt he does; but you,
Bishop! could surely teach us what God knows.
Ride back and order some score handicrafts
To fix them in their places.
 Bishop.   The command
Of our most gracious king shall be obeyed.
(*Riding off.*) Malisons on the atheist! Who can tell
Where are my squires and other men! confused
Among the servitors of temporal lords!
I must e'en turn again and hail that brute.
Sir Walter! good Sir Walter! one half-word!
         [*Tyrrel rides toward him.*

Sir Walter! may I task your courtesy
To find me any of my followers!
 Tyrrel. Willingly.
 Rufus.   Stay with me; I want thee, Tyrrel!
What does the bishop boggle at?
 Tyrrel.   At nothing.
He seeks his people, to retrieve the damage.
 Rufus. Where are the lords?
 Tyrrel.   Gone past your Grace, bare-headed,
And falling in the rear.
 Rufus.   Well, prick them on.
I care but little for the chase to-day,
Although the scent lies sweetly. To knock down
My paling is vexatious. We must see
Our great improvements in this forest; what
Of roads blockt up, of hamlets swept away,
Of lurking dens called cottages, and cells,
And hermitages. Tyrrel! thou didst right
And dutifully, to remove the house
Of thy forefathers. 'Twas an odd request,
To leave the dovecote, for the sake of those
Flea-bitten blind old pigeons. There it stands!
But, in God's name! what mean these hives? the bees
May sting my dogs.
 Tyrrel.   They hunt not in the summer.
 Rufus. They may torment my fawns.
 Tyrrel.   Sir! not unless
Driven from their hives: they like the flowers much better.
 Rufus. Flowers! and leave flowers too?

Tyrrel.   Only some half-wild,
In tangled knots; balm, clary, marjoram.
    Rufus. What lies beyond this close briar hedge, that smells
Through the thick dew upon it, pleasantly?
    Tyrrel. A poor low cottage: the dry marl-pit shields it,
And, frail and unsupported like itself,
Peace-breathing honeysuckles comfort it
In its misfortunes.
    Rufus.   I am fain to laugh
At thy rank minstrelsy. A poor low cottage!
Only a poor low cottage! where, I ween,
A poor low maiden blesses Walter Tyrrel.
    Tyrrel. It may be so.
    Rufus.   No; it may not be so.
My orders were that all should be removed,
And, out of special favour, special trust
In thee, Sir Walter, I consigned the care
Into thy hands, of razing thy own house
And those about it; since thou hast another
Fairer and newer, and more lands around.
    Tyrrel. Hall, chapel, chamber, cellar, turret, grange,
Are level with the grass.
    Rufus.   What negligence
To leave the work then incomplete, when little
Was there remaining! Strip that roof, and start
Thy petty game from cover.
    Tyrrel.   O my liege!
Command not this!
    Rufus.   Make me no confidant
Of thy base loves.
    Tyrrel.   Nor you, my liege! nor any:
None such hath Walter Tyrrel.
    Rufus.   Thou 'rt at bay;
Thou hast forgotten thy avowal, man!
    Tyrrel. My father's house is (like my father) gone:
But in that house, and from that father's heart
Mine grew into his likeness, and held thence
Its rich possessions . . God forgive my boast!
He bade me help the needy, raise the low . .
    Rufus. And stand against thy king!
    Tyrrel.   How many yokes
Of oxen, from how many villages
For miles around, brought I, at my own charge,
To bear away the rafters and the beams
That were above my cradle at my birth,
And rang when I was christened, to the carouse
Of that glad father and his loyal friends!
    Rufus. He kept good cheer, they tell me.

Tyrrel.   Yonder thatch
Covers the worn-out woman at whose breast
I hung, an infant.
    Rufus.   Ay! and none beside?
    Tyrrel. Four sons have fallen in the wars.
    Rufus.   Brave dogs!
    Tyrrel. She hath none left.
    Rufus.   No daughter?
    Tyrrel.   One.
    Rufus.   I thought it.
Unkennel her.
    Tyrrel.   Grace! pity! mercy on her!
    Rufus. I will not have hot scents about my chase.
    Tyrrel. A virtuous daughter of a virtuous mother
Deserves not this, my liege!
    Rufus.   Am I to learn
What any subject at my hand deserves?
    Tyrrel. Happy, who dares to teach it and who can!
    Rufus. And thou, forsooth!
    Tyrrel.   I have done my duty, sire!
    Rufus. Not half: perform the rest, or bide my wrath.
    Tyrrel. What, break athwart my knee the staff of age!
    Rufus. Question me, villain!
    Tyrrel.   Villain I am none.
    Rufus. Retort my words! By all the saints! thou diest,
False traitor.
    Tyrrel.   Sire, no private wrong, no word
Spoken in angriness, no threat against
My life or honour, urge me . .
    Rufus.   Urge to what?
Dismountest?
    Tyrrel.   On my knees, as best beseems,
I ask . . not pardon, sire! but spare, oh spare
The child devoted, the deserted mother!
    Rufus. Take her; take both.
    Tyrrel.   She loves her home; her limbs
Fail her; her husband sleeps in that churchyard;
Her youngest child, born many years the last,
Lies (not half-length) along the father's coffin.
Such separate love grows stronger in the stem
(I have heard say) than others close together,
And that, where pass these funerals, all life's spring
Vanishes from behind them, all the fruits
Of riper age are shrivelled, every sheaf
Husky; no gleaning left. She would die here,
Where from her bed she looks on his, no more
Able to rise, poor little soul! than he.
    Rufus. Who would disturb them, child or father? where

Is the churchyard thou speakest of?
  Tyrrel.   Among
Yon nettles: we have levelled all the graves.
  Rufus. Right: or our horses might have stumbled on them.
  Tyrrel. Your grace oft spares the guilty; spare the innocent!
  Rufus. Up from the dew! thy voice is hoarse already.
  Tyrrel. Yet God hath heard it. It entreats again,
Once more, once only; spare this wretched house.
  Rufus. No, nor thee neither.
  Tyrrel.   Speed me, God! and judge
O thou! between the oppressor and opprest!
                          [He pierces Rufus with an arrow.

THE PARENTS OF LUTHER

[Scene: Eisleben in Mansfeld, 1483.

CHARACTERS

John Luther and his wife Margaretta Zeigler.]

John Luther. I left thee, Margaretta, fast asleep,
Thou, who wert always earlier than myself,
Yet hast no mine to trudge to, hast no wedge
To sharpen at the forge, no pickaxe loose
In handle.
            Come, blush not again: thy cheeks
May now shake off those blossoms which they bore
So thick this morning, that last night's avowal
Nestles among them stil.
                So, in few months
A noisier bird partakes our whispering bower.
Say it again.
  Margaretta. And, in my dream, I blushed!
  John. Idler! wert dreaming too? and after dawn?
  Margaretta. In truth was I.
  John.   Of me?
  Margaretta.   No, not of you.
  John. No matter; for methinks some Seraph's wing
Fann'd that bright countenance.
  Margaretta.   Methinks it did,
And stir'd my soul within.
               How could you go
And never say good-bye, and give no kiss?
  John. It might have waken'd thee. I can give more
Kisses than sleep: so thinking, I heav'd up
Slowly my elbow from above the pillow,
And, when I saw it woke thee not, went forth.

Margaretta. I would have been awaken'd for a kiss,
And a good-bye, or either, if not both.
 John. Thy dreams were not worth much then.
 Margaretta.   Few dreams are;
But . . . . .
 John. By my troth! I will intrench upon
The woman's dowry, and will contradict,
Tho' I should never contradict again.
I have got more from dreams a hundred-fold
Than all the solid earth, than field, than town,
Than (the close niggard purse that cramps my fist)
The mine will ever bring me.
 Margaretta.   So have I,
And so shall each indeed, if this be true.
 John. What was it then? for when good dreams befall
The true of heart, 'tis likely they come true . .
A vein of gold? ay? silver? copper? iron?
Lead? sulphur? alum? alabaster? coal?
Shake not those ringlets nor let down those eyes,
Tho' they look prettier for it, but speak out.
True, these are not thy dainties.
 Margaretta.   Guess again.
 John. Crystalline kitchens, amber-basted spits
Whizzing with frothy savory salamanders,
And swans that might, so plump and pleasant-looking,
Swim in the water from the mouths of knights;
And ostrich-eggs off coral woods (the nests
Outside of cinnamon, inside of saffron,
And mortar'd well, for safety-sake, with myrrh,)
Serv'd up in fern leaves green before the Flood?
 Margaretta. Stuff! you will never guess it, I am sure.
 John. No? and yet these are well worth dreaming of.
 Margaretta. Try once again.
 John.   Faith! it is kind to let me.
Under-ground beer-cascades from Nuremberg?
Rhine vintage stealing from Electoral cellars,
And, broader than sea-baths for mermaid brides,
With fluits upon the surface strides across,
Pink conchs, to catch it, and to light it down;
And music from basaltic organ-pipes
For dancing; and five fairies to one man.
 Margaretta. Oh his wild fancies! . . . Are they innocent?
 John. I think I must be near it by that shrug.
Spicy sack-posset, roaring from hot springs
And running off like mad thro' candied cliffs,
But catching now and then some fruit that drops . . . . . .
Shake thy head yet? why then thou hast the palsy.
Zooks! I have thought of all things probable

And come to my wit's end.
                       What canst thou mean?
   Margaretta. Nay, I have half a mind now not to tell.
   John. Then it is out . . . Thy whole one ill could hold it.
A woman's mind hates pitch upon its seams.
   Margaretta. Hush! one word more! and then my lips are closed.
   John. Pish! one more word! and then my lips . . .
   Margaretta.   O rare
Impudent man! . . . and such discourse from you!
I dreamt we had a boy . . .
   John.   A wench, a wench . . . .
A boy were not like thee.
   Margaretta.   I said a boy.
   John. Well, let us have him, if we miss the girl.
   Margaretta. My father told me he *must* have a boy,
And call him Martin (his own name) because
Saint Martin both was brave and cloth'd the poor.
   John. Hurrah then for Saint Martin! he shall have
Enough to work on in this house of ours.
   Margaretta. Now do not laugh, dear husband! but this dream
Seem'd somewhat more.
   John.   So do all dreams, ere past.
   Margaretta. Well, but it seems so stil.
   John.   Aye, twist my fingers,
Basketing them to hold it.
   Margaretta.   Never grave!
   John. I shall be.
   Margaretta.   That one thought should make you now.
   John. And that one tap upon the cheek to boot.
   Margaretta. I do believe, if you were call'd to Heaven
You would stay toying here.
   John.   I doubt I should.
Methinks I set my back against the gate,
Thrown open to me by this rosy hand,
And look both ways, but see more heaven than earth:
Give me thy dream: thou puttest it aside:
I must be feasted: fetch it forth at once.
   Margaretta. Husband! I dreamt the child was in my arms,
And held a sword, which from its little grasp
I could not move, nor you: I dreamt that proud
But tottering shapes, in purple filagree,
Pull'd at it, and he laught.
   John.   They frighten'd thee!
   Margaretta. Frighten'd me! no: the infant's strength prevail'd.
Devils, with angel's faces, throng'd about;
Some offer'd flowers, and some held cups behind,
And some held daggers under silken stoles.
   John. These frighten'd thee, however.

Margaretta. He knew all;
I knew he did.
    John. A dream! a dream indeed!
He knew and laught!
    Margaretta. He sought his mother's breast,
And lookt at them no longer.
                    All the room
Was fill'd with light and gladness.
                      John. He shall be
Richer than we are; he shall mount his horse . .
A feat above his father; and be one
Of the duke's spearmen.
                Margaretta. God forbid! they lead
Unrighteous lives, and often fall untimely.
    John. A lion-hearted lad shall Martin be.
    Margaretta. God willing; if *his* servant; but not else.
I have such hopes, full hopes, hopes overflowing.
    John. A grave grand man, half collar and half cross,
With chain enough to hold our mastiff by,
Thou fain would'st have him. Out of dirt so stiff,
Old Satan fashioneth his idol, Pride.
    Margaretta. If proud and cruel to the weak, and bent
To turn all blessings from their even course
To his own kind and company, may he
Never be great, with collar, cross, and chain;
No, nor be ever angel, if, O God!
He be a fallen angel at the last.
                (After a pause.)
Uncle, you know, is sacristan; and uncle
Had once an uncle who was parish priest.
    John. He was the man who sung so merrily
Those verses which few scholars understand,
Yet which they cannot hide away, nor drive
The man from memory after forty years.
    Margaretta. (sings) *Our brightest pleasures are reflected pleasures,*
And they shine sweetest from the cottage-wall.
    John. The very same.
    Margaretta. We understand them, John!
    John. An inkling. But your uncle sacristan
Hath neither sword nor spur.
                Margaretta. It was a sword,
A flaming sword, but innocent, I saw;
And I have seen in pictures such as that,
And in the hands of angels borne on clouds.
He may defend our faith, drive out the Turk,
And quench the crescent in the Danaw stream.
    John. Thou, who begannest softly, singest now
Shrill as a throstle.

Margaretta.   Have we then no cause
To sing as throstles after sign thus strange?
　John. Because it was so strange, must we believe
The rather?
　Margaretta. Yes; no fire was in the house,
No splinter, not a spark: the virgin's chin
Shone not with rushlight under it; 'twas out,
For night was almost over, if not past,
And the Count's chapel has not half that blaze
On the Count's birth-day, nor the ball at night.
Ah surely, surely fare like our's sends up
No idle fumes; nor wish nor hope of mine
Fashion'd so bright a substance to a form
So beautiful . . . . There must be truth in it.
　John. There shall be then. Your uncle's sacristy
Shall hold the armour quite invisible,
Until our little Martin some fine day
Bursts the door open, spurr'd, caparison'd,
Dukes lead his bridle, princes tramp behind.
He may be pope . . . . who knows?
　Margaretta.   Are you in earnest?
But if he should be pope, will he love *us?*
Or let us (O yes sure he would!) love *him?*
Nor slink away, ashamed? Pope, no; not pope,
But bishop (ay?) he may be? There are few
Powerfuller folks than uncle Grimmermann.
Promise he scarce would give us, but a wink
Of hope he gave, to make a chorister.
　John. If thou wilt find materials, were his words.
　Margaretta. I did not mark the words; they were too light:
And yet he never breaks his troth.
　John.   Not he:
No, he would rather break his fast ten times.
Do not look seriously . . . . when church allows,
I mean; no more; six days a week; not seven.
I *have* seen houses where the Friday cheese
Was not (in *my* mind) cut with Thursday knife.
　Margaretta. O now for shame! such houses cannot stand.
Pr'ythee talk reason . . . . As the furnace-mouth
Shows only fire, so your's shows laughter only.
Choristers have been friars . . . . our's may be . . . .
And then a father abbot.
　John.   At one leap,
As salmon up Schaffhausen.
　Margaretta.   Just the same . . . .
Then . . . .
　John. Ring the bells! Martin is pope, by Jove!

[LOVE AND FATE]

FATE! I have askt few things of thee,
    And fewer have to ask.
Shortly, thou knowest, I shall be
    No more . . . then con thy task.

If one be left on earth so late
    Whose love is like the past,
Tell her, in whispers, gentle Fate,
    Not even love must last.

Tell her, I leave the noisy feast
    Of life, a little tired;
Amidst its pleasures few possest
    And many undesired.

Tell her, with steady pace to come
    And, where my laurels lie,
To throw the freshest on the tomb
    When it has caught her sigh.

Tell her, to stand some steps apart
    From others, on that day,
And check the tear (if tear should start)
    Too precious for dull clay.

HENRY THE EIGHTH AND ANNE BOLEYN

[*Scene, Tower of London*, May 18, 1536.

CHARACTERS

ANNE BOLEYN, SIR WILLIAM KINGSTON, Constable of the Tower.]

Anne Boleyn. Is your liege ill, sir, that you look so anxious?
Constable of the Tower. Madam!
Anne.   I would not ask what you may wish
To keep a secret from me; but indeed
This right, I think, is left me . . I would know
If my poor husband is quite well to-day.
Constable. Pardon me, gracious lady! what can prompt
To this inquiry?
Anne.   I have now *my* secret.
Constable. I must report all questions, sayings, doings,
Movements, and looks of yours. His Highness may
Be ruffled at this eagerness to ask
About his health.

Anne.   I am used to ask about it.
Beside, he may remember . . .
   Constable.   For your Highness
Gladly will I remind our sovran Lord
Of any promise.
   Anne.   Oh, no! do not that!
It would incense him: he made only one,
And Heaven alone that heard him must remind him!
Last night, I do suspect, but am not sure,
He scarcely was what kings and husbands should be.
A little wine has great effect upon
Warm hearts (and Henry's heart *was* very warm)
And upon strong resentments . . . I do fear
He has those too . . But all his friends must love him.
He may have past (poor Henry!) a bad night,
Thinking upon his hasty resolution.
   Constable. Lady! I grieve to tell you, worse than that . .
Far worse!
   Anne.   Oh, mercy, then! the child! the child!
Why not have told me of all this before?
What boots it to have been a guiltless wife,
When I, who should have thought the first about it,
Am an ill mother? Not to think of thee,
My darling! my Elizabeth! whose cradle
Rocks in my ear and almost crazes me.
Is she safe? Tell me, tell me, is she living?
   Constable. Safe, lady, and asleep in rosy health,
And radiant (if there yet be light enough
To shew it on her face) with pleasant dreams,
Such as young angels come on earth to play with.
   Anne. Were I but sure that I could dream of her
As I, until last autumn, oft have done,
Joyously, blithely, only waking up
Afraid of having hurt her by my arms
Too wildly in my rapture thrown around her,
I would lay down my weary head, and sleep,
Although the pillow be a little strange,
Nor like a bridal or a childbed pillow.
   Constable. Oh, spare those words!
   Anne.   Why spare them? when I feel
Departure from this world would never be
Departure from its joys: the joys of heaven
Would mingle with them scarcely with fresh sweetness.
   Constable (falling on his knees). My queen!
   Anne.   Arise, sir constable!
   Constable.   My queen!
Heaven's joys lie close before you.
   Anne.   And you weep?

Few days, I know, are left me; they will melt
All into one, all pure, all peaceable . .
No starts from slumber into bitter tears,
No struggles with sick hopes and wild desires,
No cruel father cutting down the tree
To crush the child that sits upon its boughs
And looks abroad . . too tender for suspicion,
Too happy even for hope, maker of happiness.
I could weep too, nor sinfully, at this.
    Thou knowest, O my God! thou surely knowest
'Tis no repining at thy call or will.
              (Constable, *on his knees, presents the Writ of Execution*.)
    I can do nothing now . . take back that writing,
And tell them so, poor souls! Say to the widow
I grieve, and can *but* grieve for her; persuade her
That children, although fatherless, are blessings;
And teach those little ones, if e'er you see them,
They are not half so badly off as some.
Fold up the paper . . put it quite aside . .
I am no queen; I have no almoner . .
Ah, now I weep indeed! Put, put it by.
Many . . I grieve (yet, *should* I grieve?) to think it,
Many will often say, when I am gone,
They once had a young queen to pity them.
Nay, though I mention'd I had nought to give,
Yet dash not on your head, nor grapple so
With those ungentle hands, while I am here,
A helpless widow's innocent petition.
Smoothe it; return it with all courtesy:
Smoothe it, I say again: frame some kind words
And see they find their place, then tender it
What! in this manner gentlemen of birth
Present us papers? turn they thus away,
Putting their palms between their eyes and us?
Sir! I was queen . . and you were kind unto me
When I was queen no longer . . why so changed?
Give it . . but what is now my signature?
Ignorant are you, or incredulous,
That not a clasp is left me? not a stone
The vilest; not chalcedony; not agate.
Promise her all my dresses, when . . no, no . .
I am grown superstitious; they might bring
Misfortune on her, having been Anne Boleyn's.
    Constable. Lady! I wish this scroll could suffocate
My voice. One order I must disobey,
To place it in your hand and mark you read it.
I lay it at your feet, craving your pardon
And God's, my lady!

Anne.   Rise up; give it me;
I know it ere I read it, but I read it
Because it is the king's, whom I have sworn
To love and to obey.
   Constable (aside). Her mind's distraught!
Alas, she smiles!
   Anne.   The worst hath long been over:
Henry loves courage; he will love my child
For this; although I want more than I have;
And yet how merciful at last is Heaven
To give me but thus much for her sweet sake.

SCENE IN EPPING FOREST

[May 19, 1536.]

HENRY, *Courtiers, Hounds, &c.*

   Henry. Northumberland! pray tell me, if thou canst,
Who is that young one in the green and gold?
Dost thou not see her? hast thou left both eyes
Upon the bushes?
   Northumberland. There are many, sir,
In the same livery.
   Henry.   *Her* I mean; her yonder
On the iron-gray with yellow round his ears.
Impudent wench! she turns away her cheek!
   Northumberland.   *(after inquiring.)*
The Lady Katharine Parr, an' please your Highness.
   Henry. Faith! she *doth* please me. What a sap is rising
In that young bud! how supple! yet how solid!
What palpable perfection! ay, Lord Arundel!
   Arundel. A bloom well worthy of a monarch's bower,
Where only one more lovely smiles beside him.
   Henry. Though spring is stirring, yet give me the summer . .
I can wait yet . . though, some day, not far off,
I would confer with her at Hampton-Court . .
Merely to ask her how she likes the chase:
We shall not have another all this season:
The stag alone can help us on in May:
To-morrow is the twentieth.
                   Hark! the knell
From Paul's! . . the Tower-gun, too!
                    I am right enough!
                    (Claps his hands.)
I am a widower!   *[Again claps his hands.*

By this hour to-morrow
Sunny Jane Seymour's long and laughing eyes
Shall light me to our chamber.
                              Lords! prick on!
The merry hounds are chiding! To the chase
To-day! our coronation for to-morrow.

TO IANTHE [IN VIENNA]

IANTHE! since our parting day
Pleasure and you were far away.
Leave you then all that strove to please
In proud Vienna's palaces
To soothe your Landor's heart agen
And roam once more our hazel glen?
Formerly you have held my hand
Along the lane where now I stand,
In idle sadness looking round
The lonely disenchanted ground,
And take my pencil out, and wait
To lay the paper on this gate.
About my temples what a hum
Of freshly wakened thought is come!
Ah! not without a throb or two
That shake me as they used to do.
Where alders rise up dark and dense
But just behind the wayside fence,
A stone there is in yonder nook
Which once I borrowed of the brook;
And the first hind who fain would cross
Must leap five yards or feel its loss.
You sate beside me on that stone,
Rather (not much) too wide for one.
Suggesting to our arms and knees
Most whimsical contrivances.
Unsteady stone! and never quite
(Tho' often very near it) right,
And putting to sore shifts my wit
To roll it out, then steddy it,
And then to prove that it must be
Too hard for any one but me.
Ianthe come! ere June declines
We'll write upon it all these lines.

May 27, 1838

[WHY, WHY REPINE]

Why, why repine, my pensive friend,
  At pleasures slipt away?
Some the stern Fates will never lend,
  And all refuse to stay.

I see the rainbow in the sky,
  The dew upon the grass,
I see them, and I ask not why
  They glimmer or they pass.

With folded arms I linger not
  To call them back; 'twere vain;
In this, or in some other spot,
  I know they'll shine again.

[THE EVENING STAR]

Smiles soon abate; the boisterous throes
  Of anger long burst forth;
Inconstantly the south-wind blows,
  But steadily the north.

Thy star, O Venus! often changes
  Its radiant seat above,
The chilling pole-star never ranges—
  'Tis thus with Hate and Love.

TO POETS

Patience! coy songsters of the Delphic wood,
The brightest sun tempts forth the viper brood;
And, of all insects buds and blooms enclose,
The one that stinks the most infests the rose.

[DR. WORDSWORTH]

Wordsworth has well deserved of late
A very pretty doctorate!
O Dons! I would desire no more
Could you make *me* a bachelor.

K

HOW TO READ ME

To turn my volume o'er nor find
  To chide or discommend
Some vestige of a wandering mind,
  Sweet unsuspicious friend!

Believe that all were loved like you,
  With love from blame exempt,
Believe that all my griefs were true
  And all my joys were dreamt.

[WEAKEST THOUGHTS]

THOUGHTS when they're weakest take the longest flights,
And tempt the wintry seas in darkest nights.

[FOR HIS BIRTHDAY]

WHAT, of house and home bereft,
For my birthday what is left?
Not the hope that any more
Can be blest like those of yore,
Not the wish; for wishes now
Fall like flowers from aching brow,
When the jovial feast is past,
And when heaven, with clouds o'ercast,
Strikes the colours from the scene,
And no herb on earth is green.
What is left me after all?
What, beside my funeral?
Bid it wait a little while,
Just to let one thoughtful smile
Its accustom'd time abide:
There are left two boons beside . .
Health, and eyes that yet can see
Eyes not coldly turn'd from me.

January 30, 1841

[FROM MOSCHUS]

AH! when the mallow in the croft dies down,
Or the pale parsley or the crisped anise,
Again they grow, another year they flourish;
But we, the great, the valiant, and the wise,
Once covered over in the hollow earth,
Sleep a long, dreamless, unawakening sleep.

[FROM CATULLUS: CARMEN XX]

In spring the many-colour'd crown,
The sheafs in summer, ruddy-brown,
The autumn's twisting tendrils green,
With nectar-gushing grapes between,
Some pink, some purple, some bright gold,
Then shrivel'd olive, blue with cold,
Are all for me: for me the goat
Comes with her milk from hills remote,
And fatted lamb, and calf, pursued
By moaning mother, sheds her blood.

THE HAMADRYAD

Rhaicos was born amid the hills wherefrom
Gnidos the light of Caria is discern'd,
And small are the white-crested that play near
And smaller onward are the purple waves.
Thence festal choirs were visible, all crown'd
With rose and myrtle if they were inborn;
If from Pandion sprang they, on the coast
Where stern Athenè raised her citadel,
Then olive was intwined with violets
Cluster'd in bosses, regular and large.   10
For various men wore various coronals;
But one was their devotion: 'twas to her
Whose laws all follow, her whose smile withdraws
The sword from Ares, thunderbolt from Zeus,
And whom in his chill caves the mutable
Of mind, Poseidon, the sea-king, reveres,
And whom his brother, stubborn Dis, hath pray'd
To turn in pity the averted cheek
Of her he bore away; with promises,
Nay, with loud oath before dread Styx itself,   20
To give her daily more and sweeter flowers
Than he made drop from her on Enna's dell.
   Rhaicos was looking from his father's door
At the long trains that hasten'd to the town
From all the valleys, like bright rivulets
Gurgling with gladness, wave outrunning wave,
And thought it hard he might not also go
And offer up one prayer, and press one hand,
He knew not whose. The father call'd him in,
And said, 'Son Rhaicos! those are idle games;   30
Long enough I have lived to find them so.'

And, ere he ended, sigh'd; as old men do
Always, to think how idle such games are.
'I have not yet,' thought Rhaicos in his heart,
And wanted proof.
            'Suppose thou go and help
Echion at the hill, to bark yon oak
And lop its branches off, before we delve
About the trunk and ply the root with axe:
This we may do in winter.'
            Rhaicos went;
For thence he could see farther, and see more   40
Of those who hurried to the city-gate.
Echion he found there, with naked arm
Swart-hair'd, strong sinew'd, and his eyes intent
Upon the place where first the axe should fall:
He held it upright. 'There are bees about,
Or wasps, or hornets,' said the cautious eld,
'Look sharp, O son of Thallinos!' The youth
Inclined his ear, afar, and warily,
And cavern'd in his hand. He heard a buzz
At first, and then the sound grew soft and clear,   50
And then divided into what seem'd tune,
And there were words upon it, plaintive words.
He turn'd, and said, 'Echion! do not strike
That tree: it must be hollow; for some God
Speaks from within. Come thyself near.' Again
Both turn'd toward it: and behold! there sat
Upon the moss below, with her two palms
Pressing it, on each side, a maid in form.
Downcast were her long eyelashes, and pale
Her cheek, but never mountain-ash display'd   60
Berries of colour like her lip so pure,
Nor were the anemonies about her hair
Soft, smooth, and wavering like the face beneath.

'What dost thou here?' Echion half-afraid,
Half-angry, cried. She lifted up her eyes
But nothing spake she. Rhaicos drew one step
Backward, for fear came likewise over him,
But not such fear: he panted, gaspt, drew in
His breath, and would have turned it into words,
But could not into one.
            'O send away   70
That sad old man!' said she. The old man went
Without a warning from his master's son,
Glad to escape, for sorely he now fear'd,
And the axe shone behind him in their eyes.

Hamadryad. And wouldst thou too shed the most innocent
Of blood? no vow demands it; no God wills
The oak to bleed.
    Rhaicos.   Who art thou? whence? why here?
And whither wouldst thou go? Among the robed
In white, or saffron, or the hue that most
Resembles dawn, or the clear sky, is none   80
Array'd as thou art. What so beautiful
As that gray robe which clings about thee close,
Like moss to stones adhering, leaves to trees,
Yet lets thy bosom rise and fall in turn,
As, toucht by zephyrs, fall and rise the boughs
Of graceful platan by the river-side.
    Hamadryad. Lovest thou well thy father's house?
    Rhaicos.   Indeed
I love it, well I love it, yet would leave
For thine, where'er it be, my father's house,
With all the marks upon the door, that show   90
My growth at every birth-day since the third,
And all the charms, o'erpowering evil eyes,
My mother nail'd for me against my bed,
And the Cydonian bow (which thou shalt see)
Won in my race last spring from Eutychus.
    Hamadryad. Bethink thee what it is to leave a home
Thou never yet hast left, one night, one day.
    Rhaicos. No, 'tis not hard to leave it; 'tis not hard
To leave, O maiden, that paternal home,
If there be one on earth whom we may love   100
First, last, for ever; one who says that she
Will love for ever too. To say which word,
Only to say it, surely is enough:
It shows such kindness! If 'twere possible,
We, at the moment, think she would indeed.
    Hamadryad. Who taught thee all this folly at thy age?
    Rhaicos. I have seen lovers, and have learnt to love.
    Hamadryad. But wilt thou spare the tree?
    Rhaicos.   My father wants
The bark; the tree may hold its place awhile.
    Hamadryad. Awhile! thy father numbers then my days! 110
    Rhaicos. Are there no others where the moss beneath
Is quite as tufty? Who would send thee forth
Or ask thee why thou tarriest? Is thy flock
Anywhere near?
    Hamadryad.   I have no flock: I kill
Nothing that breathes, that stirs, that feels the air,
The sun, the dew. Why should the beautiful
(And thou art beautiful) disturb the source

Whence springs all beauty? Hast thou never heard
Of Hamadryads?
    Rhaicos.   Heard of them I have:
Tell me some tale about them. May I sit   120
Beside thy feet? Art thou not tired? The herbs
Are very soft; I will not come too nigh;
Do but sit there, nor tremble so, nor doubt.
Stay, stay an instant: let me first explore
If any acorn of last year be left
Within it; thy thin robe too ill protects
Thy dainty limbs against the harm one small
Acorn may do. Here's none. Another day
Trust me: till then let me sit opposite.
    Hamadryad. I seat me; be thou seated, and content.   130
    Rhaicos. O sight for gods! Ye men below! adore
The Aphroditè. *Is* she there below?
Or sits she here before me? as she sate
Before the shepherd on those heights that shade
The Hellespont, and brought his kindred woe.
    Hamadryad. Reverence the higher Powers; nor deem amiss
Of her who pleads to thee, and would repay . .
Ask not how much . . but very much. Rise not:
No, Rhaicos, no! Without the nuptial vow
Love is unholy. Swear to me that none   140
Of mortal maids shall ever taste thy kiss,
Then take thou mine; then take it, not before.
    Rhaicos. Hearken, all gods above! O Aphrodite!
O Herè! let my vow be ratified!
But wilt thou come into my father's house?
    Hamadryad. Nay: and of mine I cannot give thee part.
    Rhaicos. Where is it?
    Hamadryad.   In this oak.
    Rhaicos.   Ay; now begins
The tale of Hamadryad: tell it through.
    Hamadryad. Pray of thy father never to cut down
My tree; and promise him, as well thou mayst,   150
That every year he shall receive from me
More honey than will buy him nine fat sheep,
More wax than he will burn to all the gods!
Why fallest thou upon thy face? Some thorn
May scratch it, rash young man! Rise up; for shame!
    Rhaicos. For shame I cannot rise. Oh, pity me!
I dare not sue for love . . but do not hate!
Let me once more behold thee . . not once more,
But many days: let me love on . . unloved!
I aim'd too high: on my own head the bolt   160
Falls back, and pierces to the very brain.
    Hamadryad. Go . . rather go, than make me say I love.

Rhaicos. If happiness is immortality,
(And whence enjoy it else the gods above?)
I am immortal too: my vow is heard:
Hark! on the left . . Nay, turn not from me now,
I claim my kiss.
    Hamadryad. Do men take first, then claim?
Do thus the seasons run their course with them?

    Her lips were seal'd; her head sank on his breast.
'Tis said that laughs were heard within the wood: 170
But who should hear them? and whose laughs? and why?
    Savoury was the smell, and long past noon,
Thallinos! in thy house; for marjoram,
Basil and mint and thyme and rosemary,
Were sprinkled on the kid's well-roasted length,
Awaiting Rhaicos. Home he came at last,
Not hungry, but pretending hunger keen,
With head and eyes just o'er the maple plate.
'Thou seest but badly, coming from the sun,
Boy Rhaicos!' said the father. 'That oak's bark   180
Must have been tough, with little sap between;
It ought to run; but it and I are old.'
Rhaicos, although each morsel of the bread
Increast by chewing, and the meat grew cold
And tasteless to his palate, took a draught
Of gold-bright wine, which, thirsty as he was,
He thought not of until his father fill'd
The cup, averring water was amiss,
But wine had been at all times pour'd on kid,
It was religion.
              He thus fortified,   190
Said, not quite boldly, and not quite abasht,
'Father, that oak is Jove's own tree: that oak
Year after year will bring thee wealth from wax
And honey. There is one who fears the gods
And the gods love . . that one'
                    (He blusht, nor said
What one)
           'has promised this, and may do more.
Thou hast not many moons to wait until
The bees have done their best: if then there come
Nor wax nor honey, let the tree be hewn.'
    'Zeus hath bestow'd on thee a prudent mind,'   200
Said the glad sire: 'but look thou often there,
And gather all the honey thou canst find
In every crevice, over and above
What has been promist; would they reckon that?'

Rhaicos went daily; but the nymph was oft
Invisible. To play at love, she knew,
Stopping its breathings when it breathes most soft,
Is sweeter than to play on any pipe.
She play'd on his: she fed upon his sighs:
They pleased her when they gently waved her hair,   210
Cooling the pulses of her purple veins,
And when her absence brought them out they pleased.
Even among the fondest of them all,
What mortal or immortal maid is more
Content with giving happiness than pain?
One day he was returning from the wood
Despondently. She pitied him, and said
'Come back!' and twined her fingers in the hem
Above his shoulder. Then she led his steps
To a cool rill that ran o'er level sand   220
Through lentisk and through oleander, there
Bathed she his feet, lifting them on her lap
When bathed, and drying them in both her hands.
He dared complain; for those who most are loved
Most dare it; but not harsh was his complaint.
'O thou inconstant!' said he, 'if stern law
Bind thee, or will, stronger than sternest law,
Oh, let me know henceforward when to hope
The fruit of love that grows for me but here.'
He spake; and pluckt it from its pliant stem.   230
  Hamadryad. Impatient Rhaicos! why thus interecpt
The answer I would give? There is a bee
Whom I have fed, a bee who knows my thoughts
And executes my wishes: I will send
That messenger. If ever thou art false,
Drawn by another, own it not, but drive
My bee away: then shall I know my fate,
And, for thou must be wretched, weep at thine.
But often as my heart persuades to lay
Its cares on thine and throb itself to rest,   240
Expect her with thee, whether it be morn
Or eve, at any time when woods are safe.'

Day after day the Hours beheld them blest,
And season after season: years had past,
Blest were they still. He who asserts that Love
Ever is sated of sweet things, the same
Sweet things he fretted for in earlier days,
Never, by Zeus! loved he a Hamadryad.
  The nights had now grown longer, and perhaps
The Hamadryads find them lone and dull   250
Among their woods; one did, alas! She called

Her faithful bee: 'twas when all bees should sleep,
And all did sleep but hers. She was sent forth
To bring that light which never wintry blast
Blows out, nor rain nor snow extinguishes,
The light that shines from loving eyes upon
Eyes that love back until they see no more.

   Rhaicos was sitting at his father's hearth:
Between them stood the table, not o'erspread
With fruits which autumn now profusely bore,   260
Nor anise cakes, nor odorous wine; but there
The draft-board was expanded; at which game
Triumphant sat old Thallinos: the son
Was puzzled, vext, discomfited, distraught.
A buzz was at his ear: up went his hand,
And it was heard no longer. The poor bee
Return'd (but not until the morn shone bright)
And found the Hamadryad with her head
Upon her aching wrist, and showed one wing
Half-broken off, the other's meshes marr'd,   270
And there were bruises which no eye could see
Saving a Hamadryad's.
                   At this sight
Down fell the languid brow, both hands fell down,
A shriek was carried to the ancient hall
Of Thallinos: he heard it not: his son
Heard it, and ran forthwith into the wood.
No bark was on the tree, no leaf was green,
The trunk was riven through. From that day forth
Nor word nor whisper soothed his ear, nor sound
Even of insect wing: but loud laments   280
The woodmen and the shepherds one long year
Heard day and night; for Rhaicos would not quit
The solitary place, but moan'd and died.
Hence milk and honey wonder not, O guest,
To find set duly on the hollow stone.

ON READE'S *CAIN*

THE reign of justice is return'd again:
Cain murder'd Abel, and Reade murders Cain.

[BYRON PARODIED]

WE sat down and wept by the waters
   Of Camus, and thought of the day,
When damsels would show their red garters
   In their hurry to scamper away.

[LINES FROM A DREAM]

O Friendship! Friendship! the shell of Aphrodite
Lies always at the bottom of thy warm and limpid waters.

[TO SIR SAMUEL MEYRICK]

MEYRICK! surrounded by Silurian boors,
Against that rabble shut your castle-doors;
I mean that coarser rabble which aspires
To square its shoulders in the squad of squires;
Which holds the scholar under heavy ban,
And, drunk or sober, spurns the gentleman.
Meyrick! how wide your difference! hardly wider
Your mellow claret and their musty cider.

TO MY DAUGHTER

By that dejected city, Arno runs,
Where Ugolino claspt his famisht sons.
There wert thou born, my Julia! there thine eyes
Return'd as bright a blue to vernal skies.
And thence, my little wanderer! when the Spring
Advanced, thee, too, the hours on silent wing
Brought, while anemonies were quivering round,
And pointed tulips pierced the purple ground,
Where stood fair Florence: there thy voice first blest
My ear, and sank like balm into my breast:
For many griefs had wounded it, and more
Thy little hands could lighten were in store.
But why revert to griefs? Thy sculptured brow
Dispels from mine its darkest cloud even now.
What then the bliss to see again thy face,
And all that Rumour has announced of grace!
I urge, with fevered breast, the four-month day.
O! could I sleep to wake again in May.

A CASE AT SESSIONS

YESTERDAY, at the Sessions held in Buckingham,
The Reverend Simon Shutwood, famed for tucking ham
And capon into his appointed maw,
Gravely discust a deadly breach of law,
And then committed to the county jail
(After a patient hearing) William Flail:
   For that he, Flail, one day last week,

Was seen maliciously to sneak
And bend his body by the fence
Of his own garden, and from thence
Abstract, out of a noose, a hare,
Which he unlawfully found there,
Against the peace (as may be seen
In Burn and Blackstone) of the Queen.
He, question'd thereupon, in short,
Could give no better reason for't
Than that his little boys and he
Did often in the morning see
Said hare, and sundry other hares,
Nibbling on certain herbs of theirs.
Teddy, the seventh of the boys,
Counted twelve rows, fine young savoys,
Bit to the ground by them, and out
Of ne'er a plant a leaf to sprout:
And Sam, the youngest lad, did think
He saw a couple at a pink.
'Come!' cried the Reverend, 'Come, confess!'
Flail answered, 'I will do no less.
Puss we did catch; Puss we did eat;
It was her turn to give the treat.
Nor overmuch was there for eight o' us
With a half-gallon o' potatoes:
Eight; for our Prue lay sick abed,
And poor dear Bessy with the dead.'
'We can not listen to such idle words,'
The Reverend cried: 'The hares are all my Lord's.
Have you no more, my honest friend, to say
Why we should not commit you, and straightway?'
    Whereat Will Flail
    Grew deadly pale,
And cried, 'If you are so severe on me,
An ignorant man, and poor as poor can be,
O Mister Shutwood! what would you have done
If you had caught God's blessed only Son,
When he broke off (in land not His they say)
That ear of barley on the Sabbath-day?
Sweet Jesus! in the prison he had died,
And never for our sins been crucified.'
With the least gouty of two doeskin feet
The reverend stampt, then cried in righteous heat,
    'Constable! take that man down-stairs,
    He quotes the Scripture and eats hares.'

TO ROBERT BROWNING

THERE is delight in singing, though none hear
Beside the singer; and there is delight
In praising, though the praiser sit alone
And see the prais'd far off him, far above.
Shakespeare is not *our* poet, but the world's,
Therefore on him no speech; and short for thee,
Browning! Since Chaucer was alive and hale,
No man hath walk'd along our roads with step
So active, so inquiring eye, or tongue
So varied in discourse. But warmer climes
Give brighter plumage, stronger wing; the breeze
Of Alpine heights thou playest with, borne on
Beyond Sorrento and Amalfi, where
The Siren waits thee, singing song for song.

Nov. 19, 1845.

[AN IMAGINARY CONVERSATION]

Landor. Kenyon, I've written for your delectation,
A short Imaginary Conversation.
Kenyon. Landor, I much rejoice at the report;
But only keep your promise—*be* it short.

[ON GREY CLIFFS]

NIGHT airs that make tree-shadows walk, and sheep
Washed white in the cold moonshine on grey cliffs.

[LINES BY JOHN DONNE—IMAGINARY]

SHE was so beautiful, had God but died
    For her, and none beside,
Reeling with holy joy from east to west
    Earth would have sunk down blest:
And, burning with bright zeal, the buoyant Sun
Cried thro' his worlds *well done!*

[WORDSWORTH]

DANK, limber verses, stuft with lakeside sedges,
And propt with rotten stakes from broken hedges.

129

[SHAKESPEARE]

HE lighted with his golden lamp on high
The unknown regions of the human heart,
Show'd its bright fountains, show'd its rueful wastes,
Its shoals and headlands; and a tower he rais'd
Refulgent, where eternal breakers roll,
For all to see, but no man to approach.

[WISDOM AND PLEASURE]

THE narrow mind is the discontented one.
There is pleasure in wisdom, there is wisdom in pleasure.
If thou findest no honey in thy cake,
Put thy cake into honey with thine own right-hand,
Nor think it defiled thereby.

THE PRAYER OF ORESTES

Orestes. O king Apollo! god Apollo! god
Powerful to smite and powerful to preserve!
If there is blood upon me, as there seems,
Purify that black stain (thou only canst)
With every rill that bubbles from these caves
Audibly; and come willing to the work.
No; 'tis not they; 'tis blood; 'tis blood again
That bubbles in my ear, that shakes the shades
Of thy dark groves, and lets in hateful gleams,
Bringing me . . what dread sight! what sounds abhorr'd!
What screams! They are my mother's: 'tis her eye
That through the snakes of those three furies glares,
And makes them hold their peace that she may speak.
Has thy voice bidden them all forth? There slink
Some that would hide away, but must turn back,
And others like blue lightnings bound along
From rock to rock; and many hiss at me
As they draw nearer. Earth, fire, water, all
Abominate the deed the Gods commanded!
Alas! I came to pray, not to complain;
And lo! my speech is impious as my deed!

Priestess of Apollo.

Take refuge here amid our Delphian shades,
    O troubled breast!
Here the most pious of Mycenai's maids
    Shall watch thy rest

And wave the cooling laurel o'er thy brow,
    Nor insect swarm
Shall ever break thy slumbers, nor shalt thou
    Start at the alarm
Of boys infesting (as they do) the street
    With mocking songs,
Stopping and importuning all they meet,
    And heaping wrongs
Upon thy diadem'd and sacred head,
    Worse than when base
Œgisthus (shudder not!) his toils outspread
    Around thy race.
Altho' even in this fane the fitful blast
    Thou may'st hear roar,
Thy name among our highest rocks shall last
    For evermore.
Orestes. A calm comes over me: life brings it not
With any of its tides: my end is near.
O Priestess of the purifying God
Receive her![1] and when she hath closed mine eyes,
Do thou (weep not, my father's child!) close hers.

ICARIOS AND ERIGONE

IMPROVIDENT were once the Attic youths,
As (if we may believe the credulous
And testy) various youths have been elsewhere.
But truly such was their improvidence,
Ere Pallas in compassion was their guide,
They never stowed away the fruits of earth
For winter use; nor knew they how to press
Olive or grape: yet hospitality
Sate at the hearth, and there was mirth and song.
Wealthy and generous in the Attic land,
Icarios! wert thou; and Erigonè,
Thy daughter, gave with hearty glee the milk,
Buzzing in froth beneath unsteady goat,
To many who stopt near her; some for thirst,
And some to see upon its back that hand
So white and small and taper, and await
Until she should arise and show her face.
The father wisht her not to leave his house,
Nor she to leave her father; yet there sued
From all the country round both brave and rich.
Some, nor the wealthier of her wooers, drove
Full fifty slant-brow'd kingly-hearted swine,

---

[1] Pointing to his sister.

Reluctant ever to be led aright,
Race autocratical, autochthon race,
Lords of the woods, fed by the tree of Jove.
Some had three ploughs; some had eight oxen; some
Had vines, on oak, on maple, and on elm,
In long and strait and gleamy avenues,
Which would have tired you had you reacht the end
Without the unshapen steps that led beyond
Up the steep hill to where they leaned on poles.
Yet kind the father was, and kind the maid.
And now when winter blew the chaff about,
And hens pursued the grain into the house,
Quarrelsome and indignant at repulse,
And rushing back again with ruffled neck,
They and their brood; and kids blinkt at the brand,
And bee-nosed oxen, with damp nostrils lowered
Against the threshold, stampt the dogs away;
Icarios, viewing these with thoughtful mind,
Said to Erigonè, 'Not scantily
The Gods have given us these birds and these
Short-bleating kids, and these loose-hided steers.
The Gods have given: to them will we devote
A portion of their benefits, and bid
The youths who love and honour us partake:
So shall their hearts, and so shall ours, rejoice.'
The youths were bidden to the feast: the flesh
Of kid and crested bird was plentiful:
The steam hung on the rafters, where were nail'd
Bushes of savory herbs, and figs and dates;
And yellow-pointed pears sent down long stalks
Through nets wide-mesht, work of Erigonè
When night was long and lamp yet unsupplied.
Choice grapes Icarios had; and these, alone
Of all men in the country, he preserved
For festive days; nor better day than this
To bring them from beneath his reed-thatcht roof.
He mounted the twelve stairs with hearty pride,
And soon was heard he, breathing hard: he now
Descended, holding in both arms a cask,
Fictile, capacious, bulging: cork-tree bark
Secured the treasure; wax above the mouth,
And pitch above the wax. The pitch he brake,
The wax he scraped away, and laid them by.
Wrenching up carefully the cork-tree bark,
A hum was heard. 'What! are there bees within?'
Euphorbas cried. 'They came then with the grapes,'
Replied the elder, and pour'd out clear juice
Fragrant as flowers, and wrinkled husks anon.

'The ghosts of grapes!' cried Phanor, fond of jokes
Within the house, but ever abstinent
Of such as that, in woodland and alone,
Where any sylvan God might overhear.
No few were sadden'd at the ill-omen'd word,
But sniffing the sweet odour, bent their heads,
Tasted, sipt, drank, ingurgitated: fear
Flew from them all, joy rusht to every breast,
Friendship grew warmer, hands were join'd, vows sworn.
From cups of every size, from cups two-ear'd,
From ivy-twisted and from smooth alike,
They dash the water; they pour in the wine;
(For wine it was,) until that hour unseen.
They emptied the whole cask; and they alone;
For both the father and the daughter sate
Enjoying their delight. But when they saw
Flusht faces, and when angry words arose
As one more fondly glanced against the cheek
Of the fair maiden on her seat apart,
And she lookt down, or lookt another way
Where other eyes caught hers, and did the like,
Sadly the sire, the daughter fearfully,
Upon each other fixt wide-open eyes.
This did the men remark, and, bearing signs
Different, as were their tempers, of the wine,
But feeling each the floor reel under him,
Each raging, with more thirst at every draught,
Acastor first (sidelong his step) arose,
Then Phanor, then Antyllos:
                              'Zeus above
Confound thee, cursed wretch!' aloud they cried,
'Is this thy hospitality? must all
Who loved thy daughter perish at a blow?
Not at a blow, but like the flies and wasps.'
Madness had seiz'd them all. Erigonè
Ran out for help: what help? Before her sprang
Mœra, and howl'd and barkt, and then return'd
Presaging. They had dragg'd the old man out
And murdered him. Again flew Mœra forth,
Faithful, compassionate, and seized her vest,
And drew her where the body lay, unclosed
The eyes, and rais'd toward the stars of heaven.

Raise thine, for thou hast heard enough, raise thine
And view Böotes bright among those stars,
Brighter the Virgin: Mœra too shines there.
But where were the Eumenides? Repress
Thy anger. If the clear calm stars above

Appease it not, and blood must flow for blood,
Listen, and hear the sequel of the tale.
Wide-seeing Zeus lookt down; as mortals knew
By the woods bending under his dark eye,
And huge towers shuddering on the mountain tops,
And stillness in the valley, in the wold,
And over the deep waters all round earth.
He lifted up his arm, but struck them not
In their abasement: by each other's blow
They fell; some suddenly; but more beneath
The desperate gasp of long-enduring wounds.

ALCIPHRON AND LEUCIPPE

AN ancient chestnut's blossoms threw
Their heavy odour over two:
Leucippe, it is said, was one,
The other then was Alciphron.
    'Come, come! why should we stand beneath
This hollow tree's unwholesome breath,'
Said Alciphron, 'here's not a blade
Of grass or moss, and scanty shade.
Come; it is just the hour to rove
In the lone dingle shepherds love,
There, straight and tall, the hazel twig
Divides the crooked rock-held fig,
O'er the blue pebbles where the rill
In winter runs, and may run still.
Come then, while fresh and calm the air,
And while the shepherds are not there.'
    Leucippe. But I would rather go when they
Sit round about and sing and play.
Then why so hurry me? for you
Like play and song and shepherds too.
    Alciphron. I like the shepherds very well,
And song and play, as you can tell.
But there is play I sadly fear,
And song I would not have you hear.
    Leucippe. What can it be? what can it be?
    Alciphron. To you may none of them repeat
The play that you have played with me,
The song that made your bosom beat.
    Leucippe. Don't keep your arm about my waist.
    Alciphron. Might not you stumble?
    Leucippe.   Well then, do.
But why are we in all this haste?
    Alciphron. To sing.
    Leucippe.   Alas! and not play too?

L

ENALLOS AND CYMODAMEIA

A vision came o'er three young men at once,
A vision of Apollo: each had heard
The same command; each followed it; all three
Assembled on one day before the God
In Lycia, where he gave his oracle.
Bright shone the morning; and the birds that build
Their nests beneath the column-heads of fanes
And eaves of humbler habitations, dropt
From under them and wheeled athwart the sky,
When, silently and reverently, the youths
Marcht side by side up the long steps that led
Toward the awful God who dwelt within.
Of those three youths fame hath held fast the name
Of one alone; nor would that name survive
Unless Love had sustain'd it, and blown off
With his impatient breath the mists of time.
'Ye come,' the God said mildly, 'of one will
To people what is desert in the isle
Of Lemnos. But strong men possess its shores;
Nor shall you execute the brave emprize
Unless, on the third day from going forth,
To him who rules the waters ye devote
A virgin, cast into the sea alive.'
They heard, and lookt in one another's face,
And then bent piously before the shrine
With prayer and praises and thanksgiving hymn,
And, after a short silence, went away,
Taking each other's hand and swearing truth,
Then to the ship in which they came, return'd.
Two of the youths were joyous, one was sad;
Sad was Enallos; yet those two by none
Were loved; Enallos had already won
Cymodameia, and the torch was near.
By night, by day, in company, alone,
The imagine of the maiden fill'd his breast
To the heart's brim. Ah! therefore did that heart
So sink within him.
                            They have sail'd; they reach
Their home again. Sires, matrons, maidens, throng
The plashing port, to watch the gather'd sail,
And who springs first and farthest upon shore.
Enallos came the latest from the deck.
Swift ran the rumour what the God had said,
And fearful were the maidens, who before
Had urged the sailing of the youths they loved,
That they might give their hands, and have their homes,

And nurse their children; and more thoughts perhaps
Led up to these, and even ran before.
But they persuaded easily their wooers
To sail without them, and return again
When they had seiz'd the virgin on the way.
Cymodameia dreamt three nights, the three
Before their fresh departure, that her own
Enallos had been cast into the deep,
And she had saved him. She alone embarkt
Of all the maidens, and unseen by all,
And hid herself before the break of day
Among the cloaks and fruits piled high aboard.
But when the noon was come, and the repast
Was call'd for, there they found her. Not quite stern,
But more than sad, Enallos lookt upon her.
Forebodings shook him: hopes rais'd *her*, and love
Warm'd the clear cheek while she wiped off the spray.
Kindly were all to her and dutiful;
And she slept soundly mid the leaves of figs
And vines, and far as far could be apart.
Now the third morn had risen, and the day
Was dark, and gusts of wind and hail and fogs
Perplext them: land they saw not yet, nor knew
Where land was lying. Sudden lightnings blaz'd,
Thunder-claps rattled round them. The pale crew
Howled for the victim. 'Seize her, or we sink.'
   O maid of Pindus! I would linger here
To lave my eyelids at the nearest rill,
For thou hast made me weep, as oft thou hast,
Where thou and I, apart from living men,
And two or three crags higher, sate and sang.
Ah! must I, seeing ill my way, proceed?
And thy voice too, Cymodameia! thine
Comes back upon me, helpless as thyself
In this extremity. Sad words! sad words!
'O save me! save! Let me not die so young!
Loving you so! Let me not cease to see you!'
Thou claspedest the youth who would have died
To have done less than save thee. Thus he prayed.
'O God! who givest light to all the world,
Take not from me what makes that light most blessed!
Grant me, if 'tis forbidden me to save
This hapless helpless sea-devoted maid,
To share with her (and bring no curses up
From outraged Neptune) her appointed fate!'
They wrung her from his knee; they hurl'd her down
(Clinging in vain at the hard slippery pitch)
Into the whitening wave. But her long hair

Scarcely had risen up again, before
Another plunge was heard, another form
Clove the straight line of bubbling foam, direct
As ringdove after ringdove. Groans from all
Burst, for the roaring sea ingulpht them both.
Onward the vessel flew; the skies again
Shone bright, and thunder roll'd along, not wroth,
But gently murmuring to the white-wing'd sails.
Lemnos at close of evening was in sight.
The shore was won; the fields markt out; and roofs
Collected the dun wings that seek house-fare;
And presently the ruddy-bosom'd guest
Of winter, knew the doors: then infant cries
Were heard within; and lastly, tottering steps
Pattered along the image-stationed hall,
Ay, three full years had come and gone again,
And often, when the flame on windy nights
Suddenly flicker'd from the mountain-ash
Piled high, men pusht almost from under them
The bench on which they talkt about the dead.
Meanwhile beneficent Apollo saw
With his bright eyes into the sea's calm depth,
And there he saw Enallos, there he saw
Cymodameia. Gravely-gladsome light
Environed them with its eternal green:
And many nymphs sate round: one blew aloud
The spiral shell; one drew bright chords across
Shell more expansive; tenderly a third
With cowering lip hung o'er the flute, and stopt
At will its dulcet sob, or waked to joy;
A fourth took up the lyre and pincht the strings,
Invisible by trembling: many rais'd
Clear voices. Thus they spent their happy hours.
I know them all; but all with eyes downcast,
Conscious of loving, have entreated me
I would not utter now their names above.
Behold, among these natives of the sea
There stands but one young man: how fair! how fond!
Ah! were he fond to *them!* It may not be!
Yet did they tend him morn and eve; by night
They also watcht his slumbers: then they heard
His sighs, nor his alone; for there were two
To whom the watch was hateful. In despair
Upward he rais'd his arms, and thus he prayed,
'O Phœbus! on the higher world alone
Showerest thou all thy blessings? Great indeed
Hath been thy favour to me, great to her;
But she pines inly, and calls beautiful

More than herself the Nymphs she sees around,
And asks me "Are they not more beautiful?"
Be all more beautiful, be all more blest,
But not with me! Release her from the sight;
Restore her to a happier home, and dry
With thy pure beams, above, her bitter tears!'
　She saw him in the action of his prayer,
Troubled, and ran to soothe him. From the ground,
Ere she had claspt his neck, her feet were borne.
He caught her robe; and its white radiance rose
Rapidly, all day long, through the green sea.
Enallos loost not from that robe his grasp,
But spann'd one ancle too. The swift ascent
Had stunn'd them into slumber, sweet, serene,
Invigorating her, nor letting loose
The lover's arm below; albeit at last
It closed those eyes intensely fixt thereon,
And still as fixt in dreaming. Both were cast
Upon an island till'd by peaceful men
And few (no port nor road accessible)
Fruitful and green as the abode they left,
And warm with summer, warm with love and song.
'Tis said that some, whom most Apollo loves,
Have seen that island, guided by his light;
And others have gone near it, but a fog
Rose up between them and the lofty rocks;
Yet they relate they saw it quite as well,
And shepherd-boys and credulous hinds believe.

IPHIGENEIA

IPHIGENEIA, when she heard her doom
At Aulis, and when all beside the king
Had gone away, took his right-hand, and said,
'O father! I am young and very happy.
I do not think the pious Calchas heard
Distinctly what the Goddess spake. Old age
Obscures the senses. If my nurse, who knew
My voice so well, sometimes misunderstood,
While I was resting on her knee both arms
And hitting it to make her mind my words,
And looking in her face, and she in mine,
Might not he also hear one word amiss,

Spoken from so far off, even from Olympus?'
The father placed his cheek upon her head,
And tears dropt down it, but the king of men
Replied not. Then the maiden spake once more.
'O father! sayst thou nothing? Hear'st thou not
Me, whom thou ever hast, until this hour,
Listen'd to fondly, and awaken'd me
To hear my voice amid the voice of birds,
When it was inarticulate as theirs,
And the down deadened it within the nest?'
He moved her gently from him, silent still,
And this, and this alone, brought tears from her,
Altho' she saw fate nearer: then with sighs,
'I thought to have laid down my hair before
Benignant Artemis, and not have dimm'd
Her polisht altar with my virgin blood;
I thought to have selected the white flowers
To please the Nymphs, and to have askt of each
By name, and with no sorrowful regret,
Whether, since both my parents will'd the change,
I might at Hymen's feet bend my clipt brow;
And (after these who mind us girls the most)
Adore our own Athena,[1] that she would
Regard me mildly with her azure eyes.
But father! to see you no more, and see
Your love, O father! go ere I am gone!'
Gently he moved her off, and drew her back,
Bending his lofty head far over her's,
And the dark depths of nature heaved and burst.
He turn'd away; not far, but silent still.
She now first shudder'd; for in him, so nigh,
So long a silence seem'd the approach of death,
And like it. Once again she rais'd her voice.
'O father! if the ships are now detain'd,
And all your vows move not the Gods above,
When the knife strikes me there will be one prayer
The less to them: and purer can there be
Any, or more fervent than the daughter's prayer
For her dear father's safety and success?'
A groan that shook him shook not his resolve.
An aged man now enter'd, and without
One word, stept slowly on, and took the wrist
Of the pale maiden. She lookt up, and saw
The fillet of the priest and calm cold eyes.
Then turn'd she where her parent stood, and cried
'O father! grieve no more: the ships can sail.'

---

[1] Pallas Athena was the patroness of Argos.

MENELAUS AND HELEN AT TROY

HELEN is pursued by MENELAUS up the steps of the palace: an old attendant
deprecates and intercepts his vengeance.

Menelaus. Out of my way! Off! or my sword may smite thee,[1]
Heedless of venerable age. And thou,
Fugitive! stop. Stand, traitress, on that stair . .
Thou mountest not another, by the Gods!   (*She stops: he seizes her.*)
Now take the death thou meritest, the death
Zeus who presides o'er hospitality,
And every other god whom thou hast left,
And every other who abandons thee
In this accursed city, sends at last.
Turn, vilest of vile slaves! turn, paramour
Of what all other women hate, of cowards,
Turn, lest this hand wrench back thy head, and toss
It and its odours to the dust and flames.
Helen. Welcome the death thou promisest! Not fear
But shame, obedience, duty, make me turn.
Menelaus. Duty! false harlot!
Helen.   Name too true! severe
Precursor to the blow that is to fall,
It should alone suffice for killing me.
Menelaus. Ay, weep: be not the only one in Troy
Who wails not on this day . . its last . . the day
Thou and thy crimes darken with dead on dead.
Helen. Spare! spare! O let the last that falls be me!
There are but young and old.
Menelaus.   There are but guilty
Where thou art, and the sword strikes none amiss.
Hearest thou not the creeping blood buzz near
Like flies? or wouldst thou rather hear it hiss
Louder, against the flaming roofs thrown down
Wherewith the streets are pathless? Ay, but vengeance
Springs over all; and Nemesis and Atè
Drove back the flying ashes with both hands.
I never saw thee weep till now: and now
There is no pity in thy tears. The tiger
Leaves not her young athirst for the first milk,
As thou didst. Thine could scarce have claspt thy knee
If she had felt thee leave her.
Helen.   O my child!
My only one! Thou livest: 'tis enough:
Hate me, abhor me, curse me . . these are duties . .

[1] The reader must be reminded that this is no translation from a French
tragedy: such really and truly were the manners of the Greeks in the time of the
Trojan war: they respected age, but disregarded sex.

Call me but Mother in the shades of death!
She now is twelve years old, when the bud swells
And the first colours of uncertain life
Begin to tinge it.
    Menelaus (aside). Can she think of home?
Hers once, mine yet, and sweet Hermione's!
Is there one spark that cheer'd my hearth, one left,
For thee, my last of love!
                       Scorn, righteous scorn
Blows it from me . . but thou mayst . . never, never.
Thou shalt not see her even there. The slave
On earth shall scorn thee, and the damn'd below.
    Helen. Delay not either fate. If death is mercy,
Send me among the captives; so that Zeus
May see his offspring led in chains away,
And thy hard brother, pointing with his sword
At the last wretch that crouches on the shore,
Cry, 'She alone shall never sail for Greece!'
    Menelaus. Hast thou more words?
                       Her voice is musical
As the young maids who sing to Artemis:
How glossy is that yellow braid my grasp
Seiz'd and let loose! Ah! can then years have past
Since . . but the children of the Gods, like them,
Suffer not age.
             Helen! speak honestly,
And thus escape my vengeance . . was it force
That bore thee off?
    Helen.   It was some evil God.
    Menelaus. Helping that hated man?
    Helen.   How justly hated!
    Menelaus. By thee too?
    Helen.   Hath he not made *thee* unhappy?
O do not strike.
    Menelaus.   Wretch!
    Helen.   Strike, but do not speak.
    Menelaus. Lest thou remember me against thy will.
    Helen. Lest I look up and see you wroth and sad,
Against my will; O! how against my will
They know above, they who perhaps can pity.
    Menelaus. They shall not save thee.
    Helen.   Then indeed they pity.
    Menelaus. Prepare for death.
    Helen.   Not from that hand: 'twould pain
    you.
    Menelaus. Touch not my hand. Easily dost thou drop it!
    Helen. Easy are all things, do but thou command.
    Menelaus. Look up then.

Helen.   To the hardest proof of all
I am now bidden: bid me not look up.
   Menelaus. She looks as when I led her on behind
The torch and fife, and when the blush o'erspread
Her girlish face at tripping in the myrtle
On the first step before the wreathed gate.
Approach me. Fall not on thy knees.
   Helen.   The hand
That is to slay me, best may slay me thus.
I dare no longer see the light of heaven,
Nor thine . . alas! the light of heaven to me.
   Menelaus. Follow me.
                 She holds out both arms . . and now
Drops them again . . She comes . . Why stoppest thou?
   Helen. O Meneläus! could thy heart know mine,
As once it did . . for then did they converse,
Generous the one, the other not unworthy . .
Thou wouldst find sorrow deeper even than guilt.
   Menelaus. And must I lead her by the hand again?
Nought shall persuade me. Never. She draws back . .
The true alone and loving sob like her . .
Come, Helen!   [*He takes her hand.*
   Helen.   Oh! let never Greek see this!
Hide me from Argos, from Amyclai hide me,
Hide me from all.
   Menelaus.   Thy anguish is too strong
For me to strive with.
   Helen.   Leave it all to me.
   Menelaus. Peace! peace! Thy wind, I hope, is fair for Sparta.

[ON HIS POEMS]

O FRIENDS! who have accompanied thus far
My quickening steps, sometimes where sorrow sate
Dejected, and sometimes where valour stood
Resplendent, right before us; here perhaps
We best might part; but one to valour dear
Comes up in wrath and calls me worse than foe,
Reminding me of gifts too ill deserved.
I must not blow away the flowers he gave,
Altho' now faded; I must not efface
The letters his own hand has traced for me.
   Here terminates my park of poetry.
Look out no longer for extensive woods,
For clusters of unlopt and lofty trees,
With stately animals couch under them,
Or grottoes with deep wells of water pure,

And ancient figures in the solid rock:
Come, with our sunny pasture be content,
Our narrow garden and our homestead croft,
And tillage not neglected. Love breathes round;
Love, the bright atmosphere, the vital air,
Of youth; without it life and death are one.

[THE TORCH OF LOVE: TO IANTHE]

THE torch of Love dispels the gloom
Of life, and animates the tomb;
But never let it idly flare
On gazers in the open air,
Nor turn it quite away from one
To whom it serves for moon and sun,
And who alike in night or day
Without it could not find his way.

[SO CHILLS THE MORN]

THOU hast not rais'd, Ianthe, such desire
  In any breast as thou hast rais'd in mine.
No wandering meteor now, no marshy fire,
  Leads on my steps, but lofty, but divine:
And, if thou chillest me, as chill thou dost
  When I approach too near, too boldly gaze,
So chills the blushing morn, so chills the host
  Of vernal stars, with light more chaste than day's.

[THE TIDES OF LOVE]

MY hopes retire; my wishes as before
Struggle to find their resting-place in vain:
The ebbing sea thus beats against the shore;
The shore repels it; it returns again.

[THE VIOLET]

I CAN not tell, not I, why she
Awhile so gracious, now should be
So grave: I can not tell you why
The violet hangs its head awry.
It shall be cull'd, it shall be worn,
In spite of every sign of scorn,
Dark look, and overhanging thorn.

IANTHE'S TROUBLES

FROM you, Ianthe, little troubles pass
    Like little ripples down a sunny river;
Your pleasures spring like daisies in the grass,
    Cut down, and up again as blithe as ever.

[THE INCENSE]

ART thou afraid the adorer's prayer
    Be overheard? that fear resign.
He waves the incense with such care
    It leaves no stain upon the shrine.

[LOVE]

YOU see the worst of love, but not the best,
Nor will you know him till he comes your guest.
Tho' yearly drops some feather from his sides,
In the heart's temple his pure torch abides.

[FAME AND DEATH]

ACCORDING to eternal laws
('Tis useless to inquire the cause)
The gates of fame and of the grave
Stand under the same architrave,
So I would rather some time yet
Play on with you, my little pet!

[ADMONITION TO IANTHE]

RETIRED this hour from wondering crowds
And flower-fed poets swathed in clouds,
Now the dull dust is blown away,
Ianthe, list to what I say.
Verse is not always sure to please
For lightness, readiness, and ease;
Romantic ladies like it not
Unless its steams are strong and hot
As Melton-Mowbray stables when
Ill-favored frost comes back again.
Tell me no more you feel a pride
To be for ever at my side,
To think your beauty will be read
When all who pine for it are dead.

I hate a pomp and a parade
Of what should ever rest in shade;
What not the slenderest ray should reach,
Nor whispered breath of guarded speech:
There even Memory should sit
Absorbed, and almost doubting it.

[IANTHE'S DEPARTURE]

HAVE I, this moment, led thee from the beach
Into the boat? now far beyond my reach!
Stand there a little while, and wave once more
That 'kerchief; but may none upon the shore
Dare think the fond salute was meant for him!
Dizzily on the plashing water swim
My heavy eyes, and sometimes can attain
Thy lovely form, which tears bear off again.
In vain have they now ceast; it now is gone
Too far for sight, and leaves me here alone.
O could I hear the creaking of the mast!
I curse it present, I regret it past.

[BE SILENT]

YE walls! sole witnesses of happy sighs,
   Say not, blest walls, one word.
Remember, but keep safe from ears and eyes
   All you have seen and heard.[1]

[THE OLIVE]

ON the smooth brow and clustering hair
   Myrtle and rose! your wreath combine;
The duller olive I would wear,
   Its constancy, its peace, be mine.

[COLOURLESS SANDS]

No, thou hast never griev'd but I griev'd too;
Smiled thou hast often when no smile of mine
Could answer it. The sun himself can give
But little colour to the desert sands.

---

[1] First pencilled thus,
      O murs! temoins des plus heureux soupirs,
      N'en dites mot: gardez nos souvenirs.

[TWENTY YEARS HENCE]

TWENTY years hence my eyes may grow
If not quite dim, yet rather so,
Still yours from others they shall know
                Twenty years hence.
Twenty years hence tho' it may hap
That I be call'd to take a nap
In a cool cell where thunder-clap
                Was never heard.
There breathe but o'er my arch of grass
A not too sadly sigh'd *Alas*,
And I shall catch, ere you can pass,
                That winged word.

[SUMMER TO WINTER]

REMAIN, ah not in youth alone,
  Tho' youth, where you are, long will stay,
But when my summer days are gone,
  And my autumnal haste away.
'Can I be always by your side?'
  No; but the hours you can, you must,
Nor rise at Death's approaching stride,
  Nor go when dust is gone to dust.

[IS IT NO DREAM?]

Is it no dream that I am he
  Whom one awake all night
Rose ere the earliest birds to see,
  And met by dawn's red light;

Who, when the wintry lamps were spent
  And all was drear and dark,
Against the rugged pear-tree leant
  While ice crackt off the bark;

Who little heeded sleet and blast,
  But much the falling snow;
Those in few hours would sure be past,
  His traces *that* might show;

Between whose knees, unseen, unheard,
  The honest mastiff came,
Nor fear'd he; no, nor was he fear'd:
  Tell me, am I the same?

O come! the same dull stars we'll see,
 The same o'er-clouded moon.
O come! and tell me am I he?
 O tell me, tell me soon.

[SILENT, YOU SAY]

Silent, you say, I'm grown of late,
Nor yield, as you do, to our fate?
Ah! that alone is truly pain
Of which we never can complain.

[YOU SMILED]

You smiled, you spoke, and I believed,
By every word and smile deceived.
Another man would hope no more;
Nor hope I what I hoped before:
But let not this last wish be vain;
Deceive, deceive me once again!

[FOUR WORDS]

Proud word you never spoke, but you will speak
 Four not exempt from pride some future day.
Resting on one white hand a warm wet cheek
 Over my open volume you will say,
'This man loved *me!*' then rise and trip away.

[THE LOVES]

The Loves who many years held all my mind,
A charge so troublesome at last resign'd.
Among my books a feather here and there
Tells what the inmates of my study were.
Strong for no wrestle, ready for no race,
They only serve to mark the left-off place.
'Twas theirs to dip in the tempestuous waves,
'Twas theirs to loiter in cool summer caves;
But in the desert where no herb is green
Not one, the latest of the flight, is seen.

CALLED PROUD

If I am proud, you surely know,
Ianthe! who has made me so,
And only should condemn the pride
That can arise from aught beside.

[ON THE STRAND]

ALONG this coast I led the vacant Hours
   To the lone sunshine on the uneven strand,
And nipt the stubborn grass and juicier flowers
   With one unconscious inobservant hand,
While crept the other by degrees more near
   Until it rose the cherisht form around,
And prest it closer, only that the ear
   Might lean, and deeper drink some half-heard sound.

[DULL IS MY VERSE]

DULL is my verse: not even thou
   Who movest many cares away
From this lone breast and weary brow,
   Canst make, as once, its fountain play;
No, nor those gentle words that now
   Support my heart to hear thee say:
'The bird upon its lonely bough
   Sings sweetest at the close of day.'

[NOVEMBER]

NOVEMBER! thou art come again
With all thy gloom of fogs and rain,
Yet woe betide the wretch who sings
Of sadness borne upon thy wings.
The gloom that overcast my brow,
The whole year's gloom, depart, but now;
And all of joy I hear or see,
November! I ascribe to thee!

[TIME]

ALL poets dream, and some do nothing more.
   When you have turn'd this paper o'er,
   You then may tell me, if you please,
   Which I resemble most of these.
   One morning as outstretcht I lay,
   Half-covered by the new-mown hay,
   I saw a bird high over-head,
   And round him many smaller fled.
   To me he seem'd a hawk or kite,
The little birds (who should be in a fright,
Yet never are, as you must oft have found)
   Flew many after, many round.

Unable at full stretch to keep
My eyes, they wearied into sleep:
And, soon as I had sunk upon the grass,
   I saw the large and little pass
All into other shapes; the great one grew
Like Time; like full-grown Loves the smaller flew;
All kept their course, as they had done before;
But soon the less quite vanisht; he, the great,
   Moved on in slow and solemn state,
Until I thought at last he reacht the skies;
And then I opened (somewhat late) my eyes.

[ON MILTON]

WILL mortals never know each other's station
Without the herald? O abomination!
Milton, even Milton, rankt with living men!
Over the highest Alps of mind he marches,
And far below him spring the baseless arches
Of Iris, coloring dimly lake and fen.

[AUTUMN NOTES]

VERY true, the linnets sing
Sweetest in the leaves of spring:
You have found in all these leaves
That which changes and deceives,
And, to pine by sun or star,
Left them, false ones as they are.
But there be who walk beside
Autumn's, till they all have died,
And who lend a patient ear
To low notes from branches sere.

[FIRST BRING ME RAFFAEL]

FIRST bring me Raffael, who alone hath seen
In all her purity Heaven's virgin queen,
Alone hath felt true beauty; bring me then
Titian, ennobler of the noblest men;
And next the sweet Correggio, nor chastise
His wicked Cupids for those wicked eyes.
I want not Rubens's pink puffy bloom,
Nor Rembrandt's glimmer in a dusty room.
With those, and Poussin's nymph-frequented woods,
His templed highths and long-drawn solitudes
I am content, yet fain would look abroad
On one warm sunset of Ausonian Claude.

Walter Savage Landor: Pastel by R. Faulkner

National Portrait Gallery

[COLUMN AND STATUE]

HE who sees rising from some open down
  A column, stately, beautiful, and pure,
Its rich expansive capital would crown
  With glorious statue, which might long endure,
And bring men under it to gaze and sigh
  And wish that honour'd creature they had known,
Whose name the deep inscription lets not die.
  I raise that statue and inscribe that stone.

[THERE IS, ALAS, A CHILL]

THERE is, alas! a chill, a gloom,
About my solitary room
That will not let one flowret bloom
    Even for you:
The withering leaves appear to say,
'Shine on, shine on, O lovely May!
But we meanwhile must drop away.'
    Light! life! adieu.

[TERNISSA]

TERNISSA! you are fled!
  I say not to the dead,
But to the happy ones who rest below:
    For, surely, surely, where
    Your voice and graces are,
Nothing of death can any feel or know.
    Girls who delight to dwell
    Where grows most asphodel,
Gather to their calm breasts each word you speak:
    The mild Persephone
    Places you on her knee,
And your cool palm smoothes down stern Pluto's cheek.

[THE ROADS OF LIFE]

VARIOUS the roads of life; in one
  All terminate, one lonely way.
We go; and 'Is he gone?'
  Is all our best friends say.

M

[THE MYRTLE AND THE BAY]

No, my own love of other years!
  No, it must never be.
Much rests with you that yet endears,
  Alas! but what with me?
Could those bright years o'er me revolve
  So gay, o'er you so fair,
The pearl of life we would dissolve
  And each the cup might share.
You show that truth can ne'er decay,
  Whatever fate befals;
I, that the myrtle and the bay
  Shoot fresh on ruin'd walls.

[THE STREAM IN WINTER]

The brightest mind, when sorrow sweeps across,
Becomes the gloomiest; so the stream, that ran
Clear as the light of heaven ere autumn closed,
When wintry storm and snow and sleet descend,
Is darker than the mountain or the moor.

[PRIDE AND MEMORY]

'Do you remember me? or are you proud?'
Lightly advancing thro' her star-trimm'd crowd,
  Ianthe said, and lookt into my eyes,
'A *yes*, a *yes*, to both: for Memory
Where you but once have been must ever be,
  And at your voice Pride from his throne must rise.'

[AGE]

No charm can stay, no medicine can assuage,
The sad incurable disease of age;
Only the hand in youth more warmly prest
Makes soft the couch and calms the final rest.

TO J. S. [IANTHE]

Many may yet recal the hours
That saw thy lover's chosen flowers
Nodding and dancing in the shade
Thy dark and wavy tresses made:
On many a brain is pictured yet

Thy languid eye's dim violet:
But who among them all foresaw
How the sad snows which never thaw
Upon that head one day should lie,
And love but glimmer from that eye!

WITH AN ALBUM

I know not whether I am proud,
But this I know, I hate the crowd:
Therefore pray let me disengage
My verses from the motley page,
Where others far more sure to please
Pour out their choral song with ease.
And yet perhaps, if some should tire
With too much froth or too much fire,
There is an ear that may incline
Even to words so dull as mine.

GOOD-BYE

Loved, when my love from all but thee had flown,
Come near me; seat thee on this level stone;
And, ere thou lookest o'er the churchyard wall,
To catch, as once we did, yon waterfall,
Look a brief moment on the turf between,
And see a tomb thou never yet hast seen.
My spirit will be sooth'd to hear once more
Good-bye as gently spoken as before.

[THE LEAVES ARE FALLING]

The leaves are falling; so am I;
The few late flowers have moisture in the eye;
So have I too.
Scarcely on any bough is heard
Joyous, or even unjoyous, bird
The whole wood through.

Winter may come: he brings but nigher
His circle (yearly narrowing) to the fire
Where old friends meet:
Let him; now heaven is overcast,
And spring and summer both are past,
And all things sweet.

152

[AFTER AUTUMN]

SUMMER has doft his latest green,
 And Autumn ranged the barley-mows.
So long away then have you been?
 And are you coming back to close
 The year? It sadly wants repose.

[FOR A TOMB IN WIDCOMBE CHURCH-YARD]

THE place where soon I think to lie,
In its old creviced wall hard-by
 Rears many a weed.
Whoever leads you there, will you
Drop slily in a grain or two
 Of wall-flower seed?

I shall not see it, and (too sure)
I shall not ever know that your
 Dear hand was there;
But the rich odor some fine day.
Shall (what I can not do) repay
 That little care.

[INTERLUDE]

MY guest! I have not led you thro'
 The old footpath of swamp and sedges;
But .. mind your step .. you're coming to
 Shingle and shells with sharpish edges.
Here a squash jelly-fish, and here
 An old shark's head with open jaw
We hap may hit on: never fear
 Scent rather rank and crooked saw.
Step forward: we shall pass them soon,
 And then before you will arise
A fertile scene; a placid moon
 Above, and star-besprinkled skies.
And we shall reach at last (where ends
 The fields of thistles, sharp and light)
A dozen brave and honest friends,
 And there wish one and all good-night.

SENT WITH POEMS

LITTLE volume, warm with wishes,
 Fear not brows that never frown!
After Byron's peppery dishes
 Matho's mild skim-milk goes down.

Change she wants not, self-concenter'd,
   She whom Attic graces please,
She whose Genius never enter'd
   Literature's gin-palaces.

THE PERFIDIOUS

Go on! go on! and love away!
Mine was, another's is, the day.
Go on, go on, thou false one! now
Upon his shoulder rest thy brow,
And look into his eyes until
Thy own, to find them colder, fill.

[SNOWFLAKES]

Ten thousand flakes about my windows blow,
Some falling and some rising, but all snow.
Scribblers and statesmen! are ye not just so?

TO LEIGH HUNT, ON AN OMISSION IN HIS
FEAST OF THE POETS

Leigh Hunt! thou stingy man, Leigh Hunt!
May Charon swamp thee in his punt,
For having, in thy list, forgotten
So many poets scarce half rotten,
Who did expect of thee at least
A few cheese-parings from thy *Feast*.
Hast thou no pity on the men
Who suck (as babes their tongues) the pen,
Until it leaves no traces where
It lighted, and seems dipt in air.
At last be generous, Hunt! and prythee
Refresh (and gratis too) in Lethe
Yonder sick Muse, surcharged with poppies
And heavier presentation-copies.
She *must* grow livelier, and the river
More potent in effect than ever.

[FRANCE]

If hatred of the calm and good,
And quenchless thirst of human blood,
Should rouse a restless race again,
And new Napoleons scour the plain,

Ye arbiters of nations, spare
The land of Rabelais and Molière,
But swing those panthers by the ears
Across the grating of Algiers.

[THE FIRE]

PLEASANT it is to wink and sniff the fumes
The little dainty poet blows for us,
Kneeling in his soft cushion at the hearth,
And patted on the head by passing maids.
Who would discourage him? who bid him off?
Invidious or morose! Enough, to say
(Perhaps too much unless 'tis mildly said)
That slender twigs send forth the fiercest flame,
Not without noise, but ashes soon succeed,
While the broad chump leans back against the stones,
Strong with internal fire, sedately breathed,
And heats the chamber round from morn till night.

COTTAGE LEFT FOR LONDON

THE covert walk, the mossy apple-trees,
    And the long grass that darkens underneath,
I leave for narrow streets and gnats and fleas,
    Water unfit to drink and air to breathe.

[ON THE POET MATHO]

DEEP forests hide the stoutest oaks;
Hazels make sticks for market-folks;
He who comes soon to his estate
Dies poor; the rich heir is the late.
Sere ivy shaded Shakespeare's brow;
But Matho is a poet now.

FLOWERS SENT IN BAY-LEAVES

I LEAVE for you to disunite
    Frail flowers and lasting bays:
One, let me hope, you'll wear to-night,
    The other all your days.

[ON SPENCER PERCEVAL, IRVINGITE]

'FEAR God!' says Percival: and when you hear
Tones so lugubrious, you perforce must fear:
If in such awful accents he should say,
'Fear lovely Innocence!' you'd run away.

[AGAINST SONNETS]

DOES it become a girl so wise,
So exquisite in harmonies,
To ask me when do I intend
To write a sonnet? What? my friend!
A sonnet? Never. Rhyme o'erflows
Italian, which hath scarcely prose;
And I have larded full three-score
With *sorte, morte, cuor, amor.*
But why should we, altho' we have
Enough for all things, gay or grave,
Say, on your conscience, why should we
Who draw deep seans along the sea,
Cut them in pieces to beset
The shallows with a cabbage-net?
Now if you ever ask again
A thing so troublesome and vain,
By all your charms! before the morn,
To show my anger and my scorn,
First I will write your name a-top,
Then from this very ink shall drop
A score of sonnets; every one
Shall call you star, or moon, or sun,
Till, swallowing such warm-water verse,
Even sonnet-sippers sicken worse.

[DESSERT]

IDLE and light are many things you see
In these my closing pages: blame not me.
However rich and plenteous the repast,
Nuts, almonds, biscuits, wafers, come at last.

[TO APOLLO]

I WOULD give something, O Apollo!
Thy radiant course o'er earth to follow,
And fill it up with light and song,
But rather would be always young.
Since that perhaps thou canst not give,
By me let those who love me live.

TO SOUTHEY

THERE are who teach us that the depths of thought
Engulph the poet; that irregular
Is every greater one. Go, Southey! mount
Up to these teachers; ask, submissively,
Who so proportioned as the lord of day?
Yet mortals see his stedfast stately course
And lower their eyes before him. Fools gaze up
Amazed at daring flights. Does Homer soar
As hawks and kites and weaker swallows do?
He knows the swineherd; he plants apple-trees
Amid Alcinous's cypresses;
He covers with his aged black-vein'd hand
The plumy crest that frighten'd and made cling
To its fond-mother the ill-fated child;
He walks along Olympus with the Gods,
Complacently and calmly, as along
The sands where Simöis glides into the sea.
They who step high and swing their arms, soon tire.
The glorious Theban then?
                              The sage from Thebes,
Who sang his wisdom when the strife of cars
And combatants had paus'd, deserves more praise
Than this untrue one, fitter for the weak,
Who by the lightest breezes are borne up
And with the dust and straws are swept away;
Who fancy they are carried far aloft
When nothing quite distinctly they descry,
Having lost all self-guidance. But strong men
Are strongest with their feet upon the ground.
Light-bodied Fancy, Fancy plover-winged,
Draws some away from culture to dry downs
Where none but insects find their nutriment;
There let us leave them to their sleep and dreams.
  Great is that poet, great is he alone,
Who rises o'er the creatures of the earth,
Yet only where his eye may well discern
The various movements of the human heart,
And how each mortal differs from the rest.
Although he struggle hard with Poverty.
He dares assert his just prerogative
To stand above all perishable things,
Proclaiming *this* shall live, and *this* shall die.

TO MICHELET
ON HIS *PEOPLE*

I prais'd thee, Michelet, whom I saw
At Reason's Feast, by Right and Law.
Must then, when Discord's voice hath ceast,
And when the faggot fails the priest,
All present Frenchmen, like all past,
Cry for a lap of blood at last?

TO MACAULAY

The dreamy rhymer's measured snore
Falls heavy on our ears no more;
And by long strides are left behind
The dear delights of woman-kind,
Who win their battles like their loves,
In satin waistcoats and kid gloves,
And have achieved the crowning work
When they have truss'd and skewer'd a Turk.
Another comes with stouter tread,
And stalks among the statelier dead.
He rushes on, and hails by turns
High-crested Scott, broad-breasted Burns,
And shows the British youth, who ne'er
Will lag behind, what Romans were,
When all the Tuscans and their Lars
Shouted, and shook the towers of Mars.

TO A BRIDE, FEB. 17, 1846

A still, serene, soft day; enough of sun
To wreathe the cottage smoke like pine-tree snow,
Whiter than those white flowers the bride-maids wore;
Upon the silent boughs the lissom air
Rested; and, only when it went, they moved,
Nor more than under linnet springing off.
Such was the wedding-morn: the joyous Year
Lept over March and April up to May.
   Regent of rising and of ebbing hearts,
Thyself borne on in cool serenity,
All heaven around and bending over thee,
All earth below and watchful of thy course!
Well hast thou chosen, after long demur
To aspirations from more realms than one.
Peace be with those thou leavest! peace with thee!
Is that enough to wish thee? not enough,

But very much: for Love himself feels pain,
While brighter plumage shoots, to shed last year's;
And one at home (how dear that one!) recalls
Thy name, and thou recallest one at home.
Yet turn not back thine eyes; the hour of tears
Is over; nor believe thou that Romance
Closes against pure Faith her rich domain.
Shall only blossoms flourish there? Arise,
Far-sighted bride! look forward! clearer views
And higher hopes lie under calmer skies.
Fortune in vain call'd out to thee; in vain
Rays from high regions darted; Wit pour'd out
His sparkling treasures; Wisdom laid his crown
Of richer jewels at thy reckless feet.
Well hast thou chosen. I repeat the words,
Adding as true ones, not untold before,
That incense must have fire for its ascent,
Else 'tis inert and can not reach the idol.
Youth is the sole equivalent of youth.
Enjoy it while it lasts; and last it will;
Love can prolong it in despite of Years.

CUPID AND PAN

CUPID saw Pan stretcht at full length asleep.
He snatcht the goatskin from the half-covered limbs,
And, now in *this* place now in *that* twitcht up
A stiff curv'd hair: meanwhile the slumberer
Blew from his ruddy breast all care about
His flock, all care about the snow, that hung
Only where creviced rocks rose bleak and high,
And felt .. what any cork-tree's bark may feel.
His hemlock pipe lay underneath his neck:
But even this the wicked boy stole out,
And unperceived .. save that he twinkled once
His hard sharp ear, and laid it down again.
'Jupiter! is there any God' said Love,
'Sluggish as this prick-ear one! verily
Not thy own wife could stir or waken him.'
  Between his rosy lips he laid the pipe
And blew it shrilly: that loud sound did wake
The sleeper: up sprang then two ears at once
Above the grass; up sprang the wrathful God
And shook the ground beneath him with his leap.
But quite as quickly and much higher sprang
The audacious boy, deriding him outright.

'Down with those arrows, wicked imp! that bow,
Down with it; then what canst thou do?'
                                        'What then,
Pan, I can do, soon shalt thou see . . There! there!'
   He spake, and threw them at Pan's feet: the bow,
The golden bow, sprang up again, and flowers
Cradled the quiver as it struck the earth.
' 'Twould shame me.'
                        'In my conflicts shame is none,
Even for the vanquisht: check but wrath: come on:
Come, modest one! close with me, hand to hand.'
   Pan rolled his yellow eyes, and suddenly
Snatcht (as a fowler with his net, who fears
To spoil the feathers of some rarer bird)
Love's slender arm, taunting and teasing him
Nearer and nearer. Then, if ne'er before,
The ruddy color left his face; 'tis said
He trembled too, like one whom sudden flakes
Of snow have fallen on, amidst a game
Of quoits or ball in a warm day of spring.
   'Go! go!' the Arcadian cried 'and learn respect
To betters, at due distance, and hold back
Big words, that suit such littleness but ill.
Why, anyone (unless thou wert a God)
Would swear thou hast not yet seen thrice five years
And yet thou urgest . . nay, thou challengest
Me, even me, quiet, and half-asleep.
Off! or beware the willow-twig, thy due.'
   Now shame and anger seized upon the boy;
He raised his stature, and he aim'd a blow
Where the broad hairy breast stood quite exposed
Without the goatskin, swifter than the bird
Of Jove, or than the lightning he has borne.
Wary was the Arcadian, and he caught
The coming fist: it burnt as burns the fire
Upon the altar. The wise elder loost
His hold, and blew upon his open palm
From rounded cheeks a long thin breath, and then
Tried to encompass with both arms the neck
And waist of the boy God: with tremulous pulse
He fain would twist his hard long leg between
The smoother, and trip up, if trip he might,
The tenderer foot, and fit and fit again
The uncertain and insatiate grasp upon
A yielding marble, dazzling eye and brain.
He could not wish the battle at an end,
No, not to conquer; such was the delight;
But glory, ah deceitful glory, seized

(Or somewhat did) one born not to obey.
When Love, unequal to such strength, had nigh
Succumbed, he made one effort more, and caught
The horn above him: he from Arcady
Laught as he tost him up on high: nor then
Forgot the child his cunning. While the foe
Was crying 'Yield thee,' and was running o'er
The provinces of conquest, now with one
Now with the other hand, their pleasant change,
Losing and then recovering what they lost,
Love from his wing drew one short feather forth
And smote the eyes devouring him. Then rang
The rivers and deep lakes, and groves and vales
Throughout their windings. Ladon heard the roar
And broke into the marsh: Alphëus heard
Stymphalos, Mænalos (Pan's far-off home),
Cyllene, Pholöe, Parthenos, who stared
On Tegea's and Lycæosis affright.
The winged horse who, no long while before,
Was seen upon Parnassus, bold and proud,
Is said (it may be true, it may be false)
To have slunk down before that cry of Pan,
And to have run into a shady cave
With broken spirit, and there lain for years,
Nor once have shaken the Castilian rill
With neigh, or ruffling of that mighty mane.
'Hail, conqueror!' cried out Love: but Pan cried out
Sadder, 'Ah never shall I see again
My woodland realm! ah never more behold
The melting snow borne down and rolled along
The whirling brook; nor river full and large,
Nor smooth and purple pebble in the ford,
Nor white round cloud that rolls o'er vernal sky,
Nor the mild fire that Hesper lights for us
To sing by, when the sun is gone to rest.
Woe! woe! the blind have but one place on earth,
And blind am I . . blind, wander where I may!
Spare me! now spare me, Cupid! 'Twas not I
Began the contest; 'tis not meet for me
First to ask peace; peace, peace is all I ask;
Victory well may grant this only boon.'
Then held he out his hand; but knowing not
Whether he held it opposite his foe,
Huge tears ran down both cheeks. Love grew more mild
At seeing this, and said . .
                              'Cheer up! behold
A remedy; upon one pact applied,
That thou remove not this light monument

Of my success, but leave it there for me.'
  Amaranth was the flower he chose the first;
'Twas brittle and dropt broken; one white rose
(All roses then were white) he softly prest;
Narcissusses and violets took their turn,
And lofty open-hearted lilies their's,
And lesser ones with modest heads just rais'd
Above the turf, shaking alternate bells.
The slenderest of all myrtle twigs held these
Together, and across both eyes confined.
Smart was the pain they gave him, first applied:
He stampt, he groan'd, he bared his teeth, and heaved
To nostril the broad ridges of his lip.
After a while, however, he was heard
To sing again; and better rested he
Among the strawberries, whose fragrant leaf
Deceives with ruddy hue the searching sight
In its late season: he grew brave enough
To trill in easy song the pliant names
Of half the Dryads; proud enough to deck
His beauty out . . down went at last the band.
Renewed were then his sorrow and his shame.
He hied to Paphos: he must now implore
Again his proud subduer. At the gate
Stood Venus, and spake thus.
                  'Why hast thou torn
Our gifts away? No gentle chastisement
Awaits thee now. The bands my son imposed,
He would in time, his own good time, remove.
O goat-foot! he who dares despise our gifts
Rues it at last. Soon, soon another[1] wreath
Shall bind thy brow, and no such flowers be there.'

DRYOPE

  Famous and over famous Œta reign'd
Dryops: him beauteous Polydora bare
To the river-god Sperchios: but above
Mother and sire, far brighter in renown,
Was Dryope their daughter, the beloved
Of him who guides thro' heaven his golden car.
Showering his light o'er all things, he endues
All things with colour, grace and song gives he,
But never now on any condescends
To lower his shining locks; his roseate lips
Breathe an ambrosial sigh on none but her.

[1] After the death of Pitys he wore the pine.

He follows that shy Nymph thro' pathless ways,
Among the willows in their soft grey flowers,
In their peel'd boughs odorous, and amid
The baskets white and humid, incomplete:
He follows her along the river-side,
Soft to the foot and gladdened by the breeze;
He follows where the Nereids watch their fords
While listen the Napæan maids around.
Tending one day her father's sheep, she heard
A flute in the deep valley; then a pipe;
And soon from upright arms the tymbrel trill'd.
Dryads and Hamadryads then appear'd,
And one among them cried to her aloud
'Knowest thou not the day when all should sing
Pæan and *Io Pæan?* Shunnest thou
The lord of all, whom all the earth adores,
Giver of light and gladness, warmth and song?
And willest thou that Dryops stand above
Admetos? from thy sight thus banishing
And shutting from thy fold the son of Jove.'
   She, proud and joyous at the gay reproof,
Stood silent. They began the dance and games.
And thus the day went on. When evening came
They sang the hymn to Delios. Nigh the seat
Of Dryope, among the tufts of grass,
A lyre shone out; whose can it be, they ask;
Each saw the next with her's upon her knee;
Whether Theano's or Autonöe's gift,
Dryope takes it gratefully, and trills
The glimmering strings: and now at one she looks,
Now at another, knowingly, and speaks
(As if it heard her) to it, now on lap
And now on bosom fondly laying it.
Behold! a snake, a snake, it glides away.
They shriek: and each one as she sate reclined
Throws her whole body back. Striving to rise,
Autonöe prest upon a fragile reed
Her flattened hand, nor felt it: when she saw
The blood, she suckt the starting globe, and sought
The place it sprang from. Hither, thither, run
The maidens. But the strings, and tortoise-shell
That held them at due distance, are instinct
With life, and rush on Dryope, too slow
To celebrate the rites the sires had taught
And Delios had ordain'd. One whom the flight
Left nearest, turn'd her head, stil flying on,
Fearful til pity overcame her fear,
And thus she cried aloud.

     'Look back! look back!
See how that creature licks her lips, her eyes,
Her bosom! how it seizes! how it binds
In the thick grass her struggles! Where is now,
Where is Apollo proud of Python slain?
Whether she sinn'd thro' silliness or dread,
Poor inexperienced girl! are snakes to teach?
Are they fit bonds for love? can fear persuade?
Phœbus! come hither! aid us! Ah, what now
Would the beast do? how swells his horrid crest?'
Various and manifold the dragon brood.
Some urge their scales along the ground, and some
Their wings aloft, some yoked to fiery cars,
And some, tho' hard of body, melt in air.
  Callianira now was brave enough
To stop her flight: on the first hill she rais'd
Her eyes above the brambles, just above,
And caught and held Diaule at her side,
Who, when she stopt her, trembled more and more.
But arguments are ready to allay
Her terror; all strong arguments, like these.
'Are there not many things that may deceive
The sight at first? might not a lizard seem
A dragon? and how pleasant in hot days
To hold a lizard to the breast, and tempt
Its harmless bitings with the finger's end!
Dragon or lizard, rare the species is.
What! are they over . . Dryope's alarms?
She treats it like a sister. Lo! her hand
Upon its neck! and, far as we are off,
Lo! how it shines! as bright as any star.
Vainly exhorts she, first Autonöe,
And then Diaule, to come on; alone
She ventures; vainly would they call her back.
  And now again the creature is transform'd.
Lizard nor serpent now, nor tortoise-shell
Cheyls, is that which purple flutters round,
And which is whiter here and darker there,
Like violets drifted o'er with shifting hail.
Golden the hair that fluctuates upon neck
None of its own. A bland etherial glow
Ran over and ran thro' the calmer maid.
At last her fellow Nymphs came all around,
And Delios stood before them, manifest
No less to them than to his Dryope:
For with a radiant nod and arm outstretcht
He call'd them back; and they obey'd his call.
He lookt upon them, and with placid smile

Bespake them, drawing close his saffron vest.
Their eyes were lower'd before him as they stept
Into his presence; well they knew what fears
He shook throughout the Dryads, when he gave
His steeds and chariot to his reckless son,
When the woods crasht and perisht under him,
And when Eridanos, altho' his stream
Flows down from heaven, saw its last ripple sink.
Well they remembered how Diana fled
Among the woods and wilds, when mightier bow
Than hers was strung, and Python gaspt in death.
Potent of good they knew him, and of ill,
And closed the secret in their prudent hearts.
At first they would have pitied the hard fate
Of Dryope; but when she answered not
The words of pity, in her face they lookt
Stealthily.
            Soft the moisture of her brow,
Languid the luster of her eyes; a shame
Rosier and richer than before suffused
Her features, and her lips were tinged with flame
A God inspired, and worthy of that God.
    Each had her little question; but she stopt
As tho' she would reprove: at this they ply
Joke after joke, until they bring her home.
All they had known they would make others know,
But they had lookt too near and seen too well,
And had invoked the God with dance and hymn;
Beside, Diana would have sore avenged
Her righteous brother, who deals openly
With mortals, and new facts from them conceals.
    Dryope soon became Andræmon's wife,
And mother of Amphissos. Every spring
They chaunt her praises; her's, who trill'd so well
The plectron of Apollo; in the vale,
Of her own shady Œta do they sing.

PAN AND PITYS

Cease to complain of what the Fates decree,
Whether shall Death have carried off or (worse)
Another, thy heart's treasure: bitter Styx
Hath overflowed the dales of Arcady,
And Cares have risen to the realms above.
By Pan and Boreas was a Dryad wooed,
Pitys her name, her haunt the grove and wild:
Boreas she fled from, upon Pan she gazed

With a sly fondness, yet accusing him
Of fickle mind; and this was her reproof.
   'Ah why do men, or Gods who ought to see
More clearly, think that bonds will bind for ever!
Often have stormy seas borne safely home
A ship to perish in its port at last;
Even they themselves, in other things unchanged,
Are mutable in love; even he who rules
Olympus hath been lighter than his clouds.
Alas! uncertain is the lover race,
All of it; worst are they who sing the best,
And thou, Pan, worse than all.
                    By what deceit
Beguiledst thou the Goddess of the night?
O wary shepherd of the snow-white flock!
Ay, thy reeds crackled with thy scorching flames
And burst with sobs and groans . . the snow-white flock
Was safe, the love-sick swain kept sharp look there.
Wonderest thou such report should reach my ear?
And widenest thou thine eyes, half-ready now
To swear it all away, and to conceal
The fountain of Selinos. So! thou knowest
Nothing about that shallow brook, those herbs
It waves in running, nothing of the stones
Smooth as the pavement of a temple-floor,
And how the headstrong leader of the flock
Broke loose from thy left-hand, and in pursuit
How falledst thou, and how thy knee was bound
With ivy lest white hairs betray the gash.
Denyest thou that by thy own accord
Cynthia whould share thy flock and take her choice?
Denyest thou damping and sprinkling o'er
With dust, and shutting up within a cave
Far out of sight, the better breed? the worse
Displayed upon the bank below, well washt,
Their puffy fleeces glittering in the sun.
Shame! to defraud with gifts, and such as these!'
   Pan, blushing thro both ears as ne'er before,
Cried 'Who drag'd back these fables from the past?
Juster and happier hadst thou been to scorn
The false and fugitive. With hoarse uproar
I heard thy Boreas bray his song uncouth,
And oldest goats ran from it in affright.
Thee, too beloved Pitys, then I saw
Averse: couldst ever thou believe his speech,
His, the most bitter foe to me and mine.
From Cynthia never fell such hard rebuke.
Different from thee, she pities them who mourn;

N

Whether beneath straw roof or lofty tower,
She sits by the bedside and silently
Watches, and soothes the wakeful til they sleep.
I wooed not Cynthia; me she wooed: not all
Please her; she hates the rude, she cheers the gay,
She shrouds her face when Boreas ventures near.
Above all other birds the nightingale
She loves; she loves the poplar of the Po
Trembling and whispering; she descends among
The boxtrees on Cytoros; night by night
You find her at the olive: it is she
Who makes the berries of the mountain-ash
Bright at her touch: the glassy founts, the fanes
Hoary with age, the sea when Hesper comes
To Tethys, and when liquid voices rise
Above the shore . . but Boreas . . no, not she.'
Then Pitys, with a smile.

                 'Ha! what a voice!
My lover Boreas could not roar his name
More harshly. Come now, cunning lightfoot! say
How was it thou couldst take the Goddess in,
And with a charge so moderate on thy fold?'
  'Again, O Pitys, wouldst thou torture me?
Gifts not as lover but as loved I gave;
I gave her what she askt: had she askt more
I would have given it; 'twas but half the flock:
Therefor 'twas separated in two parts;
The fatter one, of bolder brow, shone out
In whiteness, but its wool was like goat-hair,
And loud its bleating for more plenteous grass;
Strong too its smell: my Goddess heeded not
The smell or bleat, but took the weightier fleece.
Why shakest thou thy head, incredulous?
Why should I urge the truth on unbelief?
Or why so fondly sue to scorn and hate?
Pitys! a time there was when I was heard
With one long smile, and when the softest hand
Stroked down unconsciously the lynx-skin gift
of Bacchus on my lap, and blushes rose
If somewhat, by some chance, it was removed.
In silence or in speech I then could please,
I then at times could turn my face aside,
Forgetting that my awkward hand was placed
Just where thy knees were bending for a seat:
Then could I at another hour look up
At the sun's parting ray, and draw the breath
Of fresher herbs, while clouds took living forms
Throwing their meshes o'er the azure deep,

And while thy gaze was on the flight of crows
Hoarse overhead, winging their beaten way
At regular and wonted intervals.
Then, never doubting my sworn love, anew
Thou badest me swear it: pleasure lay secure
On its full golden sheaf.
                    Now, alas, now
What comfort brings me on the barren shore
Pale oleaster, or gay citisus
That hides the cavern, or pellucid vein
Of wandering vine, or broom that once betray'd
The weak twin fawns! how could I join the glee
Of babbling brook, or bear the lull of grove,
Or mind the dazzling vapor from the grass,
Unless my Pitys told me, and took up
The faltering reed or interrupted song?'
Thus he, enclosing with his arm hirsute
Her neck, and stroking slow her auburn hair.
   'Up with the pipe' said she 'O Pan! and since
It seems so pleasant to recall old times,
Run over those we both enjoy'd alike,
And I will sing of Boreas, whom I hate.
He boasts of oaks uprooted by his blast,
Of heaven itself his hailstones have disturb'd,
Of thy peculiar heritage afire,
And how thy loftiest woods bow'd down beneath
His furious pennons black with bale and dread.
He boasts of ships submerged, and waves up-piled
High as Olympus, and the trident torn
From Jove's own brother: worst of all, he boasts
How often he deluded with his voice,
Under the rocks of Ismaros, that true
And hapless lover when his eyes sought sleep,
And made his wandering mind believe the sound
Rose from the Manes at his wife recall'd.
His pleasure is to drive from lids fresh-closed
Fond dreams away, and draw false forms about,
And where he finds one terror to bring more.
Can such a lover ever be beloved?'
   Boreas heard all: he stood upon the cliff
Before, now crept he into the near brake;
Rage seiz'd him; swinging a huge rock around
And, shaking with one stamp the mountain-head,
Hurld it . . and cried
                'Is Boreas so contemn'd?'
It smote the Dryad, sprinkling with her blood
The tree they sat beneath: there faithful Pan
Mused often, often call'd aloud the name

Of Pitys, and wiped off tear after tear
From the hoarse pipe, then threw it wildly by,
And never from that day wore other wreath
Than off the pine-tree darkened with her gore.

SILENUS

SILENUS, when he led the Satyrs home,
Young Satyrs, tender-hooft and ruddy-horn'd,
With Bacchus equal-aged, sat down sometimes
Where softer herbs invited, then releast
From fawn-skin pouch a well-compacted pipe,
And sprinkled song with wisdom.
       Some admired
The graceful order of unequal reeds;
Others cared little for the melody
Or what the melody's deep bosom bore,
And thought Silenus might have made them shine.
They whisper'd this: Silenus overheard,
And mildly said ' 'Twere easy: thus I did
When I was youthful: older, I perceive
No pleasure in the buzzes of the flies,
Which like what *you* like, O my little ones!'
 Some fancied he reproved them, and stood still,
Until they saw how grave the Satyr boys
Were looking; then one twicht an upright ear
And one a tail recurv'd, or stroked it down.
Audacious innocence! A bolder cried
'Sound us a song of war;' a timider,
'Tell us a story that will last til night.'
 Silenus smiled on both, and thus replied.
'Chromis hath sung fierce battles, swords of flame,
Etherial arrows wing'd with ostrich-plumes,
Chariots of chrysolite and ruby reins,
And horses champing pearls and quaffing blood.
Mnasylos tells wide stories: day is short,
Night shorter; they thro months and years extend.
When suns are warm, my children, let your hearts
Beat, but not beat for battles; when o'ercast,
Mnasylos and his tepid fogs avoid.
 'I hear young voices near us; they are sweet;
Go where they call you; I am fain to rest;
Leave me, and ask for no more song to-day.'

GUIZOT'S DISGUISE

GUIZOT, in haste to cut and run,
A lackey's livery has put on;
But whosoever calls *disguise*
In him the lackey's livery, lies.

ODE TO SICILY

1

FEW mortal hands have struck the heroic string,
Since Milton's lay in death across his breast.
    But shall the lyre then rest
With vilest dust upon it? This of late
    Hath been its fate.

2

But thou, O Sicily! art born again.
Far over chariots and Olympic steeds
I see the heads and the stout arms of men,
And will record (God gives me power) their deeds.

3

Hail to thee first, Palermo! hail to thee
Who callest with loud voice, '*Arise! be free,
Weak is the hand and rusty is the chain.*'
    Thou callest; nor in vain.

4

Not only from the mountains rushes forth
    The knighthood of the North,
    In whom my soul elate
    Owns now a race cognate,
But even the couch of Sloth, 'mid painted walls,
Swells up, and men start forth from it, where calls
The voice of Honour, long, too long, unheard.

5

    Not that the wretch was fear'd,
Who fear'd the meanest as he fear'd the best,
    But that around all kings
    For ever springs
A wasting vapour that absorbs the fire
    Of all that would rise higher.

6

Even free nations will not let there be
        More nations free.
Witness (O shame!) our own,
Of late years viler none . .

7

        To gratify a brood,
Swamp-fed amid the Suabian wood,
The sons of Lusitania were cajoled,
        And bound and sold,
And sent in chains where we unchain the slave
        We die with thirst to save.

8

Ye too, Sicilians, ye too gave we up
        To drain the bitter cup,
Which ye dash from ye in the despot's face . .
        O glorious race!

9

Which Hiero, Gelon, Pindar, sat among
And prais'd for weaker deeds in deathless song;
One is yet left to laud ye. Years have marr'd
My voice, my prelude for some better bard,
When such shall rise; and such your deeds create.

10

        In the lone woods, and late,
Murmurs swell loud and louder, till at last
        So strong the blast
That the whole forest, earth and sea and sky
        To the loud surge reply.

11

Within the circle of six hundred years,
Show me a Bourbon on whose brow appears
        No brand of traitor. Change the tree,
From the same stock for ever will there be
The same foul canker, the same bitter fruit.
        Strike, Sicily, uproot
        The cursed upas. Never trust
That race again: down with it; dust to dust.

[FEW POETS BECKON TO THE CALMLY GOOD]

I

Few poets beckon to the calmly good,
Few lay a hallowing hand upon the head
Which lowers its barbarous for our Delphic crown:
But loose strings rattle on unseasoned wood,
And weak words whiffle round, where Virtue's meed
Shines in a smile or shrivels in a frown.

II

He shall not give it, shall not touch it, he
Who crawls into the gold mine, bending low
And bringing from its dripples with much mire
One shining atom. Could it ever be,
O God of light and song? The breast must glow
Not with thine only, but with Virtue's fire.

III

I stand where Tiber rolls his turbid wave
And see two men rise up; in purple one
And holding in his grasp the golden wards;
The other, not less stately, nor more brave,
Clad modestly. Pass! By your hands be done
God's work, creators of immortal bards!

[MILTON]

I

I told ye, since the prophet Milton's day
Heroic song hath never swept the earth
To soar in flaming chariot up to Heaven.
Taunt, little children! taunt ye while ye may.
Natural your wonder, natural is your mirth,
Natural your weakness. Ye are all forgiven.

II

One man above all other men is great,
Even on this globe, where dust obscures the signs.
God closed his eyes to pour into his heart
His own pure wisdom. In chill house he sate,
Fed only on those fruits the hand divine
Disdain'd not, thro' his angels, to impart.

172

III

He was despised of those he would have spilt
His blood to ransom. How much happier we,
Altho' so small and feeble! We are taught
There may be national, not royal guilt,
And, if there has been, then there ought to be,
But 'tis the illusion of a mind distraught.

IV

This with a tiny hand of ductile lead
Shows me the way; this takes me down his slate,
Draws me a line and teaches me to write;
Another pats me kindly on the head,
But finds one letter here and there too great,
One passable, one pretty well, one quite.

V

No wonder I am proud. At such award
The Muse most virginal would raise her chin
Forth from her collar-bone. What inward fire
Must swell the bosom of that favored bard
And wake to vigorous life the germ within,
On whom such judges look with such regard!

DYING SPEECH OF AN OLD PHILOSOPHER

I strove with none, for none was worth my strife:
    Nature I loved, and, next to Nature, Art:
I warm'd both hands before the fire of Life;
    It sinks; and I am ready to depart.

A RAILROAD ECLOGUE

Father. WHAT brought thee back, lad?
Son.   Father! the same feet
    As took me brought me back, I warrant ye.
Father. Couldst thou not find the rail?
Son.   The deuce himself,
    Who can find most things, could not find the rail.
Father. Plain as a pike-staff miles and miles it lies.
Son.   So they all told me. Pike-staffs in your day
    Must have been hugely plainer than just now.
Father. What didst thou ask for?
Son.   Ask for? Tewkesbury
    Thro' Defford opposite to Breedon-hill.
Father. Right: and they set ye wrong?

Son.   Me wrong? not they;
The best among 'em should not set me wrong,
Nor right, nor anything; I'd tell 'em that.—
Father. Herefordshire's short horns and shorter wits
Are known in every quarter of the land,
Those blunt, these blunter. Well! no help for it!
Each might do harm if each had more of each . . .
Yet even in Herefordshire there are some
Not downright dolts . . before the cidar's broacht,
When all are much alike . . yet most could tell
A railroad from a parish or a pike.
How thou couldst miss that railroad puzzles me,
Seeing there lies none other round about.
Son. I found the rails along the whole brook-side
Left of that old stone bridge across yon Avon.
Father. That is the place.
Son.   There was a house hard-by,
And past it ran a furnace upon wheels,
Like a mad bull, tail up in air, and horns
So low ye might not see 'em. On it bumpt,
Roaring, as strait as any arrow flits,
As strait, as fast too, ay, and faster went it,
And, could it keep its wind up and not crack,
Then woe betide the eggs at Tewkesbury
This market-day, and lambs, and sheep! a score
Of pigs might be made flitches in a trice,
Before they well could knuckle.
                      Father! father!
If they were ourn, thou wouldst not chuckle so,
And shake thy sides, and wipe thy eyes, and rub
Thy breeches-knees, like Sunday shoes, at that rate.
Hows'ever . . . .
Father.   'Twas the train, lad, 'twas the train.
Son. May-be: I had no business with a train.
'*Go thee by rail*, you told me; *by the rail
At Defford*' . . and didst make a fool of me.
Father. Ay, lad, I did indeed: it was methinks
Some twenty years agone last Martinmas.

TO THE AUTHOR OF *FESTUS*

ON THE CLASSICK AND ROMANTICK

PHILIP! I know thee not, thy song I know:
It fell upon my ear among the last
Destined to fall upon it: but while strength
Is left me, I will rise to hail the morn
Of the stout-hearted who begin a work

Wherin I did but idle at odd hours.
 The Faeries never tempted me away
From higher fountains and severer shades;
Their rings allured me not from deeper tracks
Left by Olympick wheels on ampler plains,
Yet could I see them and can see them now
With pleasurable warmth, and hold in bonds
Of brotherhood men whom their gamesome wreath
In youth's fresh slumber caught, and still detains.
I wear no cestus; my right-hand is free
To point the road few seem inclined to take.
Admonish thou, with me, the starting youth,
Ready to seize all nature at one grasp,
To mingle earth, sea, sky, woods, cataracts,
And make all nations think and speak alike.
 Some see but sunshine, others see but gloom,
Others confound them strangely, furiously;
Most have an eye for colour, few for form.
Imperfect is the glory to *create*,
Unless on our creation we can look
And see that all is good; we then may rest.
In every poem train the leading shoot;
Break off the suckers. Thought erases thought,
As numerous sheep erase each other's print
When spungy moss they press or sterile sand.
Blades thickly sown want nutriment and droop,
Altho' the seed be sound, and rich the soil.
Thus healthy-born ideas, bedded close,
By dreaming fondness, perish overlaid.
A rose or sprig of myrtle in the hair
Pleases me better than a far-sought gem.
I chide the flounce that checks the nimble feet,
Abhor the cruel piercer of the ear,
And would strike down the chain that cuts in two
The beauteous column of the marble neck.
Barbarous and false are all such ornaments,
Yet such hath poesy in whim put on.
Classical hath been deem'd each Roman name
Writ on the roll-call of each pedagogue
In the same hand, in the same tone pronounced;
Yet might five scanty pages well contain
All that the Muses in fresh youth would own
Between the grave at Tomos, wet with tears
Rolling amain down Getick beard unshorn,
And that grand priest whose purple shone afar
From his own Venice o'er the Adrian sea.
We talk of schools .. unscholarly; of schools.
Part the romantick from the classical.

The classical like the heroick age
Is past; but Poetry may reassume
That glorious name with Tartar and with Turk,
With Goth or Arab, Sheik or Paladin,
And not with Roman and with Greek alone.
   The name is graven on the workmanship.
The trumpet-blast of *Marmion* never shook
The walls of God-built Ilion; yet what shout
Of the Achaians swells the heart so high?
Nor fainter is the artillery-roar that blooms
From Hohenlinden to the *Baltick* strand.
Shakespeare with majesty benign call'd up
The obedient classicks from their marble seats,
And led them thro dim glens and sheeny glades,
And over precipices, over seas
Unknown by mariners, to palaces
High-archt, to festival, to dance, to joust,
And gave them golden spurs and vizors barred,
And steeds that Pheidias had turn'd pale to see.
The mighty man who opened Paradise,
Harmonious far above Homerick song,
Or any song that human ears shall hear,
Sometimes was classical and sometimes not.
Rome chain'd him down, the younger Italy
Dissolved, not fatally, his Sampson strength.
   I leave behind me those who stood around
The throne of Shakespeare, sturdy, but unclean;
To hurry past the opprobrious courts and lanes
Of the loose pipers at the Belial feasts,
Past mimes obscene and grinders of lampoons . .
Away the petty wheel, the callous hand!
Goldsmith was classical, and Gray almost.
So was poor Collins, heart bound to Romance:
Shelley and Keats, those southern stars, shone higher.
Cowper had more variety, more strength,
Gentlest of bards! stil pitied, stil beloved!
Shrewder in epigram than polity
Was Canning; Frere more graceful; Smith more grand;[1]
A genuine poet was the last alone.
Romantick, classical, the female hand
That chain'd the cruel Ivan down for ever,
And followed up, rapt in his fiery car
The boy of Casabianca to the skies.
Other fair forms breathe round us, which exert
With Paphian softness Amazonian power,
And sweep in bright array the Attick field.

[1] Bobus Smith.

To *men* turn now, who stand or lately stood
With more than Royalty's gilt bays adorn'd.
Wordsworth, in sonnet, is a classick too,
And on that grass-plot sits at Milton's side;
In the long walk he soon is out of breath
And wheezes heavier than his friends could wish.
Follow his pedlar up the devious rill,
And, if you faint not, you are well repaid.
Large lumps of precious metal lie engulpht
In gravelly beds, whence you must delve them out,
And thirst sometimes and hunger; shudder not
To wield the pickaxe and to shake the sieve.
Well shall the labour be (tho hard) repaid.
Too weak for ode or epick, and his gait
Somewhat too rural for the tragick pall,
Which never was cut out of duffel grey,
He fell, entangled, 'on the grunsel-edge'
Flat on his face, 'and shamed his worshipers.'
Classick in every feature was my friend
The genial Southey: none who ruled around
Held in such order such a wide domain . .
But often too indulgent, too profuse.
The ancients see us under them, and grieve
That we are parted by a rank morass,
Wishing its flowers more delicate and fewer.
Abstemious were the Greeks; they never strove
To look so fierce: their muses were sedate,
Never obstreperous: you heard no breath
Outside the flute; each sound ran clear within.
The Fauns might dance, might clap their hands, might shout,
Might revel and run riotous; the Nymphs
Furtively glanced, and fear'd, or seem'd to fear:
Descended on the lightest of light wings,
The graceful son of Maia mused apart
Graceful, but strong; he listen'd; he drew nigh;
And now with his own lyre and now with voice
Tempered the strain; Apollo calmly smiled.

TO THE REVEREND CUTHBERT SOUTHEY

CUTHBERT! whose father first in all our land
Sate in calm judgment on poetic peer,
Whom hatred never, friendship seldom, warpt . .
Agen I read his page and hear his voice;
I heard it ere I knew it, ere I saw
Who uttered it, each then to each unknown.
Twelve years had past, when upon Avon's cliff,
Hard-by his birthplace, first our hands were joined;
After three more he visited my home.

Along Lantony's ruined ailes we walkt
And woods then pathless, over verdant hill
And ruddy mountain, and aside the stream
Of sparkling Hondy.
                    Just at close of day
There by the comet's light we saw the fox
Rush from the alders, nor relax in speed
Until he trod the pathway of his sires
Under the hoary crag of Comioy.
Then both were happy.
                     War had paus'd: the Loire
Invited me. Again burst forth fierce War.
I minded not his fury: there I staid,
Sole of my countrymen, and foes abstain'd
(Tho' sore and bleeding) from my house alone.
But female fear impelld me past the Alps,
Where, loveliest of all lakes, the Lario sleeps
Under the walls of Como.
                         There he came
Again to see me; there again our walks
We recommenced . . less happy than before.
Grief had swept over him; days darkened round:
Bellagio, Valintelvi, smiled in vain,
And Monterosa from Helvetia far
Advanced to meet us, mild in majesty
Above the glittering crests of giant sons
Stationed around . . . in vain too, all in vain.
    Perhaps the hour may come when others, taught
By him to read, may read my page aright
And find what lies within it; time enough
Is there before us in the world of thought.
The favor I may need I scorn to ask.
What sovran is there able to reprieve,
How then to grant, the life of the condemned
By Justice, where the Muses take their seat?
Never was I impatient to receive
What any man could give me: when a friend
Gave me my due, I took it, and no more . .
Serenely glad because that friend was pleased.
I seek not many, many seek not me.
If there are few now seated at my board,
I pull no children's hair because they munch
Gilt gingerbread, the figured and the sweet,
Or wallow in the innocence of whey;
Give *me* wild-boar, the buck's broad haunch give *me*,
And wine that time has mellowed, even as time
Mellows the warrior hermit in his cell.

Jan. 17 [1850]

ENGLISH HEXAMETERS

Askest thou if in my youth I have mounted, as others have mounted,
Galloping Hexameter, Pentameter cantering after,
English by dam and by sire; bit, bridle, and saddlery, English;
English the girths and the shoes; all English from snaffle to crupper;
Everything English about, excepting the tune of the jockey?
Latin and Greek, it is true, I have often attacht to my phaeton
Early in life, and sometimes have I ordered them out in its evening,
Dusting the linings, and pleas'd to have found them unworn and
    untarnisht.
Idle! but Idleness looks never better than close upon sunset.
Seldom my goosequill, of goose from Germany, fatted in England,
(Frolicksome though I have been) have I tried on Hexameter,
    knowing
Latin and Greek are alone its languages. We have a measure
Fashion'd by Milton's own hand, a fuller, a deeper, a louder.
Germans may flounder at will over consonant, vowel, and liquid,
Liquid and vowel but one to a dozen of consonants, ending
Each with a verb at the tail, tail heavy as African ram's tail.
Spenser and Shakspeare had each his own harmony; each an en-
    chanter
Wanting no aid from without. *Chevy Chase* had delighted their
    fathers,
Though of a different strain from the song on the *Wrath of Achilles*.
Southey was fain to pour forth his exuberant stream over regions
Near and remote: his command was absolute; every subject,
Little or great, he controll'd; in language, variety, fancy,
Richer than all his compeers, and wanton but once in dominion;
'T was when he left the full well that for ages had run by his home-
    stead,
Pushing the brambles aside which encumber'd another up higher,
Letting his bucket go down, and hearing it bump in descending,
Grating against the loose stones 'til it came but half-full from the
    bottom.
Others abstain'd from the task. Scott wander'd at large over
    Scotland;
Reckless of Roman and Greek, he chaunted the *Lay of the Minstrel*
Better than ever before any minstrel in chamber had chaunted.
Marmion mounted his horse with a shout such as rose under Ilion;
Venus, who sprang from the sea, had envied the *Lake and its Lady*.
Never on mountain or wild hath echo so cheerily sounded,
Never did monarch bestow such glorious meed upon knighthood,
Never had monarch the power, liberality, justice, discretion.
Byron liked new-papered rooms, and pull'd down old wainscoat of
    cedar;
Bright-color'd prints he preferr'd to the graver cartoons of a
    Raphael,

Sailor and Turk (with a sack), to Eginate and Parthenon marbles.
Splendid the palace he rais'd—the gin-palace in Poesy's purlieus;
Soft the divan on the sides, with spittoons for the qualmis hand
    queesy.
Wordsworth, well pleas'd with himself, cared little for modern or
    ancient.
His was the moor and the tarn, the recess in the mountain, the
    woodland
Scatter'd with trees far and wide, trees never too solemn or lofty,
Never entangled with plants overrunning the villager's foot-path.
Equable was he and plain, but wandering a little in wisdom,
Sometimes flying from blood and sometimes pouring it freely.
Yet he was English at heart. If his words were too many; if Fancy's
Furniture lookt rather scant in a whitewasht and homely apartment;
If in his rural designs there is sameness and tameness; if often
Feebleness is there for breadth; if his pencil wants rounding and
    pointing;
Few of this age or the last stand out on the like elevation.
There is a sheepfold he rais'd which my memory loves to revisit,
Sheepfold whose wall shall endure when there is not a stone of the
    palace.
Keats, the most Grecian of all, rejected the meter of Grecians;
Poesy breath'd over *him*, breath'd constantly, tenderly, freshly;
Wordsworth she left now and then, outstretcht in a slumberous
    languor,
Slightly displeased . . but return'd, as Aurora return'd to Tithonus.
Still there are walking on earth many poets whom ages hereafter
Will be more willing to praise than we now are to praise one another:
Some do I know, but I fear, as is meet, to recount or report them,
For, be whatever the name that is foremost, the next will run over,
Trampling and rolling in dust his excellent friend the precursor.
Peace be with all! but afar be ambition to follow the Roman,
Led by the German uncomb'd, and jigging in dactyl and spondee,
Lumbering shapeless jackboots which nothing can polish or supple.
Much as old metres delight me, 'tis only where first they were
    nurtured,
In their own clime, their own speech: than pamper them here I
    would rather
Tie up my Pegasus tight to the scanty-fed rack of a sonnet.

LOVE AND AGE

LOVE flies with bow unstrung when Time appears,
    And trembles at the approach of heavy years.
    A few bright feathers leaves he in his flight,
    Quite beyond call, but not forgotten quite.

DANTE

ERE blasts from northern lands
Had covered Italy with barren sands,
  Rome's Genius, smitten sore,
Wail'd on the Danube, and was heard no more.
  Centuries twice seven had past
And crusht Etruria rais'd her head at last.
  A mightier Power she saw,
Poet and prophet, give three worlds the law.
  When Dante's strength arose
Fraud met aghast the boldest of her foes;
  Religion, sick to death,
Lookt doubtful up, and drew in pain her breath.
  Both to one grave are gone;
Altars still smoke, still is the God unknown.
  Haste, whoso from above
Comest with purer fire and larger love,
  Quenchest the Stygian torch,
And leadest from the *Garden* and the *Porch*,
  Where gales breathe fresh and free,
And where a Grace is call'd a Charity,
  To Him, the God of peace,
Who bids all discord in his household cease . .
  Bids it, and bids again,
But to the purple-vested speaks in vain.
  Crying, 'Can this be borne?'
The consecrated wine-skins creak with scorn;
  While, leaving tumult there,
To quiet idols young and old repair,
  In places where is light
To lighten day . . and dark to darken night.

REMONSTRANCE AND REPLY

So then, I feel not deeply! if I did,
I should have seized the pen, and pierced therewith
The passive world!
And thus thou reasonest?
Well hast thou known the lover's, not so well
The poet's heart: While that heart bleeds, the hand
Presses it close. Grief must run on, and pass
Near Memory's more quiet shade,
Before it can compose itself in song.
He who is agonised and turns to show
His agony to those who sit around,

Seizes the pen in vain: thought, fancy, power,
Rush back into his bosom; all the strength
Of genius can not draw them into light
From under mastering Grief; but Memory,
The Muse's mother, nurses, rears them up,
Informs, and keeps them with her all her days.

REPROOF OF THANKS

NAY, thank me not again for those
Camelias, that untimely rose;
But if, whence you might please the more,
And win the few unwon before,
I sought the flowers you loved to wear,
O'erjoy'd to see them in your hair,
Upon my grave, I pray you, set
One primrose or one violet.
. . . Stay . . . I can wait a little yet.

NIL ADMIRARI, ETC.

HORACE and Creech,
Thus do ye teach?
What idle speech!

Pope! and could you
Sanction it too?
'Twill never do.

One idle pen
Writes it, and ten
Write it agen.

Sages require
Much to admire;
Nought to desire.

God! grant thou me,
Nature to see
Admiringly.

Lo! how the wise,
Read in her eyes,
Thy mysteries!

FABLE TO BE LEARNT BY BEGINNERS

THERE lived a diver once whose boast
Was that he brought up treasures lost,
However deep, beneath the sea
Of glossy-hair'd Parthenope.
To try him, people oft threw in
A silver cross or gold zecchin.
Down went the diver 'fathoms nine',
And you might see the metal shine
Between his lips or on his head,
While lazy Tethys lay abed,
And not a Nereid round her heard
The green pearl-spangled curtain stirr'd.
One day a tempting fiend threw down,
Where whirl'd the waves, a tinsel crown,
And said, 'O diver, you who dive
Deeper than any man alive,
And see, where other folks are blind,
And, what all others miss, can find,
You saw the splendid crown I threw
Into the whirlpool: now can you
Recover it? thus won, you may
Wear it . . not once, but every day,
So may your sons.' Down, down he sprang . .
A hundred Nereids heard the clang,
And closed him round and held him fast . .
The diver there had dived his last.

TO YOUTH

WHERE art thou gone, light-ankled Youth?
  With wing at either shoulder,
And smile that never left thy mouth
  Until the Hours grew colder:

Then somewhat seem'd to whisper near
  That thou and I must part;
I doubted it; I felt no fear,
  No weight upon the heart:

If aught befell it, Love was by
  And roll'd it off again;
So, if there ever was a sigh,
  'Twas not a sigh of pain.

I may not call thee back; but thou
   Returnest, when the hand
Of gentle Sleep waves o'er my brow
   His poppy-crested wand;

Then smiling eyes bend over mine,
   Then lips once prest invite;
But Sleep hath given a silent sign
   And both, alas! take flight.

TO AGE

WELCOME, old friend! These many years
   Have we lived door by door:
The Fates have laid aside their shears
   Perhaps for some few more.

I was indocil at an age
   When better boys were taught,
But thou at length hast made me sage,
   If I am sage in aught.

Little I know from other men,
   Too little they from me,
But thou hast pointed well the pen
   That writes these lines to thee.

Thanks for expelling Fear and Hope,
   One vile, the other vain;
One's scourge, the other's telescope,
   I shall not see again:

Rather what lies before my feet
   My notice shall engage . .
He who hath braved Youth's dizzy heat
   Dreads not the frost of Age.

ON SWIFT JOINING AVON NEAR RUGBY

SILENT and modest Brook! who dippest here
Thy foot in Avon as if childish fear
Witheld thee for a moment, wend along;
   Go, follow'd by my song,
Sung in such easy numbers as they use
Who turn in fondness to the Tuscan Muse,
And such as often have flow'd down on me
   From my own Fiesole.
I watch thy placid smile, nor need to say
   That Tasso wove one looser lay,

And Milton took it up to dry the tear
    Dropping on Lycidas's bier.
In youth how often at thy side I wander'd!
What golden hours, hours numberless, were squander'd
    Among thy sedges, while sometimes
    I meditated native rhymes,
And sometimes stumbled upon Latian feet;
        Then, where soft mole-built seat
        Invited me, I noted down
        What must full surely win the crown,
But first impatiently vain efforts made
On broken pencil with a broken blade.
        Anon, of lighter heart, I threw
        My hat where circling plover flew,
And once I shouted til, instead of plover,
There sprang up half a damsel, half a lover.
I would not twice be barbarous; on I went . .
And two heads sank amid the pillowing bent.
        Pardon me, gentle Stream, if rhyme
Holds up these records in the face of Time:
Among the falling leaves some birds yet sing,
And Autumn hath his butterflies like Spring.
Thou canst not turn thee back, thou canst not see
        Reflected what hath ceast to be:
        Haply thou little knowest why
        I check this levity, and sigh.
Thou never knewest her whose radiant morn
    Lighted my path to Love; she bore thy name,
She whom no Grace was tardy to adorn,
    Whom one low voice pleas'd more than louder fame:
She now is past my praises: from her urn
        To thine, with reverence due, I turn.
O silver-braided Swift! no victim ever
        Was sacrificed to thee,
Nor hast thou carried to that sacred River
Vases of myrrh, nor hast thou run to see
A band of Mænads toss their timbrels high
Mid *io-evohes* to their Deity.
But holy ashes have bestrewn thy stream
        Under the mingled gleam
Of swords and torches, and the chaunt of Rome,
        When Wiclif's lowly tomb
        Thro its thick briars was burst
        By frantic priests accurst;
For he had enter'd and laid bare the lies
That pave the labyrinth of their mysteries.
        We part . . but one more look!
        Silent and modest Brook!

PARAPHRASE OF HORACE'S PYRRHA

WHAT slender youth perfused with fresh macassar
Wooes thee, O England, in St. Stephen's bower?
For whom unlockest thou the chest that holds thy dower?

Simple as ever! Is there a deluder
Thou hast not listen'd to, thou hast not changed,
Laughing at one and all o'er whom thy fancy ranged?

The last that won thee was not overhappy,
And people found him wavering like thyself:
The little man looks less now laid upon the shelf.

While the big waves against the rock are breaking,
And small ones toss and tumble, fume and fret,
Along the sunny wall I have hung up my net.

[AFTER WELLINGTON]

Now from the chamber all are gone
Who gazed and wept o'er Wellington,
Derby and Dis do all they can
To emulate so great a man.
If neither can be quite so great,
Resolved is each to LIE *in state.*

[SISYPHUS]

YE whom your earthly gods condemn to heave
    The stone of Sisyphus uphill for ever,
Do not, if ye have heard of him, believe,
    As your forefathers did, that he was clever.

Strength in his arm, and wisdom in his head,
    He would have hurl'd his torment higher still,
And would have brought them down with it, instead
    Of thus turmoiling at their wanton will.

TO THE RIVER AVON

Avon! why runnest thou away so fast?
Rest thee before that Chancel where repose
The bones of him whose spirit moves the world.
I have beheld thy birthplace, I have seen
Thy tiny ripples where they played amid
The golden cups and ever-waving blades.

I have seen mighty rivers, I have seen
Padus, recovered from his firy wound,
And Tiber, prouder than them all to bear
Upon his tawny bosom men who crusht
The world they trod on, heeding not the cries
Of culprit kings and nations many-tongued.
What are to me these rivers, once adorn'd
With crowns they would not wear but swept away?
Worthier art thou of worship, and I bend
My knees upon thy bank, and call thy name,
And hear, or think I hear, thy voice reply.

EPIGRAMS

EPIGRAMS must be curt, nor seem
Tail-pieces to a poet's dream.
If they should anywhere be found
Serious, or musical in sound
Turn into prose the two worst pages
And you will rank among the sages.

[THE BEE ABOUT THE ROSE]

THE richest flowers have not most honey-cells.
You seldom find the bee about the rose,
Oftener the beetle eating into it.
The violet less attracts the noisy hum
Than the minute and poisonous bloom of box.
Poets know this; Nature's invited guests
Draw near and note it down and ponder it;
The idler sees it, sees unheedingly,
Unheedingly the rifler of the hive.

TO ONE WHO QUOTES AND DETRACTS

ROB me and maim me! Why, man, take such pains
On your bare heath to hang yourself in chains?

[POETRY]

POET! I like not mealy fruit; give me
Freshness and crispness and solidity;
Apples are none the better overripe,
And prime buck-venison I prefer to tripe.

ON CATULLUS

TELL me not what too well I know
About the bard of Sirmio . .
    Yes, in Thalia's son
Such stains there are . . as when a Grace
Sprinkles another's laughing face
    With nectar, and runs on.

[MARRIAGE]

THERE falls with every wedding chime
A feather from the wing of Time.
You pick it up, and say 'How fair
To look upon its colours are!'
Another drops day after day
Unheeded; not one word you say.
When bright and dusky are blown past,
Upon the herse there nods the last.

[OUR FORTUNES]

ACROSS, up, down, our fortunes go,
Like particles of feathery snow,
Never so certain or so sound
As when they're fallen to the ground.

[BEAUTY]

EARLY I thought the worst of lies
In poets was, that beauty dies;
I thought not only it must stay,
But glow the brighter every day:
Some who then bloom'd on earth are gone,
In some the bloom is overblown.

[TO TENNYSON]

I ENTREAT you, Alfred Tennyson,
Come and share my haunch of venison.
I have too a bin of claret,
Good, but better when you share it.
Tho 'tis only a small bin,
There's a stock of it within,
And as sure as I'm a rhymer,
Half a butt of Rudesheimer.
Come; among the sons of men is one
Welcomer than Alfred Tennyson?

188

[WHY DO I SMILE?]

'*Why do I smile?*' To hear you say
'*One month, and then the shortest day!*'
The shortest, whate'er month it be,
Is the bright day you pass with me.

[A POET AND HIS POEMS]

ALAS! 'tis very sad to hear,
Your and your Muse's end draws near:
I only wish, if this be true,
To lie a little way from you.
The grave is cold enough for me
Without you and your poetry.

TO POETS

My children! speak not ill of one another;
    I do not ask you not to hate;
Cadets must envy every elder brother,
    The little poet must the great.

[CRITICS AND POETS]

MATTHIAS, Gifford, men like those,
Find in great poets but great foes;
In Wordsworth but a husky wheeze,
In Byron but a foul disease,
In Southey one who softly bleats,
And one of thinnest air in Keats.
Yet will these live for years and years,
When those have felt the fatal shears.

[WIFE AND HUSBAND]

IN the odor of sanctity Miriam abounds,
Her husband's is nearer the odor of hounds,
With a dash of the cess-pool, a dash of the sty,
And the water of cabbages running hard-by.

[AUTUMN LEAF]

THOU needst not pitch upon my hat,
    Thou wither'd leaf! to show how near
    Is now the winter of my year;
Alas! I want no hint of that.

Prythee, ah prythee get along!
   Whisper as gently in the ear,
   I once could whisper in, to fear
No change, but live for dance and song.

[PRAISE]

NEITHER in idleness consume thy days,
Nor bend thy back to mow the weeds of praise.

[THE PLANETS]

How many ages did the planets roll
  O'er sapient heads that nightly watcht their course,
Ere the most sapient betwixt pole and pole
  Believed them fleeter than the dustman's horse!

[CYPRESS AND CEDAR]

CYPRESS and Cedar! gracefullest of trees,
Friends of my boyhood! ye, before the breeze,
As lofty lords before an eastern throne,
Bend the whole body, not the head alone.

[SLEEPER'S SOUNDS]

PEOPLE may think the work of sleep
   That deep-indented frown;
Its post of honor let it keep,
   Nor draw the nightcap down.
Acknowledge that at every wheeze,
   At every grunt and groan,
You hear his verses; do not these
   Proclaim them for his own?

YOUNG

THOU dreariest droll of puffy short-breath'd writers!
All thy *night-thoughts* and day-thoughts hung on miters.

[DEATH AND SLEEP]

DEATH, in approaching, brings me sleep so sound
I scarcely hear the dreams that hover round;
One cruel thing, one only, he can do . .
Break the bright image (Life's best gift) of you.

A QUARRELSOME BISHOP

To hide her ordure, claws the cat;
You claw, but not to cover that.
Be decenter, and learn at least
One lesson from the cleanlier beast.

[MARRIAGE BELL]

BLYTHE bell, that calls to bridal halls,
  Tolls deep a darker day;
The very shower that feeds the flower
  Weeps also its decay.

THE DUKE OF YORK'S STATUE

ENDURING is the bust of bronze,
And thine, O flower of George's sons,
Stands high above all laws and duns.

As honest men as ever cart
Convey'd to Tyburn took thy part
And raised thee up to where thou art.

[TO-DAY'S POETRY]

WHY do the Graces now desert the Muse?
They hate bright ribbons tying wooden shoes.

[DEATH'S CHASM]

BIDDEN by Hope the sorrowful and fond
Look o'er the present hour for hours beyond.
Some press, some saunter on, until at last
They reach that chasm which none who breathe hath past.
Before them Death starts up, and opens wide
His wings, and wafts them to the farther side.

[IRELAND]

IRELAND never was contented . .
Say you so? you are demented.
Ireland was contented when
All could use the sword and pen,
And when Tara rose so high
That her turrets split the sky,

And about her courts were seen
Liveried Angels robed in green,
Wearing, by Saint Patrick's bounty,
Emerald's big as half a county.

[ROMANCE OF LIFE]

THERE is a time when the romance of life
Should be shut up, and closed with double clasp:
Better that this be done before the dust
That none can blow away falls into it.

[EDWARD YOUNG'S *JOB*]

'*A Paraphrase on Job*' we see
    By Young: it loads the shelf:
He who can read one half must be
    Patient as Job himself.

TO JOHN FORSTER

CENSURED by her who stands above
The Sapphic Muse in song and love,
'*For minding what such people do,*'
I turn in confidence to you.
Now, Forster, did you never stop
At orange-peel or turnip-top,
To kick them from your path, and then
Complacently walk on agen?

[SCATTERED BEAUTY]

GOD scatters beauty as he scatters flowers
O'er the wide earth, and tells us all are ours.
A hundred lights in every temple burn,
And at each shrine I bend my knee in turn.

[DEATH]

DEATH stands above me, whispering low
    I know not what into my ear:
Of his strange language all I know
    Is, there is not a word of fear.

[QUOTING MY FAULTS]

WEARERS of rings and chains!
Pray do not take the pains
   To set me right.
In vain my faults ye quote;
I write as others wrote
   On Sunium's hight.

[TO HIMSELF]

COME forth, old lion, from thy den,
Come, be the gaze of idle men,
Old lion, shake thy mane and growl,
Or they will take thee for an owl.

[ENVY'S TORCH]

ENVY ne'er thrust into my hands her torch,
The robe of those who mount up higher to scorch.
On old Greek idols I may fix my eyes
Oftener, and bring them larger sacrifice,
Yet on the altar where are worship ours
I light my taper and lay down my flowers.

[CARLYLE]

STRIKE with Thor's hammer, strike agen
The skulking heads of half-form'd men,
And every northern God shall smile
Upon thy well-aim'd blow, Carlyle!

[DARK DAY]

OLD MAN

WHAT wouldst thou say,
   Autumnal day,
Clothed in a mist akin to rain?

DARK DAY

Thus I appear,
   Because next year,
Perhaps we may not meet again.

[BYRON]

CHANGEFUL! how little do you know
Of Byron when you call him so!
True as the magnet is to iron
Byron hath ever been to Byron.
His color'd prints, in gilded frames,
Whatever the designs and names,
One image set before the rest,
In shirt with falling collar drest,
And keeping up a rolling fire at
Patriot, conspirator, and pirate.

[THE FLIGHT OF LOVE]

LOVE, flying out of sight, o'ershadows me,
And leaves me cold as cold can be;
Farewell *alasses!* and *no-mores!* and you,
Sweetest and saddest word, *adieu!*

[HER NAME]

ONE lovely name adorns my song,
And, dwelling in the heart,
For ever falters at the tongue,
And trembles to depart.

[THE STEERS]

ALTHO my soberer ear disdains
The irksome din of tinkling chains,
I pat two steers more sleek than strong
And yoke them to the car of Song.

[FALL OF LEAVES]

LEAF after leaf drops off, flower after flower,
Some in the chill, some in the warmer hour:
Alike they flourish and alike they fall,
And Earth who nourisht them receives them all.
Should we, her wiser sons, be less content
To sink into her lap when life is spent?

[REST OF MY HEART]

REST of my heart! no verse can tell
My blissful pride, beloved by you;
Yet could I love you half so well
Unless you once had grieved me too?

194

[BEETLE AND ROSE]

No insect smells so fulsome as that hard
   Unseemly beetle which corrodes the rose.
Bring forth your microscope; about the bard
   One very like it (only less) it shows.

SEPARATION

THERE is a mountain and a wood between us,
Where the lone shepherd and late bird have seen us
Morning and noon and even-tide repass.
Between us now the mountain and the wood
Seem standing darker than last year they stood,
And say we must not cross, alas! alas!

[HOLINESS IN ROME]

KNOW ye the land where from its acrid root
The sweet nepenthè rears her ripen'd fruit,
Which whoso tastes forgets his house and home?
Ye know it not: come on then; come to Rome.
Behold upon their knees with cord and scourge
Men, full-grown men, pale puffy phantasts urge!
Holiness lies with them in fish and frogs,
Mid squealing eunuchs and mid sculptured logs,
Mid gaudy dresses changed for every scene,
And mumbled prayers in unknown tongue between.
These wrongs imposed on them they call their rights!
For these the poor man toils, the brave man fights!
Exclaiming 'Saints above! your triumphs o'er,
Shall roasted Ridleys crown the feast no more?
Shall all our candles gutter into gloom,
And faith sit still, or only sweep the room?'

[TEARS OF THE DYING]

OUR youth was happy: why repine
That, like the Year's, Life's days decline?
'Tis well to mingle with the mould
When we ourselves alike are cold,
And when the only tears we shed
Are of the dying on the dead.

[NATURE'S COMMAND]

WHY do our joys depart
For cares to seize the heart?
I know not. Nature says,
Obey; and man obeys.
   I see, and know not why
Thorns live and roses die.

AGE

DEATH, tho I see him not, is near
And grudges me my eightieth year.
Now, I would give him all these last
For one that fifty have run past.
Ah! he strikes all things, all alike,
But bargains: those he will not strike.

[GREECE WITH CALM EYES I SEE]

   WHY do I praise a peach
Not on my wall, no, nor within my reach?
   Because I see the bloom
And scent the fragrance many steps from home.
   Permit me stil to praise
The higher Genius of departed days.
   Some are there yet who, nurst
In the same clime, are vigorous as the first,
   And never waste their hours
(Ardent for action) among meadow flowers.
   Greece with calm eyes I see,
Her pure white marbles have not blinded me,
   But breathe on me the love
Of earthly things as bright as things above:
   There is (where is there not?)
In her fair regions many a desart spot;
   Neither is Dircè clear,
Nor is Ilissus full throughout the year.

ON MOORE'S DEATH

IDOL of youths and virgins, Moore!
Thy days, the bright, the calm, are o'er!
No gentler mortal ever prest
His parent Earth's benignant breast.
What of the powerful can be said
They did for thee? They *edited*.
What of that royal gourd? Thy verse

Excites our scorn and spares our curse.
Each truant wife, each trusting maid,
All loves, all friendships, he betraid.
Despised in life by those he fed,
By his last mistress left ere dead,
Hearing her only wrench the locks
Of every latent jewel-box.
There spouse and husband strove alike,
Fearing lest Death too soon should strike,
But fixt no plunder to forego
Til the gross spirit sank below.
    Thy closing days I envied most,
When all worth losing had been lost.
Alone I spent my earlier hour
While thou wert in the roseate bower,
And raised to thee was every eye,
And every song won every sigh.
One servant and one chest of books
Follow'd me into mountain nooks,
Where shelter'd from the sun and breeze
Lay Pindar and Thucydides.
There antient days come back again,
And British kings renew'd their reign;
There Arthur and his knights sat round
Cups far too busy to be crown'd;
There Alfred's glorious shade appear'd,
Of higher mien than Greece e'er rear'd.
I never sought in prime or age
The smile of Fortune to engage,
Nor rais'd nor lower'd the telescope
Erected on the tower of Hope.
From Pindus and Parnassus far
Blinks cold and dim the Georgian star.

[THERE ARE SOME WORDS]

There are some words in every tongue
That come betimes and linger long:
In every land those words men hear
When Youth with rosebud crown draws near;
Men hear those words when life's full stream
Is rushing to disturb their dream;
When slowly swings life's vesper bell
Between its throbs they hear it well,
Fainter the sound, but stil the same,
Recalling one beloved name;
And graven on ice that name they find
When Age hath struck them almost blind.

[O PLAINS OF TOURS]

MEN will be slaves; let them; but force them not;
To force them into freedom is stil worse;
In one they follow their prone nature's bent,
But in the other stagger all awry,
Blind, clamorous, and with violence overthrow
The chairs and tables of the untasted feast.
Bastiles are reconstructed soon enough,
Temples are long in rising, once cast down,
And ever, when men want them, there are those
Who tell them they shall have them, but premise   10
That they shall rule within them and without.
Their voices, and theirs only, reach to heaven,
Their sprinkler cleanses souls from inborn sin
With its sow-bristles shaken in the face,
Their surplice sanctifies the marriage-bed,
Their bell and candle drive the devil off
The deathbed, and their purchast prayers cut short
All pains that would await them after death.
　O plains of Tours that rang with Martel's arms
Victorious! these are then the fruits ye bear   20
From Saracenic blood! one only God
Had else been worshipt . . but that one perhaps
Had seen less fraud, less cruelty, below.

EXPOSTULATION

Now yellowing hazels fringe the greener plain
And mountains show their unchain'd necks again,
And little rivulets beneath them creep
And gleam and glitter in each cloven steep;
Now, when supplanted by insidious snow
The huge stone rolls into the lake below,
What in these scenes, her earlier haunts, to roam,
What can detain my lovely friend from home?
'Tis that mid fogs and smoke she hears the claim
And feels the love of Freedom and of Fame:
Before these two she bends serenely meek . .
They also bend, and kiss her paler cheek.

JEALOUSY ACKNOWLEDGED

Too happy poet! true it is indeed
That I am jealous of thee. Bright blue eyes
(Half eye half heaven) look up into thy face
From Tuscan bonnet of such sunny straw,
In wonderment . . Glorious is poetry;

P

But give me pretty girls, give youth, give joy;
If not *my* youth, another's; not *my* joy,
Then too another's. I, alas! have lost
My quailpipe: I must not approach thy marsh,
To lift the yellow goslings off the ground
And warm them in my bosom with my breath.
Sorely this vexes me; not all thy wares.
I have mill'd verses somewhat solider
And rounder and more ringing: what of that?
Meanwhile the bevy flutters home again,
And thou canst blandly lower thy head to one,
Murmuring the sonnet, whispering the roundelay,
Or haply . . such things *have* been done before . .
Give her, as from thy pantry, not from mine,
The crumbs of my seed-cake, all soakt in milk.

LEDA

WONDER we that the highest star above
    Sprang forth to thy embrace,
O Leda! wonder we, when daring Love
    Turn'd thy averted face?

Smiles he had seen in Hebè, such as won
    Him of the poplar crown.
Jove, until then half-envious of his son,
    Then threw his scepter down.

Loose hung his eagle's wings; on either side
    A dove thrust in her head:
Eagle had lost his fierceness, Jove his pride . .
    And Leda what? . . her dread.

[THE WARWICKSHIRE AVON]

AVON that never thirsts, nor toils along,
Nor looks in anger, listen'd to my song,
So that I envied not the passing names
Whose gilded barges burnisht prouder Thames,
Remembering well a better man than I,
Whom in these meads the giddy herd ran by,
What time the generous Raleigh bled to death,
And Lust and Craft play'd for Elizabeth.
While murder in imperial robe sat by
To watch the twinkling of that sharp stern eye,
Til when a sister-queen was call'd to bleed,
Her fingers cased in jewels sign'd the deed!

TO SHELLEY

Shelley! whose song so sweet was sweetest here,
We knew each other little; now I walk
Along the same green path, along the shore
Of Lerici, along the sandy plain
Trending from Lucca to the Pisan pines,
Under whose shadow scatter'd camels lie,
The old and young, and rarer deer uplift
Their knotty branches o'er high-feather'd fern.
Regions of happiness! I greet ye well;
Your solitudes, and not your cities, stay'd
My steps among you; for with you alone
Converst I, and with those ye bore of old.
He who beholds the skies of Italy
Sees ancient Rome reflected, sees beyond,
Into more glorious Hellas, nurse of Gods
And godlike men: dwarfs people other lands.
Frown not, maternal England! thy weak child
Kneels at thy feet and owns in shame a lie.

HELLAS TO AUBREY DE VERE ON HIS DEPARTURE

Traveler! thou from afar that explorest the caverns of Delphi,
Led by the Muses, whose voice thou rememberest, heard over ocean,
Tell the benighted at home that the spirit hath never departed
Hence, from these cliffs and these streams: that Apollo is stil *King*
    Apollo,
And that no other should rule where Olympus, Parnassus, and
    Pindus
Are what they were, ages past; that, if barbarous bands have invaded
Temple and shrine heretofore, it is time the reproach be abolisht,
Time that the wrong be redrest, and the stranger no more be the
    ruler.
Whether be heard or unheard the complaint of our vallies and
    mountains,
From the snow-piles overhead to the furthermost iland of Pelops,
Peace be to thee and to thine! And, if Deities hear under water,
Blandly may Panopè clasp and with fervor the knee of Poseidon!
Blandly may Cymodameia prevail over Glaucos, dividing
With both her hands his white beard and kissing it just in the middle,
So that the seas be serene which shall carry thee back to thy country
Where the sun sinks to repose. But ever be mindful of Hellas!

[A DREAM]

A VOICE in sleep hung over me, and said
'Seest thou him yonder?' At that voice I raised
My eyes: it was an Angel's: but he veil'd
His face from me with both his hands, then held
One finger forth, and sternly said agen,
'Seest thou him yonder?'
       On a grassy slope
Slippery with flowers, above a precipice,
A slumbering man I saw: methought I knew
A visage not unlike it; whence the more
It troubled and perplext me.
         'Can it be
My own?' said I.
      Scarce had the word escaped
When there arose two other forms, each fair,
And each spake fondest words, and blamed me not,
But blest me, for the tears they shed with me
Upon that only world where tears are shed,
That world which they (why without me?) had left.
Another now came forth, with eye askance:
That she was of the earth too well I knew,
And that she hated those for loving me
(Had she not told me) I had soon divined.
Of earth was yet another; but more like
The heavenly twain in gentleness and love:
She from afar brought pity; and her eyes
Fill'd with the tears she fear'd must swell from mine:
Humanest thoughts with strongest impulses
Heav'd her fair bosom; and her hand was raised
To shelter me from that sad blight which fell
Damp on my heart; it could not; but a blast,
Sweeping the southern sky, blew from beyond
And threw me on the ice-bergs of the north.

INCONSISTENCY

SPRING smiles in Nature's face with fresh delight,
 With early flowers her mother's brow adorning;
When morning comes, I wish again for night,
 And when night comes, I wish again for morning.

[FOR AN EPITAPH]

HERE lies Landor,
 Whom they thought a goose,
 But he proved a gander.

THE PHILOSOPHER

HE who sits thoughtful in a twilight grot
Sees what in sunshine other men see not.
I walk away from what they run to see,
I know the world, but the world knows not me.

[INVITATION]

FORSTER! come hither, I pray, to the Fast of our Anglican Martyr.
Turbot our Church has allow'd, and perhaps (not without dispen-
    sation)
Pheasant; then strawberry cream, green-gages, and apricot-jelly,
Oranges housewives call *pot*, and red-rinded nuts of Avella,
Filberts we name them at home—happy they who have teeth for
    the crackers!
Blest, but in lower degree, whose steel-arm'd right-hand overcomes
    them!
I, with more envy than spite, look on and sip sadly my claret.

January 1854

GIBBON

GIBBON! if sterner patriots than thyself
With firmer foot have stampt our English soil;
If Poesy stood high above thy reach,
She stood with only one on either hand
Upon the cliffs of Albion tall and strong:
Meanwhile gregarious songsters trampt around
On plashy meadow-land, mid noisome flowers
Sprung from the rankness of flush city-drains.
In other regions graver History
Meets her own Muse; nor walk they far below.
   The rivulets and mountain-rills of Greece
Will have dried up while Avon stil runs on;
And those four rivers freshening Paradise
Gush yet, tho' Paradise had long been lost
Had not one man restored it; he was ours.
Not song alone detain'd him, tho' the song
Came from the lips of Angels upon his,
But strenuous action when his country call'd
Drew him from those old groves and that repose
In which the enchantress Italy lulls all.
No Delphic laurel's trembling glimmery leaves
Checkered thy gravel walk; 'twas evener ground,
Altho' mid shafts and cornices o'ergrown

With nettles, and palatial caverns choakt
With rubbish from obliterated names.
   There are who blame thee for too stately step
And words resounding from inflated cheek.
Words have their proper places, just like men.
I listen to, nor venture to reprove,
Large language swelling under gilded domes,
Byzantine, Syrian, Persepolitan,
Or where the world's drunk master lay in dust.
Fabricius heard and spake another tongue,
And such the calm Cornelia taught her boys,
Such Scipio, Cæsar, Tullius, marshaling,
Cimber and wilder Scot were humanized,
And, far as flew the Eagles, all was Rome.
   Thou lookedst down complacently where brawl'd
The vulgar factions that infest our streets,
And turnedst the black vizor into glass
Thro which men saw the murderer and the cheat
In diadem and cowl. Erectly stood,
After like work with fiercer hand perform'd,
Milton, as Adam pure, as Michael strong,
When brave Britannia struck her bravest blow,
When monstrous forms, half-reptile and half-man,
Snatcht up the hissing snakes from off Hell's floor
And flung them with blind fury at her crest.
Two valiant men sprang up, of equal force,
Protector and *Defender* each alike.
Milton amid the bitter sleet drove on,
Shieldbearer to the statelier one who struck
That deadly blow which saved our prostrate sires
And gave them (short the space!) to breathe once more.
   History hath beheld no pile ascend
So lofty, large, symmetrical, as thine,
Since proud Patavium gave Rome's earlier chiefs
To shine again in virtues and in arms.
Another rises from the couch of pain,
Wounded, and worne with service and with years,
To share fraternal glory, and ward off
(Alas, to mortal hand what vain essay!)
The shafts of Envy.
             May Thucydides,
Recall'd to life among us, close his page
Ere come the Pestilence, ere come the shame
Of impotent and Syracusan war!
Lately (how strange the vision!) o'er my sleep
War stole, in bandages untinged with wounds,
Wheezing and limping on fat nurse's arm
To take a draught of air before the tent,

And for each step too fast or wide rebuked.
Peace stood with folded arms nor ventured near,
But Scorn ran closer, and a shout went up
From north and south above the Euxine wave.

August 22 [1854]

APOLOGY FOR *GEBIR*

SIXTY the years since Fidler bore
My grouse bag up the Bala moor,
Above the lake, along the lea
Where gleams the darkly yellow Dee;
Thro' crags, o'er cliffs, I carried there
My verses with paternal care,
But left them, and went home again,
To wing the birds upon the plain.
With heavier luggage half-forgot,
For many months they followed not.
When over Tawey's sands they came,
Brighter flew up my winter flame;
And each old cricket sang alert
With joy that they had come unhurt.
Gebir! men shook their heads in doubt
If we were sane: few made us out,
Beside one stranger; in his heart
We after held no niggard part.
The songs of every age he knew,
But only sang the pure and true.
Poet he was, yet was his smile
Without a tinge of gall or guile.
Such lived, 'tis said, in ages past;
Who knows if Southey was the last?
Dapper, who may perhaps have seen
My name in some late magazine,
Among a dozen or a score
Which interest wise people more,
Wonders if I can be the same
To whom poor Southey augured fame;
Erring as usual, in his choice
Of one who mocks the public voice,
And fancies two or three are worth
Far more than all the rest on earth.
Dapper, in tones benign and clear
Tells those who treasure all they hear,
'Landor would have done better far,
Had he observed the northern star;
Or Bloomfield might have shown the way
To one who always goes astray;

He might have tried his pen upon
The living, not the dead and gone.
Are turban'd youths and muffled belles
Extinct along the Dardanelles?
Is there no scimeter, no axe?
Daggers and bow-strings, mutes and sacks,
Are they all swept away for ever
From that sky-blue resplendent river?
Do heroes of old times surpass
Cardigan, Somerset, Dundas?
Do the Sigæan mounds inclose
More corses than Death swept from those?'
  No, no: but let me ask in turn,
Whether, whene'er Corinthian urn,
With ivied Faun upon the rim
Invites, I may not gaze on him?
I love all beauty: I can go
At times from Gainsboro' to Watteau;
Never from Titian's Alpine scene
To Morland's stye, however clean.
Even after Milton's thorough-bass
I bear the rhymes of Hudibras,
And find more solid wisdom there
Than pads professor's easy chair:
But never sit I quiet long
Where broidered cassock floats round Young;
Whose pungent essences perfume
And quirk and quibble trim the tomb;
Who thinks the holy bread too plain,
And in the chalice pours champaign.
I love old places and their climes,
Nor quit the syrinx for the chimes.
Manners have changed; but hearts are yet
The same, and will be while they beat.
Ye blame not those who wander o'er
Our earth's remotest wildest shore,
Nor scoff at seeking what is hid
Within one-chambered pyramid;
Let me then, with my coat untorn
By your acacia's crooked thorn,
Follow from Gades to the coast
Of Egypt, men thro' ages lost.
Firm was my step on rocky steeps;
Others slipt down loose sandhill heaps.
I knew where hidden fountains lay;
Hoarse was their thirsty camels' bray;
And presently fresh droves had past
The beasts expiring on the waste.

OBSERVING A VULGAR NAME ON THE PLINTH
OF AN ANCIENT STATUE

BARBARIANS must we always be?
　Wild hunters in pursuit of fame?
Must there be nowhere stone or tree
　Ungasht with some ignoble name?
O Venus! in thy Tuscan dome
　May every God watch over thee!
Apollo! bend thy bow o'er Rome
　And guard thy sister's chastity.
Let Britons paint their bodies blue
　As formerly, but touch not you.

MARCH 24

SHARP crocus wakes the froward year;
In their old haunts birds reappear;
From yonder elm, yet black with rain,
The cushat looks deep down for grain
Thrown on the gravel-walk; here comes
The redbreast to the sill for crumbs.
Fly off! fly off! I can not wait
To welcome ye, as she of late
The earliest of my friends is gone.
Alas! almost my only one!
The few as dear, long wafted o'er,
Await me on a sunnier shore.

[KINGS AND MATRIMONY]

NATIONS by violence are espous'd to kings,
And men are hammer'd into wedding-rings.

[LORD ABERDEEN]

DOOM'D to the gallows, once a lord
Craved hanging by a silken cord:
On the same errand, Aberdeen
Receives the garter of our Queen.
He who hath long played *fast and loose*,
Leaves Riga hemp for vulgar use;
Low rogues on rougher rope may swing,
But lords, . . 'tis quite another thing.

THE GEORGES

GEORGE the First was always reckoned
Vile, but viler George the Second;
And what mortal ever heard
Any good of George the Third?
When from earth the Fourth descended
(God be praised!) the Georges ended.

BOURBONS

ISABELLA spits at Spain,
  Bomba strips and scourges Naples:
Are there not then where they reign
  Addled eggs or rotten apples?

Treadmills, pillories, humbler stocks!
  Ye repeat your lessons yet.
Halters, gibbets, axes, blocks!
  Your old textbook ye forget.

Men have often heard the thunder
  Roll at random; where, O where
Rolls it now? I smell it under
  That fat priest in that foul chair.

Never was there poet wanting
  Where the lapdog licks the throne;
Lauds and hymns we hear them chanting,
  Shame if I were mute alone!

Let me then your deeds rehearse,
  Gem of kings and flower of queens!
Tho' I may but trail a verse
  Languider than Lamartine's.

LEADERS AND ASPIRANTS

PALMERSTON 'lies and gives the lie
With equal volubility.'
Even the 'artful Dodger,' little John,
Is scarce a match for Palmerston.
Who next? Jim Crow; he prigs our letters,
And parries Freedom like his betters.

[TWO MISERIES]

THERE are two miseries in human life;
To live without a friend, and with a wife.

THOMAS PAINE

MOBS I abhor, yet bear a crowd
Which speaks its mind, if not too loud.
Willingly would I hear again
The honest words of pelted Payne.
Few dared such homely truths to tell,
Or wrote our English half so well.

ANTONY AND OCTAVIUS

SCENES FOR THE STUDY

THE SCENES
ARE DEDICATED TO
EDWARD CAPERN,
POET AND DAY-LABORER AT BIDEFORD, DEVON.

We are fellow-laborers; you work in two fields, I in one only; you incessantly, I intermittently. Well do I know the elevation of your mind above your worldly condition, and that in Christian humility there walks with you a spirit conscious of its divine descent. This shall not deter me from offering what may be eventually of some service, however small; and I offer it with confidence, because it is not personally to yourself, but to your children. Should there be at the close of the year any small profit accruing from the sale of this first, and perhaps last, edition of *Scenes for the Study*, accept it for their benefit. Little is to be expected from so old-fashioned and obsolete a style of composition, and that little will be owing to the virtues and genius, not of the author, but of EDWARD CAPERN. Rely on your own exertions, and on that Supreme Power whence is derived whatever is worth possessing. Depend not on the favor of Royalty; expect nothing from it; for you are not a hound or a spaniel or a German prince.

PREFACE

Few have obtained the privilege of entering Shakespeare's garden, and of seeing him take turn after turn, quite alone, now nimbly now gravely, on his broad and lofty terrace.

Let us never venture where he is walking, whether in deep meditation or in buoyant spirits. Enough is it for us to ramble and loiter in the narrower paths below, and to look up at the various images which, in the prodigality of his wealth, he has placed in every quarter.

Before you, reader, are some scattered leaves gathered from under them: carefuller hands may arrange and compress them in a book of their own, and thus for a while preserve them, if rude children do not finger them first and tamper with their fragility.

SCENE THE FIRST

[*Near Actium, 31 B.C.*]

SOOTHSAYER AND ANTONY

Soothsayer. Speak it I must. Ill are the auguries.
Antony. Ill ever are the auguries, O priest,
To those who fear them: at one hearty stroke
The blackest of them scud and disappear.
Now, not a word of any less than good
To Cleopatra.
Soothsayer. 'Twas at her command
I hasten'd to consult them.
Antony. Rightly done
To follow her commands; not rightly comes
Whate'er would grieve her; this thou must withhold.
Soothsayer. Not this, not this: her very life may hang
Upon the event foretold her.
Antony. What is that?
Announced then is the accursed augury
So soon?
Soothsayer. She waited at the temple-door
With only one attendant, meanly drest,
That none might know her; or perhaps the cause
Was holier; to appease the offended Gods.
Antony. Which of them can she ever have offended?
She who hath lavisht upon all of them
Such gifts, and burnt more incense in one hour
Before her Isis, than would wrap in smoke
A city at mid-day! The keenest eye
Of earth or heaven could find in her no guile,
No cruelty, no lack of duty.
Soothsayer. True;
Yet fears she one of them, nor knows she which,
But Isis is the one she most suspects.
Antony. Isis! her patroness, her favourite?
Soothsayer. Even so! but they who patronize may frown
At times, and draw some precious boon away.

Antony. I deem not thus unworthily of Gods;
Indeed I know but Jupiter and Mars;
Each hath been ever on my side, and each
Alike will prosper me, I trust, to-morrow.
    Soothsayer. But there are others, guardian Gods of Egypt;
Prayers may propitiate them, with offerings due.
    Antony. I have forgotten all my prayers.
    Soothsayer.   No need,
When holier lips pronounce them.
    Antony.   As for offerings,
There shall be plenty on the day's success.
    Soothsayer. Merit it.
    Antony.   Do your Gods or ours mind that?
Merit! and where lies merit?
    Soothsayer.   In true faith
On auguries.
    Antony.   Birds hither thither fly,
And heard there have been from behind the veil
Voices not varying much from yours and mine.

SCENE THE SECOND
[Before the battle of Actium 31 B.C.]

SOOTHSAYER AND CLEOPATRA

Soothsayer. Our lord Antonius wafts away all doubt
Of his success.
    Cleopatra. What! against signs and tokens?
    Soothsayer. Even so!
    Cleopatra.   Perhaps he trusts himself to Hercules,
Become of late progenitor to him.
    Soothsayer. Ah! that sweet smile might bring him back; he once
Was flexible to the bland warmth of smiles.
    Cleopatra. If Hercules is hail'd by men below
For strength and goodness, why not Antony?
Why not succede as lawful heir? why not
Exchange the myrtle for the poplar crown?

ANTONY *enters.* SOOTHSAYER *goes.*

Cleopatra. Antony! is not Cæsar now a god?
    Antony. We hear so.
    Cleopatra.   Nay, we know it. Why not thou?
Men would not venture then to strike a blow
At thee: the laws declare it sacrilege.
    Antony. Julius, if I knew Julius, had been rather
First among men than last among the Gods.
    Cleopatra. At least put on thy head a kingly crown.

Antony. I have put on a laurel one already;
As many kingly crowns as should half-cover
The Lybian desert are not worth this one.
    Cleopatra. But all would bend before thee.
    Antony.   'Twas the fault
Of Cæsar to adopt it; 'twas his death.
    Cleopatra. Be then what Cæsar is.
                                 O Antony!
To laugh so loud becomes not state so high.
    Antony. He is a star, we see; so is the hair
Of Berenice: stars and Gods are rife.
What worth, my love, are crowns? Thou givest pearls,
I give the circlet that encloses them.
Handmaidens don such gear, and valets snatch it
Sportively off, and toss it back again.
    Cleopatra. But graver men gaze up with awful eyes . .
    Antony. And never gaze at that artificer
Who turns his wheel and fashions out his vase
From the Nile clay! 'Tis easy work for him;
Easy was mine to turn forth kings from stuff
As vile and ductile: he stil plies his trade,
But mine, with all my customers, is gone.
Ever by me let enemies be awed,
None else: bring round me many, near me few,
Keeping afar those shaven knaves obscene
Who lord it with humility, who press
Men's shoulders down, glue their two hands together,
And cut a cubit off, and tuck their heels
Against the cushion mother Nature gave.
    Cleopatra. Incomprehensible! incorrigible!
O wretch! if queens were ever taught to blush,
I should at such unseemly phrase as thine.
I think I must forgive it.
                         What! and take
Before I grant? Again! You violent man!
Will you for ever drive me thus away?

SCENE THE THIRD

[after the battle of Actium]

ANTONY AND CLEOPATRA

    Antony. What demon urged thy flight?
    Cleopatra.   The demon Love.
I am a woman, with a woman's fears,
A mother's, and, alas O Antony!
More fears than these.

Antony. Of whom?
Cleopatra. Ask not *of* whom
But ask *for* whom, if thou must ask at all,
Nor knowest nor hast known. Yes, I did fear
For my own life . . ah! lies it not in thine?
How many perils compast thee around!
   Antony. What are the perils that are strange to me?
   Cleopatra. Mine thou couldst not have seen when swiftest oars,
Attracted by the throne and canopy,
Pounced at me only, numerous as the waves;
Couldst not have seen my maidens throwing down
Their fans and posies (piteous to behold!)
That they might wring their hands more readily.
I was too faint myself to still their cries.
   Antony (*aside*). I almost thought her blameable.

            (*To* CLEOPATRA.) The Gods
So will'd it. Thou despondest . . too aware
The day is lost.
   Cleopatra. The day may have been lost,
But other days, and happier ones, will come.
   Antony. Never: when those so high once fall, their weight
Keeps them for ever down.
   Cleopatra. Talk reasonably,
And love me as . . til now . . it should be more,
For love and sorrow mingle where they meet.
   Antony. It shall be more. Are these last kisses cold?
   Cleopatra. Nor cold are they nor shall they be the last.
   Antony. Promise me, Cleopatra, one thing more.
   Cleopatra. 'Tis promist, and now tell me what it is.
   Antony. Rememberest thou this ring?
   Cleopatra. Dost thou remember
The day, my Antony, when it was given?
   Antony. Day happiest in a life of many happy,
And all thy gift.
   Cleopatra. 'Tis call'd the richest ruby,
The heaviest, and the deepest, in the world.
   Antony. The richest certainly.
   Cleopatra. And not the deepest
And broadest? Look! it hides all this large nail,
And mine are long ones, if not very wide;
Now let me see if it don't cover yours
As wide again! there! it would cover two.
Why smile you so?
   Antony. Because I know its story.
   Cleopatra. Ha! then you have not lost all memory quite.
I told it you. The king of Pontus sent it
When dying to my father, warning him

By letter that there was a charm in it
Not to be trifled with.

Antony.   It shall not be.

Cleopatra. But tell me now the promise I must make;
What has the ring to do with it?

Antony.   All, all.
Know, Cleopatra, this is not one ruby.

Cleopatra. The value then is smaller.

Antony.   Say not so,
Remark the rim.

Cleopatra.   The gold is thin, I see.

Antony. And seest thou it will open? It contains
Another jewel, richer than itself.

Cleopatra. Impossible! my Antony! for rubies
Are richer than all other gems on earth.

Antony. Now, my sweet trifler, for thy promise.

Cleopatra.   Speak.
By all the Powers above and all below,
I will perform thy bidding, even to death.

Antony. To death it goes; not until after mine.

Cleopatra. I kiss the precious charm. Methinks an odor
Of almond comes from it. How sweet the flower
Of death!

Antony. 'Tis painless death, 'tis sudden too.

Cleopatra. Who could wish more, even were there more to wish?
With us there is not.

Antony.   Generous, pious girl!
Daughter of Ptolemies! thou hast not won
A lower man than they. Thy name shall rise
Above the pyramids, above the stars,
Nations yet wild shall that name civilize,
And glorious poets shake their theaters,
And stagger kings and emperors with applause.

Cleopatra. I was not born to die; but I was born
To leave the world with Antony, and will.

Antony. The greatest of all eastern kings died thus,
The greater than all eastern kings thus died.
O glorious forgeman who couldst rivet down
Refractory crowds by thousands, and make quake
Scepters like reeds! we want not here thy voice
Or thy example. Antony alone
And queenly pride, tho' Love were dumb, would do.

SCENE THE FOURTH

[At Alexandria, after arrival of Octavius, 30 B.C.]

CLEOPATRA.   CHARMIAN.   IRAS

Cleopatra. At the first entrance of your lord, before
He ordered you, before he spake a word,
Why did ye run away?
Charmian.   I was afraid,
Never so in my life; he lookt so fierce
He fear'd his own wild eyes, he placed one hand
(His right) across them on lowered brow, his left
Waved us away as would a hurricane
A palm-tree on the desert.
Cleopatra (to IRAS).   And wert thou,
Iras, so terrified?
Iras.   Not I indeed;
My lady, never man shall frighten *me*.
Cleopatra. Thou silly creature! I have seen a mouse
Do it.
Iras. A mouse is quite another thing.
Charmian (hesitating). Our lord and master . .
Cleopatra.   What of Antony?
Charmian. Octavius . .
Cleopatra.   Who? Our lord and master he?
He never shall be mine . . that is to say . .
Charmian. What! lady?
Cleopatra.   I forget . . 'twas not worth saying.
Charmian! where hast thou been this last half-hour?
Charmian. In my own room.
Cleopatra.   So fearful?
Charmian.   Far more sad.
Cleopatra. Where, Iras, thou?
Iras.   I wanted to report
To my sweet lady what I might espy.
Cleopatra. And what have those long narrow eyes espied?
Iras. All.
Cleopatra. 'Twas done speedily; but what is all?
Army and fleet from any terrace-roof
Are quite discernible, the separate men
Nowhere.
Iras. My heart had told me what delight
Its queen would feel to hear exactly how
The leaders look.
Cleopatra.   And how then did they look?
Tell me: some might have ridden near enough
The town to judge by, where the sight is sharp.

Q

Iras. Merciful Isis! ridden! and so close!
Horses are frightful, horses kick and rear
And whinny, full of wickedness; 'twere rash
To venture nigh them.
  Cleopatra.   There are things more rash.
  Iras. Quieter creatures than those generals are
Never were seen.
  Cleopatra.   Barbarians! not a word
About them, Iras, if thou lovest me;
They would destroy my city, seize my realm,
And ruin him we live for.
  Iras.   Surely no;
It were a pity; none are so unkind;
Cæsar the least of all.
  Cleopatra.   Ah simple child!
Thou knowest not his heart.
  Iras.   I do indeed.
  Cleopatra. No, nor thy own.
  Iras.   His better; for of mine
I never askt a question. He himself
Told me how good he would be.
  Cleopatra.   He told *thee?*
What! hast thou seen him?
  Iras.   Aye, and face to face,
Close as our lord's to yours.
  Cleopatra.   O impudence!
  Iras. But he would have it so; just like our lord.
  Cleopatra. Impudent girl! thou shalt be whipt for this.
  Iras. I am too old; but lotuses don't hurt
Like other things; they cool the strokes they give.
  Cleopatra. I have no patience with thee. How I hate
That boy Octavius!
      Dared he touch thy cheek?
  Iras. He could; he only whispered in my ear,
Holding it by the ring.
  Cleopatra.   Whispered? what words?
  Iras. The kindest.
  Cleopatra.   Ah! no doubt! but what were they?
  Iras. He said, The loveliest creature in the world . .
  Cleopatra. The vulgar brute! Our ferrymen talk so:
And couldst thou listen, Iras, to such speech?
  Iras. Only when people praise our gracious queen.
  Cleopatra. Me? this of me? Thou didst thy duty, child:
He might have fail'd in what he would express.
The birds have different voices, yet we bear
To hear those sing which do not sing the best.
Iras! I never thought thee half so wise.
And so, he said those gentle words of *me?*

Iras. All, and forgot to kiss me when I vow'd
I would report them faithfully.

 Cleopatra.   Is there
Resemblance in him to that marble image
I would have broken, but my Antony
Seiz'd both my hands?

 Iras.   Alas! that image wants
The radiant eyes, and hair more radiant stil,
Such as Apollo's may have been if myrrh
Were sprinkled into its redundant waves.

 Cleopatra. He must be tenderer than I fancied him
If this be true.

 Iras.   He spoke those very words.

 Cleopatra. Iras! 'tis vain to mind the words of men;
But if he lookt as thou hast said he lookt,
I think I may put trust in him.

 Iras.   And see him?

 Cleopatra. I am not hasty.

 Iras.   If you could but see him.

 Cleopatra. Call Charmian: I am weary: I must rest
Awhile.

 Iras. My sweetest lady! could not I,
Who have been used to it almost a year,
Help you as well as Charmian? While you sleep
Could I not go again and bid him haste
To comfort you?

 Cleopatra.   Is the girl mad? Call Charmian.

      (*To* CHARMIAN.)

Charmian! hath Iras tickled thee away
From moping in thy chamber? thou hast sped.

 Charmian. Iras is growing bold.

 Cleopatra.   I was bold too
While I was innocent as Iras is.

 Charmian. Our lady looks more flurried than deprest.

 Cleopatra. I am not flurried, I am not deprest.

           [*After a pause.*

Believest thou in Cæsar's generosity?

 Charmian. I know it.

 Cleopatra.   In what matter?

 Charmian.   Half the guards
And half the ministers of state have shown
Signs of his bounty to the other half.

 Cleopatra. Gifts are poor signs of bounty. Do not slaves
Slip off the gold-black pouches from their necks
Untied but to buy other slaves therewith?
Do not tame creatures lure into the trap
Their wilder brethren with some filthy bait?

All want companions, and the worst the most.
I am much troubled: even hope troubles me.
   Charmian. I dare not ask our lady why she weeps.
   Cleopatra. Cæsarion, my first-born, my dearest one,
Is safely shielded by his father's name:
He loves his brothers, he may save them both,
He only can: I would fain take the advice
Of Dolabella, fain would venture him
In Cæsar's camp: the father's voice and look
Must melt him, for his heart is not so hard
That he could hurt so beautiful a child;
Nay, what man's is?
   Charmian.   But trust not the two younger;
Their father will not help them in their need.
   Cleopatra. Cæsarion in fit hour will plead for them.
Charmian, what ponderest thou? what doubtest thou?
   Charmian. Cæsar I doubt, and Dolabella more;
And what I pondered were your words: *It may be*
That givers are not always benefactors.
   Cleopatra. I have one secret, but keep none from thee:
He loves me!
   Charmian.   All do.
   Cleopatra.   Yes, but some have power.
   Charmian. Power, as most power is, gain'd by treachery.
   Cleopatra.   Whom
In Egypt, Europe, Asia, can I trust?
   Charmian. Few, nor those few too far, nor without watch.
   Cleopatra. Not Charmian?
   Charmian.   Bid her die; here; now; and judge.

SCENE THE FIFTH

OCTAVIUS. MECÆNAS. GALLUS.

   Octavius. Is Dolabella to be trusted?
   Mecænas.   Youth
There is on Dolabella's side; with youth
Comes always eloquence where women are.
   Octavius. Gallus is honester and prudenter.
   Mecænas. But Gallus is the older by some years.
   Octavius. A poet says, Love at odd hours hath smiled
And covered with his pinions sportively,
Where he espied some hairs that seem'd like Time's
Rather than his.
   Mecænas.   There must have been but few,
Or else the poet dreamt it.
   Octavius.   Who comes hither?
   Mecænas. Not Dolabella, but the better man.

Octavius. Welcome, brave Gallus, opportunely met.
We were debating how to lure that dove
Of Antony's, now in her cote, a tower,
From which we would not frighten her away,
But tempt her down.
    Gallus.   It might be difficult.
    Octavius. Unless thou aidest us, indeed it might.
    Mecænas. What sport 'twould be to see her mate descend
And catch him too!
    Gallus.   Nor this more easily.
    Octavius. To Gallus all is easy.
    Mecænas.   Pleasant too
Would such task be.
    Gallus.   No better judge of pleasures
Than Cilnius here; but ours are not alike.
    Octavius. Gallus! one word apart. We need thee much.
    Gallus. What! after Egypt won?
    Octavius.   Antony lives!
    Gallus. Beaten, disgraced, imprisoned, his own jailer.
    Mecænas. Defying us, however, by the power
The queen his mistress gives him with her name . .
    Gallus. Worthless as his.
    Mecænas.   Were she within our reach
We soon might bright him down.
    Gallus.   What! lower?
    Octavius.   Even yet?
    Gallus. She might succumb, and must, by promising
That Cæsar's son, after her death, shall reign.
    Mecænas. A prudent thought. But will she give up Antony
Unless she hear it from the giver's mouth?
There is one anxious to deserve the grace
Of princes. Dolabella could persuade
The queen to trust herself to him for Cæsar.
    Gallus. I doubt it.
    Mecænas.   Doubt his honor, not his skill.
He could not keep the secret that he loves
And that he often in times past hath seen her.
    Gallus. He loves her? then, by all the Gods! he never
Will win her for another than himself.
Beside, he was the friend of Antony
And shared with him the toils at Mutina.
Altho' no eagle, he would soar aloft
Rather than bow for others, like an owl,
The smallest of the species, hooded for it.
Who knows not Dolabella?
    Mecænas.   Thou hast sense,
Comeliness, courage, frankness. Antony
Tore from thy couch the fairest girl in Rome.

Gallus. And let him have her, let him have her, man.
What then?
    Mecænas. There are who would retaliate.
    Gallus. The girl hath left no mark upon my memory ..
    Mecænas. Or mine, beside a few soft lines; but mine
Retains them, mindful of a friend who sang,
Unless my singing mars the harmony,

> I thought it once an idle tale
> That lovely woman's faith could fail;
> At last I said, It may be true,
> Lycoris, of them all but you.
> And now you leave me! and you go
> O'er pinnacles of Alpine snow.
> Another leads you (woe is me!)
> Across that grim and ghastly sea!
> Let him protect those eyes from sleet,
> And guide and chafe those tender feet,
> And fear for every step you tread,
> Then hardly will I wish him dead.
> If ice-barb'd shafts that ring around
> By his neglect my false one wound,
> O may the avenging Gods for this
> Freeze him to death in the abyss!

    Gallus. They have reserved him for a sadder fate.
Sleep, without painful dreams that crush the breast,
Sleep, without any joyous ones that come
Only to mock the awaken'd, comes unfelt
And unsolicited among those cliffs
Of ice perennial.
                  Antony hath dreamt
His broken dream, and wakened to despair:
I never wisht him that; the harm I wisht him
Was when my youth was madder than his age.
He stood a prouder and a better man
At Mutina, when Famine walkt the camp,
When I beheld him climb up painfully
A low and crumbling crag, where servises
Hung out above his head their unripe fruit:
That was my day. Some grains of sodden maize
I brought and offered him: he struck them down.
    Octavius. Rejoice at pride so humbled.
    Gallus.   I rejoice
At humbled pride, at humbled valor no.
    Octavius. But those avenging Gods whom thou invokedst
Stand now before thee and demand why call'd.
    Gallus. They know: they pardon such irresolution
As pity, and not cowardice, persuades.
One woman has betraid me; not one woman
Will I betray.
    Mecænas.   O that poetic mind!

Gallus. Where others sneer, Mecænas only smiles.

Mecænas. Such is my nature, and I widely err,
Gallus, if such be not thy nature too.

Octavius. Did then Lycoris, that wild girl, prefer
The unworthy to the worthy, the most rude
To the most gentle, scampering beyond reach?
Let her repair her fault: no danger here
That angry skies turn coral lips to slate
Or icicles make limp the runaway.

Gallus. Those days are over. He who won the prize
May say as much and add a little more.

Octavius. Laughest thou not to see the tables turn'd?
The little queen who fascinates her fool
Is now as lovely as Lycoris was,
And never ran away from any man:
Fain would I see that roysterer's spirit broken,
And she alone can do it: help her on.

Gallus. In any such attempt, in such a place
Fortune would baffle me.

Octavius.   Then baffle *her*;
She baffles only those who hesitate.

Gallus. The queen, we hear, takes refuge in the depths
Below the palace, where but reptiles lie.

Octavius. Indeed! what! scorpions, serpents?

Gallus.   Haply these.

Octavius. Poor woman! they may bite her! let my fears
Prove not prophetic!
                    Now, my friend, adieu!
Reflect upon our project; turn it over.   [GALLUS *goes.*
These poets look into futurity
And bring us glimpses from it more than dreams.
Asps! But the triumph then without the queen!
Alas! was ever mortal so perplext!
I doubt if your friend Gallus can be won.

Mecænas. All may be won, well handled; but the ear
Is not the thing to hold by. Show men gold,
Entangle them in Gallic torquises,
Tie stubborn necks with ropes of blushing pearls,
Seat them on ivory from the realms of Ind,
Augur them consulates, proconsulates,
Make their eyes widen into provinces,
And, gleaming further onward, tetrarchies.

Octavius. It strikes me now that we may offer Gallus
The prefecture of Egypt.

Mecænas.   Some time hence:
Better consult Agrippa.

Octavius. None more trusty.
Yet our Agrippa hath strange whims; he dotes
Upon old Rome, the Rome of matted beards
And of curt tunics; of old Rome's old laws,
Worm-eaten long, now broken and swept off. [*Pausing.*
He stands forth high in station and esteem.

 Mecænas. So should the man who won the world for thee.

 Octavius. I must not play with him who won so much
From others; he might win as much from me:
I fear his fortunes.

 Mecænas. Bind them with your own.
Becoming are thy frowns, my dear Octavius,
Thy smiles alone become thee better: trust
Thy earliest friend and fondest: take not ill
My praises of Agrippa, tried in war
And friendship.

 Octavius. And for this wouldst thou, my Cilnius,
Send him away from me?

 Mecænas. Thyself did fear
His popularity: all Rome applauds
His valor, justice, moderation, mercy.

 Octavius. Not one word more.

 Mecænas. One word I have to speak,
And speak it I will now. He must away.

 Octavius. Can Cilnius then be jealous of Agrippa?

 Mecænas. No; crown him king and give him provinces,
But give him not to clench the heart of Rome.

 Octavius. I could make kings and unmake kings by scores,
But could not make nor unmake one Agrippa.

 Mecænas. Well spoken! wisely! worthily! No praise
Can equipoise his virtues, kings may lay
Their tributes on the carpet of his throne
And cities hope to honor whom they serve,
The royal mantle would obscure Agrippa.

 Octavius. I would be generous, but be cautious too.

 Mecænas. Then grant him all beyond the sight of Rome;
Men's eyes would draw him thither tho' his will
Hung back: thus urged the steddiest might give way.

 Octavius. I hate suspicion and suspicious men.
Gallus I fancied was the bitterest foe
Of Antony, his rival, and successful,
Then he should hate him worse than I.

 Mecænas. But empire
Is more worth hatred than a silly girl,
Every day to be won and lost again.

 Octavius. Our Gallus is weak-minded to forgive
So easily.

Mecænas. I find that on the hearth
Where lie love's embers there lie hatred's too,
Equally cold and not to be stir'd up.
   Octavius. I do not think, my Cilnius, thou hast felt
Love but for me; I never knew thee hate.
   Mecænas. It is too troublesome; it rumples sleep,
It settles on the dishes of the feast,
It bites the fruit, it dips into the wine;
Then rather let my enemy hate *me*
Than I hate him.
   Octavius.   We must look round. What think you?
Is Dolabella to be trusted?
   Mecænas.   Try.
   Octavius. I wish this country settled, us return'd.
Resolved am I to do what none hath done,
And only Julius ever purposed doing;
Resolved to render Rome, beneath my rule,
A second Alexandria. Corinth, Carthage,
One autumn saw in stubble; not a wreath
Enough to crown a capital was left,
Nor capital to crown its pillar, none;
But here behold what glorious edifices!
What palaces! what temples! what august
Kings! how unmoved is every countenance
Above the crowd! And so it was in life.
No other city in the world, from west
To east, seems built for rich and poor alike.
In Athens, Antioch, Miletus, Rhodes,
The richest Roman could not shelter him
Against the dogstar; here the poorest slave
Finds refuge under granite, here he sleeps
Noiseless, and, when he wakens, dips his hand
Into the treasured waters of the Nile.
   Mecænas. I wish, Octavius, thou wouldst carry hence
For thy own worship one of those mild Gods,
Both arms upon the knees: 'tis time that all
Should imitate this posture.
   Octavius.   We will close
The gates of Janus.
   Macænas.   Janus looks both ways;
He may like best the breezy air abroad
And knock too hard against the bolted brass.
   Octavius (*to* a Guard). Call Gallus hither.
   Gallus.   Cæsar! what commands?
   Octavius. I would entrust a legion, more than one,
To our friend Gallus: I would fix him here
In Egypt: none is abler to coerce
The turbulent.

222

Gallus.　　　　Let others flap their limbs
With lotus-leaves when Sirius flames above,
Give me the banks of Anio, where young Spring,
Who knows not half the names of her own flowers,
Looks into Summer's eyes and wakes him up
Alert, and laughs at him until he lifts
His rod of roses and she runs away.
　　Octavius. And has that lovely queen no charms for thee?
　　Gallus. If truth be spoken of her, and it may,
Since she is powerless and deserted now,
Tho' more than thrice seven[1] years have come and stolen
Day after day a leaf or two of bloom,
She has but changed her beauty; the soft tears
Fall, one would think, to make it spring afresh.
　　Octavius. And not for Gallus? Let one brave man more
Ascend the footstool of the regal bed.
　　Gallus. As the Gods will! but may they not will *me*!

SCENE THE SIXTH

Antony and Dolabella

　　Antony. Welcome, my Dolabella! There is none
From yonder camp I would embrace beside.
My little queen hath given at last an audience
To thy persuasive tongue?
　　Dolabella.　　　　Most graciously.
　　Antony. I never thought she would permit Cæsarion
To leave her side; hardly can I myself
Bear separation from that brave young boy;
I love him as my own.
　　Dolabella.　　　　Your own thus stand
Safe from all peril.
　　Antony.　　　　Is not it disgrace?
A boy save *me*? for to save them is *me*.
　　Dolabella. Create a generosity of soul
In one whom conquest now hath made secure;
Bid him put forth his power, it now is greater
Than any man's: consider what a friend

---

[1] History and poetry do not always well agree. Julius Cæsar had left Egypt before the birth of Cæsarion, at which time Cleopatra was about fourteen. That she retained her freshness seven or eight years longer may be attributed in part to the care she took of it, and in a greater to her pure Macedonian blood. Beside, Alexandria is not sultry; and the architects of antiquity knew how to keep up an equable and healthy temperature.

Cæsarion hath in Julius, all whose wounds
Will bleed afresh before the assembled tribes
On the imperial robe thy hands outsprad
With its wide rents, for every God above
And every Roman upon earth to number.

    Antony. Ah! those were days worth living o'er again.

    Dolabella. Live them again then.

    Antony.   Never, stript of power,
Of dignity, of Rome's respect, of theirs
Who compass me, who fix before these eyes
The very eagles which adorn'd my tent.

    Dolabella. Brave thoughts! but are none weaker intermixt?

    Antony. Smile, Dolabella! Oh, could but that smile
Kill as it pierces me! But tread the ground
Softly and lightly where her feet have moved.
My Cleopatra! never will we part,
Thy son shall reign in Egypt.

    Dolabella.   Much I fear'd,
O Antony, thy rancour might prevail
Against thy prudence. Cæsar bears no rancour.

    Antony. Too little is that heart for honest hatred.
The serpent the most venomous hath just
Enough of venom for one deadly wound,
He strikes but once, and then he glides away.

    Dolabella. Octavius strikes not Antony.

    Antony.   One man
Alone dares strike the man whom thou hast named.
But let me hear the phrase of fraudulence.

    Dolabella. Cæsar's, I trust, will not deserve that name,
He says his reign shall be the reign of peace.

    Antony. Peace! what is that? a pleasant room to sit
Or walk about in, nor could heart desire
A cooler place wherein to spread the cates:
First, bring these cates; bring liberty, the salt
That seasons with true relish all things else.

    Dolabella. We sometimes leave but little, when we rise
From its enjoyment, for those servitors
Who toil'd for us throughout the heat of day:
Reckless we riot: never can spilt wine
Enter the golden cup it sparkled in:
Harpies above defile the half-eaten fruit.
Rome now would rest awhile.

    Antony.   Yea, long will be
Her rest; the scourge of Earth will be the scorn.

    Dolabella. We must submit.

    Antony.   Thou must; thou hast submitted;
But never I; what I have been I am.

Dolabella. Less prosperous than once, thy fortunes may
Be yet restored.
  Antony.   I would not take them back,
By any man, least by that man, bestow'd;
I would not have my portion of the world,
No, nor the whole of it, if that glib tongue
Call'd every God to ratify the gift.
Show me the foe he ever fairly met,
The friend he hath embraced, and not betray'd,
And tell me, Dolabella, for thou canst,
Who murder'd Hirtius; by whose agency
Poison was dropt into the wound of Pansa.
  Dolabella. Of this ask Glyco, ask Aquilius Niger
Of that.
  Antony. Both know the secret, both have told it:
And now will I tell thee one.
                              At the noon
Of yesterday, when fruit is most refreshing,
A countryman who brings the yellow figs
His queen is fond of, brought a basketful,
Saying to Iras:
                'These my little daughter,
Whom once you used to play with in the garden,
Bids me to give into your hands; she thinks
The queen requires some frolic; you alone
Can venture so far with her. Place within
The smooth cool linen of her bed this basket
Of cane-leaves and of rushes intertwined,
With all the fruit below, the leaves a-top;
You see it is but shallow, scarce a palm,
Mind it lie flat; yet she will find it out
Tho' it be always dusky in that room.'
What is there in the tale that thou shouldst stare?
  Dolabella. Enough. An idle rumor reacht the camp
That Cleopatra stung herself to death,
Vexing two asps held close against her bosom.
  Antony. Are Romans all so ignorant of the asp
That two are wanted? that he must be vext?
That, like domestic animals, he bites?
He bites not, but he strikes with upper jaw
As other vipers do, and the black lid
Drops, and he crawls away; one pang, one shriek,
Death hears it, nor delays: the hind knows that.
An earlier story now. So exquisite
In luxury, my queen dissolved a pearl
Above all price, and drank it in her wine.
Bid thou the tatler of the tale expound
How that same acid which dissolved the pearl

Darken'd no tooth, abbreviated no smile,
But gave her spirits for the festive song.
Ah! had she done so, Medicine had run up
In vain to help her; Death had interposed.

    Dolabella. Another tale, alike incredible.
'Tis said she shook from off her coronal
Poison into your cup, dashing it down
Just at the lip, and proving its effect
On household beast before you, thus to show
How easy were the deed to one who will'd.

    Antony. Is such a fiction workt by homespun yarn?
I doubt it: surely some Greek needle wrought
The quaint device, for poet to adorn
By metaphor, and sage by apologue.
Thou hast among thy friends one capable,
In man's attire, fresh-blooming from Hymettus,
Handmaid of Cilnius the rich Aretine.
O Romans! are your ears to falsities
Wide open, and your mouths agape for them
As are the callow sparrows for their food,
Hour after hour? Ye little know that asps
Are not mere worms of one span-length, one cubit,
But longer than the vipers in your fields,
So hideous that no woman, young or old,
Or rustic, or well train'd to monkey-gods,
But must abhor them. Your credulity
Will urge the whisper in each other's ear
That she, the daintiest of all womankind,
Would handle them, now plague them, now caress
And hug them as she might a tender babe . .
Yet even the serious may believe the tale,
For what in Rome is not believed . . but truth?

    Dolabella. To me the queen said nothing of this snare.

    Antony. Nothing she knows of it.
                           I heard a scream
From Iras, and rusht in. She threw herself
Before my feet, prayed me to strike her dead,
And ran toward the corner, where I saw
The beasts coil'd up, and cut them thro' and thro'.
Then told she all; but not until her prayer
For death was fruitless, not until I warn'd her
Her life and death, while yet we live, are ours.

    Dolabella. Might I advise . .

    Antony.   Not me: I never took
Any advice, in battle or debate:

    Dolabella. Cæsar hath urged thee sorely, and may worse;
What wouldst thou do with him were he the vanquisht?

Antony. Do with him? throw him to the fishermen
To bait their hooks with and catch crocodiles,
If crocodile feeds upon crocodile.
Take him these words: we keep no secrets here.
    Dolabella. Cæsar is lenient.
    Antony.   Never let that word
Glide o'er thy lips, no word is it for me.
Tell him no friend of mine shall ask my life,
No enemy shall give it. I am lord
Of my own honor; he has none to lose:
The money-changer's granson calculates
But badly here. He waits for thee: depart.

SCENE THE SEVENTH

ANTONY AND AGRIPPA

    Antony. And so, the victor comes to taunt the vanquisht!
Is this well done, Agrippa?
    Agrippa.   'Twere ill done,
And never done by me.
                   There have been some
Who carried to the forum and there cast
The tags and rags of mimes, and tarnisht spangles
Bag'd from the dusthole corner; gravity
Becomes me better and plain Roman garb
In action and in speech; no taunt is mine.
    Antony. What then demands the vanquisher?
    Agrippa.   I come
To ask a favor, ask a gift, of thee.
Give me thy children.
    Antony.   To adopt?
    Agrippa.   To save:
They may have enemies; they shall have friends
If thou accedest to my last request:
Lose we no time; we shall be soon at Rome.
    Antony. Ventidius may prevent it.
    Agrippa.   He hath serv'd thee
Faithfully, and is steddy to thy cause:
The sea is closed to him, the river closed,
Wide as the desert is, it is not open,
And half his army, more than half, is ours.
    Antony. But many yet are left me, brave and true.
    Agrippa. When Fortune hath deserted us, too late
Comes Valor, standing us in little stead.
They who would die for us are just the men
We should not push on death or throw away.

Antony. Too true! Octavius with his golden wand
Hath reacht from far some who defied his sword.
How little fire within warps loosen'd staves
Together, for the hoop to hold them tight!
I have too long stood balancing the world
Not to know well its weight: of that frail crust
Friends are the lightest atoms.
 Agrippa.   Not so all.
 Antony. I thought of Dolabella and the rest.
Ventidius and Agrippa, these are men
Romulus might have wrestled with nor thrown.
I have proved both.
 Agrippa.   One thou shalt prove again,
In guise more friendly than when last we met.
 Antony. To me well spoken hast thou for Ventidius,
Speak for him in that manner to another,
Tell him that he has done against the Parthian
What Julius might, perhaps might not, have done.
Triumph must follow. I shall never see it,
Nor shall I see, nor shalt thou either, one
On which cold eyes, dim even in youth to beauty,
Look forward.
    Are there not kings left enow
To drag, by brace or leash, and back to back,
Along the *Sacred Way*?
      Vile wretch! his steeds
Shall never at the cries of Cleopatra
Prance up against their trappings stiff with gold.
 Agrippa. Sad were the sight.
 Antony.   Too far hath Dolabella
Prevail'd with her.
 Agrippa.   Hath Dolabella come
Within these walls?
 Antony.   Hast thou not seen him then
Leave them within the hour?
 Agrippa.   Indeed not I.
My station is the harbor where the ships
Are riding, his lies nearer to the town.
Thou musest, Antony!
 Antony.   And well may muse.
He was my friend . . *is* he. Away with doubt!
 Agrippa. He was the friend of Tullius, friend of Brutus,
Friend too of Lepidus, akin to each,
And yet betraid he them.
     Give me the boys;
With me they enter Rome.
 Antony.   Take, take them; both?
Yes; both are safer, both are happier so.

I loved them; but I might have loved them more;
Now is too late.
                    Take them; be kind to them . .
Nay, look not back. Tears scorch the father's eyes,
The Roman should extinguish them . . and shall.
Farewell! farewell!
                    But turn thy face aside . .
No . . one word more.
    Agrippa.   Thy gladness gladdens me,
Bursting so suddenly. What happy change!
    Antony. Thou hast a little daughter, my old friend,
And I two little sons . . I had at least . .
Give her the better and the braver one,
When by thy care he comes to riper age.
    Agrippa. O Antony! the changes of our earth
Are suddener and oftener than the moon's,
On hers we calculate, not so on ours,
But leave them in the hands of wilful Gods,
Inflexible, yet sometimes not malign.
    Antony. They have done much for me, nor shall reproach
Against them pass my lips: I might have askt,
But never thought of asking, what desert
Was mine for half the blessings they bestow'd.
I will not question them why they have cast
My greatness and my happiness so low;
They have not taken from me their best gift,
A heart for ever open to my friends:
It will be cold ere long, and one will grieve.

SCENE THE EIGHTH

Octavius. Agrippa. Cæsarion. Mecænas

    Octavius. What said that obstinate and proud old thief?
Couldst thou not draw him from his den, Agrippa?
    Agrippa. I tried not.
    Octavius.   Nor perhaps desired.
    Agrippa.   'Tis true,
I entered not by stealth, and broke no confidence;
Tatius, who knew and once fought under me . .
    Octavius. And would not he who knows thy power, and who
Admitted thee within the royal hold,
Do more?
    Agrippa. Not even this would he have done
For any other, nor for me without
Permission from his general; this obtain'd,
I enter'd.

Octavius.   His audacity, no doubt,
Abated with his fortunes, and he droopt
As droops a lotus when the water fails.
   Agrippa. Neither in life nor death will that man droop;
He holds down Fortune, stil too strong for her.
   Octavius. We must then starve him out, or slay his sons
Before his eyes.
   Agrippa.   Thus nothing will remain
For him to fear, and every honest sword
Will skulk within its scabbard for mere shame.
This may not be the worst . . when brave men fall
By treachery, men like them avenge the blow;
Antonius did it . . was Antonius blamed?
   Octavius. But who will answer for our own dear lives
If these boys live?
   Agrippa.   I will . . the boys are mine.
   Octavius. Cæsarion is secure.
   Agrippa.   I do rejoice
At this.
   Octavius. I wonder he hath not arrived.
   Agrippa. Rescued from Egypt is the Roman lad?
I long to see him.
   Octavius.   Wait then, and thou shalt.
   Agrippa. Women and eunuchs and Greek parasites
Educate ill those who may one day rule.
   Octavius. True, very true . . we will bear this in mind.
   Agrippa. He must learn better soon.
   Octavius.   Be sure he shall.
   Agrippa. What are those sistrums and those tamborines
That trifle with the trumpet and intrude?
   Octavius. The very things thou wouldst provide against.
Heigh! who commanded such obstreperous shouts?
   Agrippa. The man who gave us Egypt, sir, and thee.
The sound bursts louder from his hollow tomb:
Such are the honors which attend his child.
   Octavius. Hark! the arms strike the ground!
   Agrippa.   Soldiers, well done!
Already do they know whom they salute.
   Cæsarion. Hail! hail! my cousin!
                        Let me kiss that hand
So soft and white. Why hold it back from me?
I am your cousin, boy Cæsarion.
   Octavius. Who taught you all this courtesy?
   Cæsarion.   My heart.
Beside, my mother bade me wish you joy.
   Octavius. I would myself receive it from her.
   Cæsarion.   Come,
Come then with me; none see her and are sad.

R

Octavius. Then she herself is not so?

Cæsarion.   Not a whit,
Grave as she looks, but should be merrier stil.

Octavius. She may expect all bounty at our hands.

Cæsarion. Bounty! she wants no bounty.

                                        Look around;
Those palaces, those temples, and their gods
And myriad priests within them, all are hers;
And people bring her ships, and gems, and gold.

   O cousin! do you know what some men say,
(If they do say it) that your sails ere long
Will waft all these away?

                              I wish 'twere true
What else they talk.

   Octavius.   What is it?

   Cæsarion.   That you come
To carry off her also.

                          She is grown
Paler, and I have seen her bite her lip
At hearing this. Ha! well I know my mother;
She thinks it may look redder for the bite.

   But will you really carry us to Rome
In triumph? thro' the streets, and up the hill,
And over arches . . foolish folks say under . .
With flowers all round them? O! what joy to see
The people that once loved my father so!

   Octavius. We will do all that may oblige the queen.

   Cæsarion. And yet she shudders at the very thought
Of those fresh honors which delight my heart.

   Octavius. For her, or for yourself?

   Cæsarion.   We boys, you know,
Think of ourselves the first; and yet, and yet,
If my sweet mother is averse to change,
And weary of it, I would pass my days
With her; yes, even in that lonely tower
(Which to my eyes looks like a sepulcher)
Whence she protests the Gods alone shall take her.

   Octavius. (*to a* Guard). See due attention paid this royal guest.

   Cæsarion. Unwillingly I part from one so kind.

   Octavius (*to* AGRIPPA). Agrippa, didst thou mark that comely boy?

   Agrippa. I did indeed.

   Octavius.   There is methinks in him
A somewhat not unlike our common friend.

   Agrippa. Unlike? There never was such similar
Expression. I remember Caius Julius
In youth, altho' my elder by some years;
Well I remember that high-vaulted brow,
Those eyes of eagle under it, those lips

At which the senate and the people stood
Expectant for their portals to unclose;
Then speech, not womanly but manly sweet,
Came from them, and shed pleasure as the morn
Sheds light.
    Octavius. The boy has too much confidence.
    Agrippa. Not for his prototype. When he threw back
That hair in hue like cinnamon, I thought
I saw great Julius tossing his, and warn
The pirates he would give them their desert.
    My boy, thou gazest at those arms hung round.
    Cæsarion. I am not strong enough for sword and shield,
Nor even so old as my sweet mother was
When I first rioted upon her knee
And seiz'd whatever sparkled in her hair.
Ah! you had been delighted had you seen
The pranks she pardon'd me. What gentleness!
What playfulness!
    Octavius.   Go now, Cæsarion.
    Cæsarion. And had you ever seen my father too!
He was as fond of her as she of me,
And often bent his thoughtful brow o'er mine
To kiss what she had kist, then held me out
To show how he could manage the refractory,
Then one long smile, one pressure to the breast.
    Octavius. How tedious the boy grows!
                        Lead him away,
Aufidius!
                  There is mischief in his mind,
He looks so guileless.
    Agrippa.   He has lived apart
From evil counsellors, with grey-hair'd men
Averse to strife, and maidens of the queen.
    Octavius. This makes me think . .
                  We will another time
Consider what is best.
           Here comes Mecænas.

          (*To* MECÆNAS.)

Cilnius! you met upon the stairs that boy?
    Mecænas. I did.
    Octavius.   What think you of him?
    Mecænas.   At one glance
'Twere rashness to decide.
    Octavius.   Seems he not proud?
    Mecænas. He smiled, and past me by.
    Octavius. What insolence! quite insupportable!

Mecænas. Perhaps he knew me not; and, if he knew me,
I have no claim on affability
From Cæsar's enemies.
    Agrippa (to himself). By Jove! the man
At first so calm begins at last to chafe.
O, the vain Tuscan of protuberant purse!
    Octavius. What said Agrippa?
    Agrippa.   That our friend here chafes,
Altho' the mildest of all mortal men.
    Octavius. Excepting one; one whom no wrongs can ruffle.
I must give orders for some small affairs,
And will rejoin you soon.
    Agrippa.   My gentle Cilnius!
Do save this lad! Octavius is so calm,
I doubt he hath some evil in his breast
Against the only scion of the house,
The orphan child of Julius.
    Mecænas.   Think, Agrippa,
If there be safety where such scion is,
Safety for you and me.
    Agrippa.   The mother must
Adorn the triumph, but that boy would push
Rome, universal Rome, against the steeds
That should in ignominy bear along
The image of her Julius. Think; when Antony
Show'd but his vesture, sprang there not tears, swords,
Curses? and swept they not before them all
Who shared the parricide? If such result
Sprang from torn garment, what must from the sight
Of that fresh image which calls back again
The latest of the Gods, and not the least,
Who nurtured every child within those walls,
And emptied into every mother's lap
Africa, Sicily, Sardinia, Gaul,
And this inheritance of mighty kings.
No such disgrace must fall on Cæsar's son.
Spare but the boy, and we are friends for ever.
    Mecænas. Friends are we, but Octavius is our master.
    Agrippa. Let him brush kings away and blow off queens,
But there are some of us who never struck
At boys, nor trampled on a prostrate head;
Some of us are there too who fain would see
Rome better than they left her, with high blood
Bounding along her veins; enough hath flowed.
    Mecænas. Here comes Octavius. We attend his will.
    Octavius. Enough that I know yours, my truest friends!
I look into your hearts and find my own.
Thy wishes, O Agrippa, I divine.

Antony was thy comrade in the wars
Of Julius; Fulvia was thy enemy
And mine: her children to the Infernal Gods
Devote I, but the born of Cleopatra
Thou shalt have saved: Cæsarion shall rest here.

SCENE THE NINTH

DOLABELLA. CÆSARION. SCOPAS.

Dolabella. Where hast thou put Cæsarion?
Scopas.   Nigh at hand.
Dolabella. What is he doing?
Scopas.   Just what lads like most;
Munching a water-melon.
                           There is good,
At least good-nature, in that simple soul.
While most were sleeping in the night of noon
I brought him hither. Thirsty were we both
And wine I offer'd him: he pusht it by
And said, 'I drink no wine; bring water-melons.'
I brought him one: he cut it fairly thro',
And gave me half before he toucht the other,
Saying, 'but keep the seeds, the round and black,
That I may plant them, when we get to Rome,
With my own hands in garden all my own.'
  Dolabella. Poor innocent!
Scopas.   I could not help but smile.
  Dolabella. For once I envy thee.
                        But call him in.
  Scopas. Ho! youngster! here!
  Cæsarion.   What means that loud rude speech?
This man seems civiler; I may converse
With him, but never more, thou churl, with thee.
  Dolabella. I would, my fair young friend, his voice less **rough**,
But honest Romans are sometimes abrupt.
Scopas is sorry.
  Cæsarion.   Honest! sorry too!
I then was wrong, and am more vext than he.
  Scopas. Boy! I could wish I never saw thy face
Nor heard thy tongue.
  Cæsarion.   What can he mean?
  Dolabella.   He feels
The offence he gave.
  Cæsarion.   Good man, be comforted,
And let my hand atone for face and tongue.
  Scopas (*to* DOLABELLA). That smile disarms me.

Dolabella.   My sweet prince, observe
How he repents.
                    I have some words to speak
In private to him: but I first would hear
How fare your little brothers.
    Cæsarion.   They are gone,
Both gone: two maidens carried them away
Before a noble-looking man they call
Agrippa.
    Dolabella. Gone? say you? and with Agrippa?
O that I could have seen them ere they went!
    Cæsarion. No matter; I will tell you all about them,
It is not much, if you desire to know.
One can not talk, the other talks all day,
One smiles at me, the other pulls my hair,
But he smiles too, and then runs off as fleet
As my gazelle, yet easier to be caught.
You have heard all, and now will I return
And leave you, as you wish: I know my way.
    Dolabella. The duty must be done; 'tis Cæsar's will.
    Scopas. Then done it shall be.
    Dolabella.   Take this token: here;
Take this too; ninety golden of like weight
Lie in the leather.
    Scopas.   Thanks; the deed is done.   [*Alone.*
What do these letters, bright and sharp, denote?
CÆSAR DICTATOR; and what else beneath?
PERPETUO.
                Gods above! PERPETUO too!
Ashes may be perpetual: nothing more
Remains of our dictator. Take the urn,
Empty it, weigh its inwards: poise the two,
This inch-broad coin with it; and what I toss
On my forefinger is the solider.
    I must go in.
    Cæsarion.   'Tis very kind in you
To visit me again: you bear no malice.
I know at once who loves me.
    Scopas.   And do I?
    Cæsarion. One moment yes, one moment no. My handsome
And gentle cousin does not love me quite;
I wish he did, I want so to love *him.*
How cool and quiet is this small dim room!
It wants no cushion: I begin to think
The hard stone-seat refreshes more the limbs.
Will you not try?
    Scopas.   Not yet; but presently.

Cæsarion. My mother is not here; you need not mind.
People must not sit down before a queen;
But before boys, whatever boys they are,
Men may, and should.
                       Oh! what can I have done?
And did you strike me? Would you strike again?
What runs into my sandals from my breast?
Oh! it begins to pain me .. sadly, sadly!
  Scopas. By all the Gods and Goddesses above!
I have no strength to strike the boy again.
  Cæsarion. O father! father! where is now that face
So gravely fond that bent o'er your Cæsarion?
And, mother! thou too gone! In all this gloom
Where shall I find thee? Scopas! Scopas! help!
  Scopas. Away with me! Where is the door? Against it
Stands he? or follows he? Crazed! I am crazed!
O had but he been furious! had he struck me!
Struggled, or striven, or lookt despitefully!
Anything, anything but call my name
So tenderly. O had that mild reproach
Of his been keener when his sense return'd,
Only to leave him ever-lastingly,
I might not have been, what I now am, frantic.
Upturn'd to me those wandering orbs, outspred
Those quivering arms, falling the last of him,
And striking once, and only once, the floor,
It shook my dagger to the very hilt,
And ran like lightning up into my brain.

SCENE THE TENTH

Eros and Antony

Antony. Eros! I speak thee welcome.
Eros.   Hail, our lord!
  Antony. Thou hast been ever faithful to thy trust,
And spoken freely, but decorously,
On what concern'd the household and the state.
My glory is gone down, and life is cold
Without it. I have known two honest men
Among the senators and consulars ..
  Eros. None among humbler?
  Antony.   By the Powers above!
I thought but of the powerful, men of birth.
  Eros. All men are that. Some sink below their cradle,
Others rise higher than parental roof,
And want no scepter to support their steps.

Antony. Such there may be whom we have all past by.

Eros. Men cast long shadows when their life declines,
Which we cross over without noticing;
We met them in the street and gave not way,
When they were gone we lifted up both hands,
And said to neighbors *These were men indeed!*

Antony. Reflections such as thine had wearied me
Erewhile, and from another even now;
But what is that thou bringest me wrapt up,
Tardy in offering it as worth too little?

Eros. I bring a ruby and a hollow ring
Whereon it fitted.

Antony. Gods of Rome! at last
Ye make me grateful. Thanks, and thanks alone,
Have I to give, and one small sacrifice;
I vow it you before this hour is past.
My heart may beat against its bars awhile,
But shall not leave me yet.
Go, Eros, go,
I must lie down and rest, feeble and faint.
But come back presently.

Eros (after some absence). How fares our lord?

Antony. Recovered, sound again, more sound than ever.

Eros. And yet our lord looks more like other men.

Antony (smiling). We can not always swagger; always act
A character the wise will never learn:
When Night goes down, and the young Day resumes
His pointed shafts, and chill air breathes around,
Then we put on our own habiliments
And leave the dusty stage we proudly trod.
I have been sitting longer at life's feast
Than does me good; I will arise and go.
Philosophy would flatten her thin palm
Outspred upon my sleeve; away with her!
Cuff off, cuff out, that chattering toothless jade!
The brain she puzzles, and she blunts the sword:
Even she knows better words than that word *live.*
Cold Cato, colder Brutus, guide not me;
No, nor brave Cassius.
Thou hast brought me balm.

Eros. Our lord may have some message for the giver,
Which will console her.

Antony. She expected none:
I did; and it is come.
Say, lookt she pale?
Spake she no word?

Eros. Alas, most noble sir,
She would not see me. Charmian said her face

Was indeed pale, yet grew less pale than usual
After she gave the ring, and then she spake
Amid some sighs (some spasms too interposed)
More cheerfully, and said she fain would sleep.
  Antony. The fondest heart, the truest, beats no more.
She listened to me, she hath answered me,
She wanted no entreaty, she obeyed,
She now commands: but no command want I.
Queen of my soul! I follow in thy train,
Thine is the triumph.
                         Eros, up! rejoice!
Tears, man! do tears become us at this hour?
I never had too many; thou hast seen
(If thou didst see) the last of them.
                                   My sword!
I will march out becomingly.
  Eros.   O sir!
Enemies watch all round, and famine waits
Within.
  Antony. Thou knowest not the prudent sons
Of Egypt; corn and wine have been supplied
Enough for many years, piled underground.
Tho' stiffened by the sludge of barbarism,
Or indolent and overgorged at home,
Briton or German would take heed that none
Who fought for him should perish for the lack
Of sustenance: the timid bird herself
Will hover round and round until she bring
The grain cried out for in the helpless nest.
Give me my sword! Is the point sharp?
  Eros.   In vain
To trust it now!
  Antony.   Come, bring it; let me try it.
  Eros. O heavens and earth! Help! help! no help is nigh,
No duty left but one: less worthily
Than willingly this duty I perform.   [*Stabs himself.*
It pains not: for that blood I see no more.

SCENE THE ELEVENTH
[Alexandria. August, 30 B.C.]

OFFICER. OCTAVIUS. MECÆNAS. GALLUS.

Officer. News! glorious news! certain news! Dead as Death!
Octavius. Who dead?
Officer.   The master of the horse to Julius,
Master too, but this morning, of this realm,
The great . .

Mecænas. Halt there! and know, where Cæsar is
There is none great but Cæsar!
    Officer.   Pardon! true!
    Octavius. And nought about his paramour?
    Officer.   The queen?
    Octavius. Yes, fellow, yes.
    Officer.   Surely our emperor knows
Of her; the story now is some days old.
The queen was poisoned by two little worms
Which people here call asps, most venomous things,
Coil'd in a yellow fig around the seeds.
Her maidens wail'd her loudly; men and maidens
Alike mourn'd over . . I had nearly slipt.
    Octavius. Many have done the same.
                              Art thou a Roman?
    Officer. I have the honor, sir, to be a Gaul,
A native of Massilia, that famed city
Inhabited by heroes, built by Gods,
Who entered it again with Caius Julius.
    Mecænas. And didst thou see them enter?
    Officer.   Not distinctly,
There were a few between: one told it me
Who saw them; which, ye know, is just the same.
    Octavius. Retire, my brave! go sure of a reward.
Lucretia hath escaped us after all!
But there is wax in Egypt, there are Greeks
Who model it, and who can bear to look
On queen or asp; this model'd to the life,
The other more like what they work upon.
No trouble in thus carrying her to Rome.
Gallus! thou lookest grave: thou art the man
Exactly to compose an epitaph.
No matter which died first: I think the asps
Rather have had the start: I may be wrong,
A bad chronologist, a worse astrologer.
    Mecænas. Where Cæsar smiles, all others smile but Gallus.
    Gallus. Not even Cæsar's smiles awaken mine
When every enemy has dropt away,
And he who made so many safe, is safe.
    Mecænas. I wish thou wert more joyous.
    Gallus.   Kind the wish,
Almost enough to make me so.
    Mecænas.   Come! come!
I know you poets: any wager now
Thou hast already forced the weeping Muse
To thy embraces. Tell us honestly;
Hast thou not turn'd the egg upon the nest
Ready for hatching?

Octavius.　　　　　Guilty; look at him,
He blushes, blushes from cheekbone to beard.
Now, Gallus, for the epitaph.
　Mecænas.　　　　　Recite it.
　Gallus. Epitaphs are but cold and chisel'd words,
Or mostly false if warmer: quite unfit
Are mine for marble or for memory.
I thought of her . . another would have said
He wept: I wept not, but I know I sigh'd.
　Mecænas. And wrote? For poet is half sigh half flame:
Sigh out thy sigh.
　Gallus.　　　　　Would Cæsar hear it?
　Octavius.　　　　　　　　　Yea.
　Gallus. I have not ventured to pronounce the name
Of her I meditated on.
　Cæsar.　　　　　My friend
Is here judicious as in all things else.
　Gallus.
　　'Thou hast been floating on the o'erswollen stream
　　　Of life these many summers; is thy last
　　Now over? hast thou dreamt out every dream?
　　　Hath horn funereal blown the pageant past?
　　Cæsar! thou too must follow: all the rods
　　　Of sternest lictor cannot scare off Death;
　　She claims the earth for heritage; our Gods
　　　Themselves have seen their children yield their breath.'
　Cæsar. Gallus! I always thought thee a brave soldier,
Never a first-rate poet: I am right.
　Gallus. Cæsar! I never heard of one who gain'd
A battle and a kingdom who was not.
　Cæsar. If there be anything on earth I know
Better than other things, 'tis poetry.
　Mecænas. My sweet Octavius! draw not under nose
The knuckle of forefinger. Gallus aim'd
A harmless arrow: Love in sport hath done it
Often and often.
　　　　　Gallus, seize his hand.
Now sing a pæan; sing a prophet's; sing
Egypt! thy pyramid of power is closed.
　Gallus. I would; but want the breath: I have but strength
For elegy: here is the last of mine.
　　'The mighty of the earth are earth,
　　　A passing gleam the brightest smile,
　　In golden beds have sorrows birth,
　　　Alas! these live the longer while.'
　Octavius. Unless we haste to supper, we shall soon
Forfeit our appetites. Come, my two friends!

SCENE THE TWELFTH

Octavius and Octavia

Octavius. Embrace me, sister; we have won; thy wrongs
Are now avenged.
  Octavia.   Speak not of wrong, but right,
And bring Rome peace and happiness once more.
'Tis kind in thee (but thou wert always kind)
To come so soon to greet me, while the altar
Is warm and damp with incense for thy safety.
  Octavius. Octavia! I have brought thee from the Nile
Two pretty little serpents.
  Octavia.   Of all beasts
The serpent is the beast I most abhor.
Take them away.
  Octavius.   I have not brought them here,
Be not afraid; beside, they are so young
They can not bite.
  Octavia. But send them off.
  Octavius.   I will.
What thinkest thou are these two reptiles call'd?
  Octavia. I know not, nor can guess.
  Octavius.   *Lucius and Marcus,*
The brood of Antony. O Heaven! she faints!
Rise, sister! let me help thee up; be sure
They shall not hurt thee. Grasp not thus my wrist,
And shoot not up those leaden bolts at me,
For such are thy stiff eyes. I said, and swear,
The little monsters never shall hurt *thee.*
I do not like those tears; but better they
Than the cold flint they fall from, and now melt.
  Octavia. Brother, I know thy purpose. On my knees . .
  Octavius. Arise! There wants not this to seal their doom.
  Octavia. This is my fault, not theirs, if fault there be.
  Octavius. I want, and I will have, security.
  Octavia. What is there now on earth to apprehend?
  Octavius. I dread lest he who guards them should adopt.
  Octavia. Let him! O let him! if an honest man.
Frown not, debate not, struggle not against
Thy better Genius; argue with him thus,
'Octavius! has there not been blood enough
Without the blood of children?'
  Octavius.   Is my safety
Not dear to thee?
  Octavia.   Thy glory, thy content,
Are . . no, not dearer, but almost as dear.
Hast thou not suffer'd pangs at every head
That fell?

Octavius. They fell that mine might not.
Octavia.   But children
Strike not so high.
     Octavius.   Are children always children?
     Octavia. O brother! brother! are men always men?
They are full-grown then only when grown up
Above their fears. Power never yet stood safe;
Compass it round with friends and kindnesses,
And not with moats of blood. Remember Thebes:
The towers of Cadmus toppled, split asunder,
Crasht: in the shadow of her oleanders
The pure and placid Dirce stil flows by.
What shatter'd to its base but cruelty,
(Mother of crimes, all lesser than herself)
The house of Agamemnon king of kings?
     Octavius. Thou art not yet, Octavia, an old woman;
Tell not, I do beseech thee, such old tales.
     Octavia. Hear later; hear what our own parents saw.
Where lies the seed of Sulla? Could the walls
Of his Præneste shelter the young Marius,
Or subterranean passages provide
Escape? he stumbled through the gore his father
Had left in swamps on our Italian plains.
We have been taught these histories together,
Neither untrue nor profitless; few years
Have since gone by, can memory too have gone?
Ay, smile, Octavius! only let the smile
Be somewhat less disdainful.
     Octavius.   'Tis unwise
To plant thy foot where Fortune's wheel runs on.
     Octavia. I lack not wisdom utterly; my soul
Assures me wisdom is humanity,
And they who want it, wise as they may seem,
And confident in their own sight and strength,
Reach not the scope they aim at.
                         Worst of war
Is war of passion; best of peace is peace
Of mind, reposing on the watchful care
Daily and nightly of the household Gods.

THE END

JOAN OF ARC AND HER JUDGE

Judge. After due hearing in our court supreme
Of temporal and spiritual lords,
Condemn'd art thou to perish at the stake
By fire, forerunner of the flames below.

Hearest thou? Art thou stunn'd? Art thou gone mad?
Witch! think not to escape and fly away,
As some the like of thee, 'tis said, have done.
 Joan. The fire will aid my spirit to escape.
 Judge. Listen, ye lords. Her spirit! Hear ye that?
She owns, then, to have her Familiar.
And whither (*to* JOAN)—whither would the spirit, witch,
Bear thee?
 Joan. To Him who gave it.
 Judge.   Lucifer?
 Joan. I never heard the name until thus taught.
 Judge. He hath his imps.
 Joan.   I see he hath.
 Judge.   My lords!
Why look ye round, and upward at the rafters?
Smile not, infernal hag! for such thou art,
Altho' made comely to beguile the weak,
By thy enchantments and accursed spells.
Knowest thou not how many brave men fell
Under thy sword, and daily?
 Joan.   God knows best
How many fell—may their souls rest in peace!
We wanted not your land, why want ye ours?
France is our country, England yours; we hear
Her fields are fruitful: so were ours before
Invaders came and burnt our yellowing corn,
And slew the labouring oxen in the yoke,
And worried, in their pasture and their fold,
With thankless hounds, more sheep than were devour'd.
 Judge. Thou wast a shepherdess. Were those sheep thine?
 Joan. Whatever is my country's is mine too—
At least to watch and guard; I claim no more.
Ye drove the flocks adrift, and we the wolves.
 Judge. Thou shouldst have kept thy station in the field,
As ours do.
 Joan.   Nobles! have I not? Speak out.
In the field too,—the field ye shared with me—
The cause alone divided us.
 Judge.   My lords!
Must we hear this from peasant girl, a witch?
Wolves we are call'd. (*To* JOAN.) Do wolves, then, fight for glory?
 Joan. No; not so wicked, tho' by nature wild,
They seek their food, and, finding it, they rest.
 Judge. Sometimes the devil prompts to speak a truth
To cover lies, and to protect his brood.
But, *we* turn'd into wolves!—*we* Englishmen!
Tell us, thou knowing one, who knowest well—
Tell us, then, who are now the vanquishers.

Joan. They who will be the vanquished, and right soon.
Judge. False prophets there have been, and thou art one,
And proud as he that sent thee here inspired.
Who ever saw thee bend before the high
And mighty men, the consecrate around—
They whom our Lord exalted, they who wear
The mitre on their brows?
Joan.   One—one alone—
Hath seen me bend, and may he soon more nigh,
Unworthy as I am! I daily fall
Before the Man (for Man he would be call'd)
Who wore no mitre, but a crown of thorns
Wore he; upon his hands no jewel'd ring,
But in the centre of them iron nails,
Half-hidden by the swollen flesh they pierced.
Judge. Alert to play the pious here at last,
Thou scoffest Mother Church in these her sons,
Right reverend, worshipful, Beatitude's
Creation, Christ's and Peter's lawful heirs.
Joan. My mother Church enforced no sacrifice
Of human blood; she never made flames drink it
Ere it boil over. Dear were all *her* sons,
Nor unforgiven were the most perverse.
Judge. Seest thou not here thy hearers sit aghast?
Joan. Fear me not, nobles! Ye were never wan
In battle; ye were brave to meet the brave.
I come not now in helm or coat of mail,
But bound with cords, and helpless. God incline
Your hearts to worthier service!
Judge.   Darest thou,
After such outrages on knight and baron,
To call on God, or name his holy name?
'Tis mockery.
Joan.   'Tis too often, not with me.
When first I heard his holy name I thought
He was my Father. I was taught to call
My Saviour so, and both my parents did
The like, at rising and at setting sun
And when they shared the oaten cake at noon.
Judge. So thou wouldst babble like an infant still?
Joan. I would be silent, but ye bade me speak.
Judge. Thou mayst yet pray—one hour is left for prayer.
Edify, then, the people in the street.
Joan. I never pray in crowds; our Saviour hears
When the heart speaks to him in solitude.
May we not imitate our blessed Lord,
Who went into the wilderness to pray?

Judge. Who taught thee tales like this? They are forbidden.
Hast thou no supplication to the court?

Joan. I never sued in vain, and will not now.

Judge. We have been patient; we have heard thee prate
A whole hour by the bell; we have endured
Impiety; we have borne worse affronts.
My lords, ye have been bantered long enough.
The sorceress would have turned us into wolves,
And hunt us down; she would be prophetess.

Joan. I am no sorceress, no prophetess;
But this, O man in ermine, I foretell:
Thou and those round thee shall ere long receive
Your due reward. England shall rue the day
She entered France—her empire totters.

           Pile,
Ye sentinels, who guard those hundred heads
Against a shepherdess in bonds—pile high
The faggots round the stake that stands upright,
And roll the barrel gently down the street,
Lest the pitch burst the hoops, and mess the way.

          (*To the court.*)
Ye grant one hour; it shall be well employed.
I will impore the pardon of our God
For you. Already hath He heard my prayer
For the deliverers of their native land.

DEDICATION OF AN ANCIENT IDYL
TO ROSE

EUROPA CARRIED OFF

FRIEND of my age! to thee belong
The plaintive and the playful song,
And every charm unites in thee
Of wisdom, wit, and modesty;
Taught hast thou been from early youth
To tread the unswerving path of truth,
And guided to trip lightly o'er
The amaranth fields of ancient lore,
Turn thou not hastily aside
From her who stems the Asian tide,
For shores henceforth to bear her name . .
Thine, thine shall be a better fame;
Lands yet more distant shall it reach
Than yonder Hellespontic beach,
Or where the bravest blood now flows
Before perfidious Delhi, Rose!

245

From boyhood have I loved old times
And loitered under warmer climes.
I never dream such dreams as there . .
Voices how sweet, and forms how fair!
The Nymphs and Graces there I find,
The Muses too, and thee behind,
All chiding thee, all asking why
Thou whom they cherish art so shy;
They will not listen when I say,
Thou hast some dearer ones than they.
'Ungrateful!' cry they, 'can it be?
We have no dearer one than she.'

THE ANCIENT IDYL

Europa and her Mother

Mother. Daughter! why roamest thou again so late
Along the damp and solitary shore?
Europa. I know not. I am tired of distaf, woof,
Everything.
Mother.   Yet thou culledst flowers all morn,
And idledst in the woods, mocking shrill birds,
Or clapping hands at limping hares, who stampt
Angrily, and scour'd off.
Europa.   I am grown tired
Of hares and birds. O mother! had you seen
That lovely creature! It was not a cow,
And, if it was an ox,[1] it was unlike
My father's oxen with the hair rubb'd off
Their necks.
Mother.   A cow it was.
Europa.   Cow it might be . .
And yet . . and yet . . I saw no calf, no font
Of milk: I wish I had; how pleasant 'twere
To draw it and to drink!
Mother.   Europa! child!
Have we no maiden for such offices?
No whistling boy? Kings' daughters may cull flowers,
To place them on the altar of the Gods
And wear them at their festivals. Who knows
But some one of these very Gods may deign
To wooe thee? maidens they have wooed less fair.
Europa. The Gods are very gracious: some of them
Not very constant.
Mother.   Hush!

---

[1] Bulls are never at large in those countries; Europa could not have seen one.

S

Europa.   Nay, Zeus himself
Hath wandered, and deluded more than one.
    Mother. Fables! profanest fables!
    Europa.   Let us hope so.
But I should be afraid of him, and run
As lapwings do when we approach the nest.
    Mother. None can escape the Gods when they pursue.
    Europa. They know my mind, and will not follow me.
    Mother. Consider: some are stars whom they have loved,
Others, the very least of them, are flowers.
    Europa. I would not be a star in winter nights,
In summer days I would not be a flower;
Flowers seldom live thro' half their time, torn off,
Twirl'd round, and indolently cast aside.
Now, mother, can you tell me what became
Of those who were no flowers, but bent their heads
As pliantly as flowers do?
    Mother.   They are gone
To Hades.
    Europa. And left there by Gods they loved
And were beloved by! Be not such my doom!
Cruel are men, but crueler are Gods.
    Mother. Peace! peace! Some royal, some heroic, youth
May ask thy father for thy dower and thee.
    Europa. I know not any such, if such there live;
Royal there may be, but heroic . . where?
O mother! look! look! look!
    Mother.   Thou turnest pale;
What ails thee?
    Europa.   Who in all the house hath dared
To winde those garlands round that grand white brow?
So mild, so loving! Mother! let me run
And tear them off him: let me gather more
And sweeter.
    Mother.   Truly 'tis a noble beast.
See! he comes forward! see, he rips them off,
Himself!
    Europa. He should not wear them if he would.
Stay there, thou noble creature! Woe is me!
There are but sandrose, tyme, and snapdragon
Along the shore as far as I can see.
O mother! help me on his back; he licks
My foot. Ah! what sweet breath! Now on his side
He lies on purpose for it. Help me up.
    Mother. Well, child! Indeed he is gentle. Gods above!
He takes the water! Hold him tight, Europa!
'Tis well that thou canst swim.

> Leap off, mad girl!

She laughs! He lows so loud she hears not me . .
But she looks sadder, or my sight is dim . .
Against his nostril fondly hangs her hand
While his eye glistens over it, fondly too.
It will be night, dark night, ere she returns.
And that new scarf! the spray will ruin it.

DEFIANCE

CATCH her and hold her if you can . .
See, she defies you with her fan,
Shuts, opens, and then holds it spred
In threat'ning guize above your head.
Ah! why did you not start before
She reacht the porch and closed the door?
Simpleton! will you never learn
That girls and time will not return;
Of each you should have made the most.
Once gone, they are for ever lost.
In vain your knuckles knock your brow,
In vain will you remember how
Like a slim brook the gamesome maid
Sparkled, and ran into the shade.

THE SHORTEST DAY

THE day of brightest dawn (day soonest flown!)
Is that when we have met and you have gone.

GEORGE THE THIRD'S STATUE

ALTHO' against thee, George the Third!
I threw sometimes a scornful word,
Against thy nape I did not nail
Characteristical pig-tail.
What is thy genus none can doubt
Who looks but at thy brow and snout.

OLIM

Do and permit whate'er you will
With others, I shall love you stil.
Heaven grant we may not love the most
When to each other we are lost!

ON LOVE

WHAT right have I to hold back Love so late,
    When we should long have gone to rest?
But we were pelted by the storms of Fate
    From where we rashly built our nest.
One there is yet who drives us not away,
But warms our hands in her's this winter day.

THE HEART'S ABYSSES

TRIUMPHANT Demons stand, and Angels start,
To see the abysses of the human heart.

INCORRIGIBLE

My hopes and glories all go down,
Before the shadow of your frown:
You smile on me, and I am then
The happiest and the first of men.
To you is given, and but to you,
To punish and to pardon too.
Grave was my fault, yet wish it less
I can not; I would stil transgress.

ON LAW

WHAT thousands, Law, thy handywork deplore!
Thou hangest many, but thou starvest more.

CONFESSION

CONFESSION soon would be discarded
If all our priests were Abeilarded;
For Faith is hardly worth a pin
Without a few good works of sin.

PARTIES

TORIES don't like me, Whigs detest;
Then in what quarter can I rest?
Among the Liberals? most of all
The liberals are illiberal.

PEOPLE AND PATRIOTS

PEOPLE like best the patriots who betray 'em;
They trusted Russell and they trusted Graham;
Past folly's last extreme they now are gone,
And pant, and halt, and cling to Palmerston.

ADVICE

AT every step of life expect
    Flings from your *Ragged School*, O bard!
Walk quietly, and recollect
    That rotten apples hit not hard.

JUSTICE AND INJUSTICE

YOU think Injustice is a curse,
But Justice you will find the worse;
Its rotten bench is stuft with thorns,
And the road to it bad for corns.
You would ride back then: well, but where
Is money left to pay the fare?

OLD-FASHIONED VERSE

IN verse alone I ran not wild
When I was hardly more than child,
Contented with the native lay
Of Pope or Prior, Swift or Gay,
Or Goldsmith, or that graver bard
Who led me to the lone churchyard.
    Then listened I to Spencer's strain,
Til Chaucer's Canterbury train
Came trooping past, and carried me
In more congenial company.
Soon my soul was hurried o'er
This bright scene: the 'solemn roar'
Of organ, under Milton's hand,
Struck me mute: he bade me stand
Where none other ambled near . .
I obey'd, with love and fear.

THE MIDDLE-SIZED

MIDDLE-SIZED men live longest, but soon dies
The phthisic poet of a middle size.

LESBIA NOSTRA! LESBIA ILLA!

Lips! that were often prest on mine,
What falsehood ever found ye there?
I scarcely call'd her half-divine,
Scarcely the fairest of the fair.
I wooed to right, I warn'd of wrong,
I taught the little lore I knew;
She paid me with a siren song . .
Better one breath of pure and true!

MORN

Sweet is the Morn where'er it shines,
Whether amid my Tuscan vines,
Or where Sorrento's shadows play
At *hide-and-seek* along the bay,
Or high Amalfi takes its turn,
Until they rest on high Salern.

And here too once the Morn was sweet,
For here I heard the tread of feet
Upon the pebbles wet with dew;
Sweet was the Morn, it breath'd of you.

MY WIT SCANTY

I have but little wit, all they
Whose brains are close and curdy say,
They relish best the broadfaced jokes
Of hearty, burly, country-folks,
And are quite certain those must judge ill
Who for the rapier drop the cudgell.

BOYS AND MEN

Leave me alone! the pettish schoolboy cries,
Leave me alone! say too the calm and wise.

HEROICS OR DACTYLICS

Force me (and force me you must if I do it) to write in heroics,
Taking (as model in English) the meter of Homer and Virgil.
Leave me, O leave me at least my own hero, my own field of battle.
Sing then, O Goddess! O Muse! or in whatever name thou delightest,
Neither a cut-throat on land nor a vagabond over the ocean,
Offering me sacksful of wind . . I can buy them as cheaply of Russell,
Palmerston, Grey, Aberdeen, Jockey Derby, or Letterman Graham.

THE MATRON

BECOME a matron, grave and sage,
You, reprehending every page
That pleas'd you not long since, seem now
To ask from under frowning brow,
'Ha! what audacity hath placed
This volume in a hand so chaste?
A volume where fictitious names
Cover, not hide, forbidden flames.'
   Be merciful! and let him pass;
He is no longer what he was:
He wrote as poets wrote before,
And loved like them . . but rather more.

THE SOLAR MICROSCOPE

YOU want a powerful lens to see
What animalcules those may be,
Which float about the smallest drop
Of water, and which never stop,
Pursuing each that goes before,
And rolling in unrest for more.

   Poets! a watery world is ours,
Where each floats after, each devours,
Its little unsubstantial prey . .
Strange animalcules . . we and they!

PIGMIES AND CRANES

I LIVE among the Pigmies and the Cranes,
Nor care a straw who loses or who gains.
Peel doffs the harness, Russell puts it on,
The late Sir Robert is the live Lord John,
Close in the corner sits the abler man,
But show me the more tricky if you can.

DIFFERENT GRACES

AROUND the child bend all the three
Sweet Graces: Faith, Hope, Charity.
Around the man bend other faces;
Pride, Envy, Malice, are his Graces.

WRITTEN IN ILLNESS

BEFORE another season comes
And frost the shrinking earth benumbs,
I think I shall be warm enough,
Like an old rat in sink or sough.
Allowing me a higher merit,
Keep off the terrier and the ferret.

LA PROMESSA SPOSA

SLEEP, my sweet girl! and all the sleep
You take away from others, keep:
A night, no distant one, will come
When those you took their slumbers from,
Generous, ungenerous, will confess
Their joy that you have slumber'd less,
And envy more than they condemn
The rival who avenges them.

SWIFT ON POPE

(Imaginary)

POPE, tho' his letters are so civil,
Wishes me fairly at the devil;
A little dentifrice and soap
Is all the harm I wish poor Pope.

THE GRATEFUL HEART

THE grateful heart for all things blesses;
　　Not only joy, but grief endears:
I love you for your few caresses,
　　I love you for my many tears.

DECLINE OF LIFE

How calm, O life, is thy decline!
　　Ah! it is only when the sun
　　His hot and headstrong course hath run,
Heaven's guiding stars serenely shine.

FASHIONS IN POETRY

THE *Swain* and *Nymph* went out together,
Now *Knight* and *Ladie* ride o'er heather:
And who comes next? Perhaps again
Will smirk and sidle *Nymph* and *Swain*.

A SENSIBLE GIRL'S REPLY TO MOORE'S

'OUR COUCH SHALL BE ROSES ALL SPANGLED WITH DEW'
IT would give me rheumatics, and so it would you.

TO A YOUNG POET

THE camel at the city-gate
Bends his flat head, and there must wait.
Thin in the desert is the palm,
And pierced the thorn to give its balm.
The Land of Promise thou shalt see,
I swear it, by myself and thee;
Rise, cheer thee up, and look around,
All earth is not for deer and hound;
Worms revel in the slime of kings,
But perish where the laurel springs.

ON SOUTHEY'S DEATH

FRIENDS! hear the words my wandering thoughts would say,
And cast them into shape some other day.
Southey, my friend of forty years, is gone,
And, shattered by the fall, I stand alone.

REFLECTION FROM SEA AND SKY

WHEN I gaze upon the sky
And the sea below, I cry,
Thus be poetry and love,
Deep beneath and bright above.

ACCUSED OF INDIFFERENCE TO PRAISE

TO SOPHIA

ACUTE in later as in earlier days
Hath ever been the poet's ear to praise;
Indifferent to its loudest voice am I,
And would exchange it for your faintest sigh.

THERMOMETER

[ON THE POEMS OF JOHN EDMUND READE]

IF the Rhætian Alps of old
Were insufferably cold,
Colder ten degrees are they
Since Reade's Poems blew that way,
And those bleak and steril scalps
Now are call'd the Readian Alps.

TRIPOS

BY THE AUTHOR OF 'DULL ESSAYS', NAMELY,
'IMAGINARY CONVERSATIONS', ETC.

I

Gaffer Lockhart! Gaffer Lockhart!
Thou no inconvenient block art,
Tho' unoil'd and coarse the stone,
To repass my razor on.

II

Lockharts who twitch my skirt may feel
Some day a buffet from my heel,
Which Nature has thought fit to place
Exactly level with their face.
Kind to his cattle, blind or lame,
Murray will feed them just the same.

III

Who would have thought the heaviest particle
That ever sank into an Article,
Blown by a whiff or two of mine,
Should cross the Ocean and the Line,
Sparkle beneath both setting sun
And rising? Yet all this is done:
Nay, more: another insect I
Quicken by electricity.
My friend the generous Crosse will own
Life-giving is not his alone.

HYPOCRICY WHY HATED

There's no hypocricy in being civil
Even to one you wish were at the devil.
It is not that you hate it, but you hate
(Don't you?) the man for somewhat good or great.
Half, more than half, the honest I have known
Feel at the heart the truth they dare not own.

A GIFT OF POEMS

Send me such poems as a treat!
By Jupiter! I'd rather eat
A mangy fox or Cheshire cheese,
Or any ordure that you please.

WHO ARE THE BEST LABORERS

You in good blinkers can see nothing shocking,
I shy and start before a crimson stocking;
I think what dippings and how deep have dyed
Those courtly trappings of unchristian pride;
Then, looking into the next field, percieve
Men work the better for less width of sleeve.

TO ONE UNEQUALLY MATCHED

Bear it, O matcht unequally, you must,
And in your strength and virtue firmly trust.
The Power that rules our destinies decreed
One heart should harden and another bleed.

LIFE HURRIES BY

Life hurries by, and who can stay
One winged Hour upon her way?
The broken trellis then restore
And train the woodbine round the door.

THE STERN BROW

You say my brow is stern and yet my smile
  (When I *do* smile) is sweet.
Seldom, ah seldom so! 'tis only while
  None see us when we meet.

It is your smile, Ianthe, and not mine,
  Altho' upon my lips;
Your's brought it thither; its pale rays decline
  Too soon in sad eclipse.

VERSES WHY BURNT

How many verses have I thrown
Into the fire because the one
Peculiar word, the wanted most,
Was irrecoverably lost.

ADVICE TO A POET

If you are jealous as pug-dog, O poet,
Button your bosom tight, and never show it.
If you are angry at the world's disdain,

What the world gives you, give the world again.
The Muses take delight in poets' sighs,
But they hear few ascending from the wise.
'*The more the merrier*' (wicked jades!) they say,
Laugh in your face, and turn their own away.

WHY NEVER SEEN

You ask me why I'm 'never seen' . .
Except by you, perhaps you mean.
Without the gazes of the crowd
I can be (while you let me) proud.
Society props slender folk,
In the deep forest swells the oak.

PHILOSOPHER AND POET

Philosopher and poet you shall find
    Each ever after his own kind:
'Tis well to watch them . . not too near perhaps . .
    One snarls at you, the other snaps.

THE BANQUET OVER

I leave the table: take my place,
Ye young, and, when ye rise, say grace.
Hence all unthankful ones, and go
Where neither vines nor myrtles grow.

THE FIRES OF LOVE

The fires of love are pure in just degree,
Like other fires, to their intensity.

FEW BUT BEND THEIR NECKS

How few there are who live content
To pass thro' life with neck unbent!
Yet the bent neck bears shame and pain,
And never comes erect again.

HEARTS-EASE

There is a flower I wish to wear,
    But not until first worne by you . .
Hearts-ease . . of all Earth's flowers most rare;
    Bring it; and bring enough for two.

THE BARK

Upon the bark of this old tree
You here and there your name will see;
You caught the blossoms where they fell,
And may you like the fruit as well.

A PAIR OF NIGHTINGALES

Cool-smelling Oleander loves the stream
And bends ripe roses over it; but whose
Are those bright eyes that look aslant at me?
And whose are those slim talons, smooth, yet sharp,
That hold an insect up?
                    She flies away,
Nor heeds my doubts and questionings.
                             Erelong
Melodious gurgles ripple from a copse
Hard-by: she seems to thank me, seems to tell
Her partner not to fear me: they defer
The song of gratitude til even-tide,
Then gushes it amain.
                  Fond pair, sing on;
I will watch near you; none shall interrupt
That deep and sparkling stream of melody.

THE PRIMROSE-BANK

It was because the seat was dry,
And many other reasons why,
O primrose-bank! Ianthe's gown
Was lifted for her to sit down,
When we both thought that harm were done
More than sufficiently by one:
So only one of us imprest
The tender turf. Why tell the rest?
Ground-ivy peer'd, and celandine
Show'd us how smartly he could shine,
And stiff-neck violets, one or two,
Pouted, and would not venture thro'.
  Forgive us, and accept our thanks,
Thou pleasantest of primrose banks!

A CRITIC

With much ado you fail to tell
The requisites for writing well;
But, what bad writing is, you quite
Have proved by every line you write.

MY HOMES

Home! I have changed thee often: on the brink
Of Arrowe early I began to think,
Where the dark alders, closing overhead,
Across the meadow but one shadow shed.
Lantony then received me for a while
And saw me musing in the ruin'd aile:
Then loitered I in Paris; then in Tours,
Where Ronsard sang erewhile his loose amours,
And where the loftier Beranger retires
To sing what Freedom, and what Mirth, inspires.
From France to Italy my steps I bent
And pitcht at Arno's side my household tent.
Six years the Medicæan palace held
My wandering Lares; then they went afield,
Where the hewn rocks of Fiesole impend
O'er Doccia's dell, and fig and olive blend.
There the twin streams in Affrico unite,
One dimly seen, the other out of sight,[1]
But ever playing in his smoothen'd bed
Of polisht stone, and willing to be led
Where clustering vines protect him from the sun,
Never too grave to smile, too tired to run.
Here, by the lake, Boccaccio's *Fair Brigade*
Beguiled the hours and tale for tale repaid.
   How happy! O how happy! had I been
With friends and children in this quiet scene!
Its quiet was not destined to be mine;
'Twas hard to keep, 'twas harder to resign.
Now seek I (now Life says, *My gates I close*)
A solitary and a late repose.

IDLE WORDS

They say that every idle word
Is numbered by the Omniscient Lord.
O Parliament! 'tis well that He
Endureth for Eternity,
And that a thousand Angels wait
To write them at thy inner gate.

[1] The scene of Boccaccio's *Ninfale* and his *Bella Brigada*.

TO LESBIA

I LOVED you once, while you loved me;
    Altho' you flirted now and then,
It only was with two or three,
    But now you more than flirt with ten.

[TO THE SAME]

I SWORE I would forget you; but this oath
    Brought back your image closer to my breast:
That oaths have little worth your broken troth
    Had taught me; teach my heart like yours to rest.

TO AN OLD POET

'TURN on the anvil twice or thrice
Your verse,' was Horace's advice:
Religiously you follow that,
And hammer it til cold and flat.

[PARADISE LOST]

AN angel from his Paradise drove Adam;
From mine a devil drove me—Thank you, Madam.

[PROEM TO *THE HELLENICS*]

COME back, ye wandering Muses, come back home,
Ye seem to have forgotten where it lies:
Come, let us walk upon the silent sands
Of Simois, where deep footmarks show long strides;
Thence we may mount perhaps to higher ground,
Where Aphroditè from Athenè won
The golden apple, and from Herè too,
And happy Ares shouted far below.
    Or would ye rather choose the grassy vale
Where flows Anapos thro anemones,
Hyacynths, and narcissuses, that bend
To show their rival beauty in the stream?
    Bring with you each her lyre, and each in turn
Temper a graver with a lighter song.

HOMER, LAERTES, AGATHA

Homer. Is this Laertes who embraces me
Ere a word spoken? his the hand I grasp?
    Laertes. Zeus help thee, and restore to thee thy sight,
My guest of old! I am of years as many,
And of calamities, as thou thyself,

I, wretched man! who have outlived my son
Odysseus, him thou knewest in this house,
A stripling fond of quoits and archery,
Thence to be call'd for counsel mid the chiefs
Who storm'd that city past the farther sea,
Built by two Gods, by more than two defended.

    Homer. He rests, and to the many toils endur'd
There was not added the worse weight of age.

    Laertes. He would be growing old had he remain'd
Until this day, tho' scarcely three-score years
Had he completed; old I seem'd to him
For youth is fanciful, yet here am I,
Stout, a full twenty summers after him:
But one of the three sisters snapt that thread
Which was the shortest, and my boy went down
When no light shines upon the dreary way.

    Homer. Hither I came to visit thee, and sing
His wanderings and his wisdom, tho' my voice
Be not the voice it was; yet thoughts come up,
And words to thoughts, which others may recite
When I am mute, and deaf as is my grave,
If any grave in any land be mine.

    Laertes. Men will contend for it in after times,
And cities claim it as the ground whereon
A temple stood, and worshippers yet stand.
Long hast thou travell'd since we met, and far.

    Homer. I have seen many cities, and the best
And wisest of the men who dwelt therein,
The children and *their* children now adult,
Nor childless they. Some have I chided, some
Would soothe, who, mounted on the higher sod,
Wept as the pebbles tinkled, dropping o'er
A form outstretcht below; they would not hear
Story of mine, which told them there were fields
Fresher, and brighter skies, but slapping me,
Cried worse, and ran away.

    Laertes.   Here sits aside thee
A child grey-headed who will hear thee out.
Here shalt thou arm my son again, in mail
No enemy, no time, can strip from him,
But first I counsel thee to try the strength
Of my old prisoner in the cave below:
The wine will sparkle at the sight of thee,
If there be any virtue left in it.
Bread there is, fitter for younger teeth than ours,
But wine can soften its obduracy.
At hand is honey in the honeycomb,
And melon, and those blushing pouting buds

That fain would hide them under crisped leaves.
Soon the blue dove and particolor'd hen
Shall quit the stable-rafter, caught at roost,
And goat shall miss her suckling in the morn;
Supper will want them ere the day decline.
    Homer. So be it: I sing best when hearty cheer
Refreshes me, and hearty friend beside.
    Laertes. Voyagers, who have heard thee, carried home
Strange stories; whether all be thy device
I know not: surely thou hadst been afraid
Some God or Goddess would have twitcht thine ear.
    Homer. They often came about me while I slept,
And brought me dreams, and never lookt morose.
They loved thy son and for his sake loved me.
    Laertes. Apollo, I well know, was much thy friend.
    Homer. He never harried me as Marsyas
Was harried by him; lest he should, I sang
His praise in my best hymn: the Gods love praise.
    Laertes. I should have thought the Gods would **more approve**
Good works than glossy words, for well they know
All we can tell them of themselves or us.
Have they enricht thee? for I see thy cloak
Is ragged.
    Homer.   Ragged cloak is songster's garb.
    Laertes. I have two better; one of them for thee.
Penelope, who died five years ago,
Spun it, her husband wore it only once,
And 'twas upon the anniversary
Of their espousal.
    Homer.   Wear it I will not,
But I will hang it on the brightest nail
Of the first temple where Apollo sits,
Golden hair'd, in his glory.
    Laertes.   So thou shalt
If so it please thee: yet we first will quaff
The gifts of Bakkos, for methinks his gifts
Are quite as welcome to the sons of song
And cheer them oftener.
          [AGATHA *enters with a cup of wine.*]
                 Maiden! come thou nigh,
And seat thee there, and thou shalt hear him sing,
After a while, what Gods might listen to:
But place that cup upon the board, and wait
Until the stranger hath assuaged his thirst,
For songmen, grasshoppers, and nightingales
Sing cheerily but when the throat is moist.
    Homer. I sang to maidens in my prime; again,
But not before the morrow, will I sing;

T

Let me repose this noontide, since in sooth
Wine, a sweet solacer of weariness,
Helps to unload the burden.

Laertes.   Lie then down
Along yon mat bestrown with rosemary,
Basil, and mint, and thyme.

                              She knows them all
And has her names for them, some strange enough.
Sound and refreshing then be thy repose!
Well may weak mortal seek the balm of sleep
When even the Gods require it, when the stars
Droop in their courses, and the Sun himself
Sinks on the swelling bosom of the sea.

    Take heed there be no knot on any sprig;
After, bring store of rushes and long leaves
Of cane sweet-smelling from the inland bank
Of yon wide-wandering river over-sea
Famed for its swans; then open and take out
From the black chest the linen, never used
These many years, which thou (or one before)
Spreadst for the Sun to bleach it; and be sure,
Be sure, thou smoothen with both hands his couch
Who has the power to make both young and old
Live throughout ages.

    Agatha.   And look well through all?
    Laertes. Aye, and look better than they lookt before.
    Agatha. I wish he would make me so, and without
My going for it anywhere below.
I am content to stay in Ithaca,
Where the dogs know me, and the ferryman
Asks nothing from me, and the rills are full
After the rain, and flowers grow everywhere,
And bees grudge not their honey, and the grape
Grows within reach, and figs, blue, yellow, green,
Without my climbing; boys, too, come at call;
And, if they hide the ripest, I know where
To find it, twist and struggle as they may;
Impudent boys! to make me bring it out,
Saying I shall not have it if I don't!
    Laertes. How the child babbles! pardon her! behold
Her strength and stature have outgrown her wits!
In fourteen years thou thyself wast not wise.
    Homer. My heart is freshen'd by a fount so pure
At its springhead; let it run on in light.
Most girls are wing'd with wishes, and can ill
Keep on their feet against the early gale
That blows impetuous on unguarded breast;
But this young maiden, I can prophecy,

Will be thy staff when other staff hath fail'd.
    Agatha. May the Gods grant it! but not grant it yet!
Blessings upon thy head!
    Homer.   May they bestow
Their choicest upon thine! may they preserve
Thy comeliness of virtue many years
For him whose hand thy master joins to thine!
    Agatha. O might I smoothen that mild wrinkled brow
With but one kiss!
    Laertes.   Take it. Now leave us, child,
And bid our good Melampos to prepare
That brazen bath wherein my rampant boy
Each morning lay full-length, struggling at first,
Then laughing as he splasht the water up
Against his mother's face bent over him.
Is this the Odysseus first at quoit and bar?
Is this the Odysseus call'd to counsel kings,
He whose name sounds beyond our narrow sea?
    Agatha. O how I always love to hear that name!
    Laertes. But linger not; pursue the task at hand:
Bethink thee 'tis for one who has the power
To give thee many days beyond old-age.
    Agatha. O tell him not to do it if he can:
He cannot make youth stay: the swallows come
And go, youth goes, but never comes again.
    Laertes. He can make heroes greater than they were.
    Agatha. By making them lay by the wicked sword?
How I shall love him when he has done that!
    Laertes. No, but he gives them strength by magic song.
    Agatha. The strength of constancy to love but one?
As did Odysseus while he lived on earth,
And when he waited for her in the shades.
    Laertes. The little jay! go, chatterer.
    Agatha to Homer.   Do not think
O stranger, he is wroth; he never is
With Agatha, albeit he stamps and frowns
And shakes three fingers at her, and forbears
To do the like to any one beside.
Hark! the brass sounds, the bath is now prepared.
    Laertes. More than the water shall her hand assuage
Thy weary feet, and lead thee back, now late.

HOMER. LAERTES. AGATHA
In the Morning

    Homer. Whose is the soft and pulpy hand that lies
Athwart the ridges of my craggy one
Out of the bed? can it be Agatha's?

Agatha. I come to bring thee, while yet warm and frothy,
A draught of milk. Rise now, rise just half-up,
And drink it. Hark! the birds, two at a time,
Are singing in the terebinth. Our king
Hath taken down his staff and gone afield
To see the men begin their daily work.

Homer. Go thou to thine: I will arise. How sweet
Was that goat's milk!

Agatha.   We have eleven below,
All milchers. Wouldst thou now the tepid bath?

Homer. Rather when thou hast laid on the left-hand
My sandals within reach; bring colder lymph
To freshen more the frame-work of mine eyes,
For eyes there are, altho their orbs be dark.

Agatha. 'Tis here; let me apply it.

Homer.   Bravely done!
Why standest thou so still and taciturn?

Agatha. The king my master hath forbidden me
Ever to ask a question: if I might,
And were not disobedience such a sin,
I would ask *thee*, so gentle and so wise,
Whether the story of that bad Calypso
Can be all true, for it would grieve me sorely
To think thou wouldst repeat it were it false,
And some ill-natured God (such Gods there are)
Would punish thee, already too afflicted.

Homer. My child! the Muses sang the tale I told,
And they know more about that wanton Nymph
Than they have uttered into mortal ear.
I do rejoice to find thee fond of truth.

Agatha. I was not always truthful. I have smarted
For falsehood, under Queen Penelope,
When I was little. I should hate to hear
More of that wicked creature who detain'd
Her lord from her, and tried to win his love.
I knew 'twas very wrong of me to listen.

Homer. A pardonable fault: we wish for listeners
Whether we speak or sing, the young and old
Alike are weak in this, unwise and wise,
Cheerful and sorrowful.

Agatha.   O! look up yonder!
Why dost thou smile? everything makes thee smile
At silly Agatha, but why just now?

Homer. What was the sight?

Agatha.   O inconsiderate
O worse than inconsiderate! cruel! cruel!

Homer. Tell me, what was it? I can see thro' speech.

Agatha. A tawny bird above; he prowls for hours,
Sailing on wilful wings that never flag
Until they drop headlong to seize the prey.
The hinds shout after him and make him soar
Eastward: our little birds are safe from kites
And idler boys.
              'Tis said (can it be true?)
In other parts men catch the nightingale
To make it food.
   Homer.   Nay, men eat men.
   Agatha.   Ye Gods!
But men hurt one another, nightingales
Console the weary with unwearied song,
Until soft slumber on the couch descends.
The king my master and Penelope
Forbade the slaughter or captivity
Of the poor innocents who trusted them,
Nor robbed them even of the tiniest grain.
   Homer. Generous and tender is thy master's heart,
Warm as the summer, open as the sky.
   Agatha. How true! how I do love thee for these words!
Stranger, didst thou not hear him wail aloud,
Groan after groan, broken, but ill supprest,
When thou recitedst in that plaintive tone
How Anticleia met her son again
Amid the shades below?
                  Thou shouldst have stopt
Before that tale was told by thee; that one
At least was true, if none were true before.
In vain, O how in vain, I smote my breast
To keep more quiet what would beat within!
Never were words so sweet, so sad, as those.
I sobb'd apart, I could not check my tears:
Laertes too, tho' stronger, could not his,
They glistened in their channels and would run,
Nor could he stop them with both hands: he heard
My sobs, and call'd me little fool for them;
Then did he catch and hold me to his bosom,
And bid me never do the like again.
   Homer. The rains in their due season will descend,
And so will tears; they sink into the heart
To soften, not to hurt it. The best men
Have most to weep for, whether foren lands
Receive them (or stil worse!) a home estranged.
   Agatha. Listen. I hear the merry yelp of dogs,
And now the ferrel'd staff drops in the hall,
And now the master's short and hurried step
Advances: here he is: turn round, turn round.

266

Laertes. Hast thou slept well, Mæonides?
Homer.   I slept
Three hours ere sunrise, 'tis my wont, at night
I lie awake for nearly twice as long.
   Laertes. Ay; singing birds wake early, shake their plumes,
And carol ere they feed. Sound was thy sleep?
   Homer. I felt again, but felt it undisturb'd,
The pelting of the little curly waves,
The slow and heavy stretch of rising billows,
And the rapidity of their descent.
I thought I heard a Triton's shell, a song
Of sylvan Nymph, and laughter from behind
Trees not too close for voices to come thro',
Or beauty, if Nymph will'd it, to be seen;
And then a graver and a grander sound
Came from the sky, and last a long applause.
   Laertes. Marvellous things are dreams! methinks we live
An age in one of them, we traverse lands
A lifetime could not reach, bring from the grave
Inhabitants who never met before,
And vow we will not leave an absent friend
We long have left, and who leaves *us* ere morn.
   Homer. Dreams are among the blessings Heaven bestows
On weary mortals; nor are they least
Altho' they disappoint us and are gone
When we awake! 'Tis pleasant to have caught
The clap of hands below us from the many,
Amid the kisses of the envious few.
There is a pride thou knowest not, Laertes,
In carrying the best strung and loudest harp.
That vibrates to deserving hearts alone.
   Laertes. Apollo, who deprived thee of thy light
When youth was fresh and nature bloom'd around,
Bestowed on thee gifts never dim with age,
And rarely granted to impatient youth.
The crown thou wearest reddens not the brow
Of him who wears it worthily; but some
Are snatcht by violence, some purloin'd by fraud,
Some dripping blood, not by the Gods unseen.
To thee, O wise Mæonides, to thee
Worthless is all that glitters and attracts
The buzzing insects of a summer hour.
The Gods have given thee what themselves enjoy,
And they alone, glory through endless days.
The Lydian king Sarpedon never swayed
Such sceptre, nor did Glaucos his compeer,
Nor Priam. Priam was about my age,
He had more sorrows than I ever had;

I lost one son, some fifty Priam lost;
This is a comfort, I may rub my palms
Thinking of this, and bless the Powers above.
    Homer. One wicked son brought down their vengeance on him,
And his wide realms invited numerous foes.
    Laertes. Alas! alas! are there not cares enow
In ruling nearly those five thousand heads,
Men, women, children; arbitrating right
And wrong, and hearing maids and mothers wail
For flax blown off the cliff when almost bleacht,
And curlew tamed in vain and fled away,
Albeit one wing was shortened; then approach
To royal ear the whisper that the bird
Might peradventure have alighted nigh,
And hist upon the charcoal, skinn'd and split.
Bounteous as are the Gods, where is the wealth
To stop these lamentations with a gift
Adequate to such losses? words are light,
And words come opposite, with heavy groans.
    Homer. The pastor of the people may keep watch,
Yet cares as wakeful creep into the fold.
    Laertes. Beside these city griefs, what mortal knows
The anxieties about my scattered sheep?
Some bleeting for lost offspring, some for food,
Scanty in winter, scantier in the drought
Of Sirius; then again the shrubs in spring;
Cropt close, ere barely budded, by the goats.
Methinks these animals are over-nice
About their food, else might they pick sea-weeds,
But these foresooth they trample on, nor deign
To taste even samphire, which their betters cull.
There also are some less solicitudes
About those rocks, when plunderers from abroad
Would pilfer eggs and nestlings; my own folk
Are abstinent, without their king's decree.
    Homer. To help thee in such troubles, and in worse,
Where is thy brave Telemakos?
    Laertes.   That youth
Is gone to rule Dulikeon, where the soil
Tho' fitter than our Ithaca for tilth,
Bears only turbulence and idleness.
He with his gentle voice and his strong arm,
Will bring into due train the restive race.
    Homer. Few will contend with gentleness and youth,
Even of those who strive against the Laws,
But some subvert them who could best defend,
And in whose hands the Gods have placed the sword.
On the mainland there are, unless report

Belie them, princes who, possessing realms
Wider than sight from mountain-head can reach,
Would yet invade a neighbour's stony croft,
Pretending danger to their citadels
From fishermen ashore, and shepherd boys
Who work for daily and but scanty bread,
And wax the reeds to pipe at festivals,
Where the dogs snarl at them above the bones.
    Laertes. What! would the cloth'd in purple, as are some,
Rip off the selvage from a ragged coat?
Accursed be the wretch, and whosoe'er
Upholds him, or connives at his misdeeds.
Away with thoughts that sadden even this hour.
    Homer. I would indeed away with 'em, but wrath
Rings on the lyre and swells above the song.
It shall be heard by those who stand on high,
But shall not rouse the lowlier, long opprest,
Who might be madden'd at his broken sleep,
And wrenching out the timbers of his gate
Batter the prince's down.
    Laertes.   Ye Gods forbid!
Thou makest the skin creep upon my flesh,
Albeit the danger lies from me afar.
Now surely this is but a songman's tale,
Yet songman never here discourst like thee,
Or whispered in low voice what thou hast sung,
Striking the lyre so that the strings all trembled.
Are people anywhere grown thus unruly?
    Homer. More are they who would rule than would be ruled,
Yet one must govern, else all run astray.
The strongest are the calm and equitable,
And kings at best are men, nor always that.
    Laertes. I have known many who have call'd me friend,
Yet would not warn me tho' they saw ten skiffs
Grating the strand with three score thieves in each.
    Curse on that chief across the narrow sea,
Who drives whole herds and flocks innumerable,
And whose huge presses groan with oil and wine
Year after year, yet fain would carry off
The crying kid, and strangle it for crying.
Alas, Mæonides, the weakest find
Strength enough to inflict deep injuries.
Much have I borne, but 'twas from those below;
Thou knowest not the gross indignities
From goat-herd and from swine-herd I endur'd
When my Odysseus had gone far away;
How they consumed my substance, how the proud
Divided my fat kine in this my house,

And wooed before mine eyes Penelope,
Reluctant and absconding til return'd
Her lawful lord, true, chaste, as she herself.
   Homer. I know it, and remotest men shall know.
If we must suffer wrong, 'tis from the vile
The least intolerable.
   Laertes.   True, my son
Avenged me: more than one God aided him,
But one above the rest; the Deity
Of wisdom, stronger even than him of war,
Guided the wanderer back, and gave the arms
And will and prowess to subdue our foes,
And their own dogs lapt up the lustful blood
Of the proud suitors. Sweet, sweet is revenge;
Her very shadow, running on before,
Quickens our pace until we hold her fast.
   Homer. Rather would I sit quiet than pursue.
   Laertes. Now art thou not, from such long talk, athirst?
Split this pomegranate then, and stoop the jar.
Hold! I can stoop it: take this cup . . 'tis fill'd.
   Homer. Zeus! God of hospitality! vouchsafe
To hear my prayer, as thou hast often done,
That, when thy lightnings spring athwart the sea,
And when thy thunders shake from brow to base
The Acrokerauneans, thy right hand protect
This Ithaca, this people, and this king![1]

LAERTES. HOMER. AGATHA
Third Day

   Laertes. And now, Mæonides, the sun hath risen
These many spans above the awaken'd earth,
Sing me that hymn, which thou hast call'd thy best,
In glory to the God who gives it light.
   First I will call the child to hear thee sing,
For girls remember well and soon repeat
What they have heard of sacred more or less.
I must forbear to join in it, although
That blessed God hath helpt to rear my grain
High as my knee, and made it green and strong.
Alas! I cackle when I aim to sing,
Which I have sometimes done at festivals,
But, ere a word were out, methought I felt
A beard of barley sticking in my throat.
                        (*Agatha enters.*)
Now, with a trail of honey down the cup

[1] It has been doubted and denied that Homer and Laertes were contemporary.

(Agatha, drop it in), commence thy chaunt.
> (*About the 500th verse Laertes falls asleep: awakening he finds Agatha in the same state, and chides her.*)

Hast thou no reverence for a song inspired?
> *Agatha* (*in a whisper*). Hush! O my king and lord, or he may hear.

You were asleep the first: I kept my eyes
Wide open, opener than they ever were,
While I do think I could have counted more
Than half a thousand of those words divine,
Had both my hands not dropt upon my lap.
> *Laertes.* Another time beware of drowsiness

When reverend men discourse about the Gods.
Now lead him forth into the cooler porch,
Entreating him that he will soon renew
His praises of Apollo.
> *Agatha.*　　　　I will bear

Your words to him; he might care less for mine,
And, sooth to say, I would much rather hear
Some other story, where more men than Gods
Shine on the field.
> *Laertes.*　　　　Of men thou know'st enough.
> *Agatha.* Too much: then why show Gods almost as bad?

They can not be . . least of all Artemis;
'Twas she directed and preserved Odysseus.
> *Laertes.* Blessings upon thee! While thou wast a babe

He fondled thee, nor saw when thou couldst walk.
Few love so early or so long: We say
We love the Gods: we lie; the seen alone
We love, to those unseen we may be grateful.
> *Agatha.* But when they are no more before our eyes . . .
> *Laertes.* That never is, altho' earth come between.

Perplex not thou thy simple little head
With what the wise were wiser to let be.
> *Agatha.* I go, and will not be again perplext.

> (*Aside.*)

He has been dozing while we have converst.
　Mæonides! rise and take this arm
To lead thee where is freshness in the porch.
My master tells me thou another time
Wilt finish that grand hymn about Apollo.
Hast thou no shorter one for Artemis?
> *Homer.* Such thou shalt have for her, but not to-day.
> *Agatha.* O, I can wait, so (I am sure) can she.
> *Homer.* Faint are the breezes here, less faint above;

Gladly then would I mount that central peak
Which overlooks the whole of Ithaca,
That peak I well remember I once clomb
(What few could do) without the help of beast.

Agatha. Here are sure-footed ones, who weed our thistles,
And give us milk, grey dappled as the dawn:
Their large and placid eyes well know that path,
And they will safely bring us to the top
And back again, treading more warily
Than up the ascent.
           I will call forth two boys
To lead them, without switches in the fist.
These two can lift thee up; I at thy side
Require no help, and can whisk off the flies.
    Homer. I know not what impels me to retrace
Scenes I can see no more: but so it is
Thro' life.
        If thou art able, lead me forth,
And let none follow; we are best alone.
    Agatha. Come forward ye.
                Now lift up carefully
The noblest guest that ever king received
And the Gods favor most.
               Well done! now rest,
Nor sing nor whistle til we all return,
And reach the chestnut and enjoy the shade.
    Homer (at the summit). I think we must be near the highest point,
For now the creatures stop, who struggled hard,
And the boys neither cheer 'em, nor upbraid.
'Tis somewhat to have mounted up so high,
Profitless as it is, nor without toil.
    Agatha. Dost thou feel weary?
    Homer.   Short as was the way
It shook my aged bones at every step;
My shoulders ache, my head whirls round and round.
    Agatha. Lean on my shoulder, place thy head on mine,
'Tis low enough.
           What were those words? . . I heard
Imperfectly . . . shame on me! Dost thou smile?
    Homer. Child! hast thou ever seen an old man die?
    Agatha. The Gods defend me from so sad a sight!
    Homer. Sad if he die in agony, but blest
If friend be nigh him, only one true friend.
    Agatha. Tho' most of thine be absent, one remains;
Is not Laertes worthy of the name?
    Homer. And Agatha, who tends me to the last.
    Agatha. I will, I will indeed, when comes that hour.
    Homer. That hour is come.
              Let me lay down my head
On the cool turf; there I am sure to rest.
    Agatha (after a pause). How softly old men sigh! Sleep, gentle soul!
He turns his face to me. Ah how composed!

Surely he sleeps already . . . hand and cheek
Are colder than such feeble breeze could make 'em.
Mæonides! hearest thou Agatha?
He hears me not . . . Can it . . . can it be . . . death?
Impossible . . . 'tis death . . . 'tis death indeed . . .
Then, O ye Gods of heaven! who would not die,
If thus to rest eternal, he descend?
  O, my dear lord! how shall I comfort thee?
How look unto thy face and tell my tale,
And kneeling clasp thy knee? to be repulst
Were hard, but harder to behold thy grief.

ÆSCHYLOS AND SOPHOCLES

Sophocles. Thou goest then, and leavest none behind
Worthy to rival thee!
  Æschylos.   Nay, say not so.
Whose is the hand that now is pressing mine?
A hand I may not ever press again!
What glorious forms hath it brought boldly forth
From Pluto's realm! The blind old Œdipos
Was led on one side by Antigone,
Sophocles propt the other.
  Sophocles.   Sophocles
Sooth'd not Prometheus chaind upon his rock,
Keeping the vultures and the Gods away;
Sophocles is not greater than the chief
Who conquered Ilion, nor could he revenge
His murder, or stamp everlasting brand
Upon the brow of that adulterous wife.
  Æschylos. Live, and do more.
                    Thine is the Lemnian ile,
And thou hast placed the arrows in the hand
Of Philoctetes, hast assuaged his wounds
And given his aid without which Greece had fail'd.
  Sophocles. I did indeed drive off the pest of flies;
We also have our pest of them which buz
About our honey, darken it, and sting;
We laugh at them, for under hands like ours,
Without the wing that Philoctetes shook,
One single feather crushes the whole swarm.
  I must be grave.
                Hath Sicily such charms
Above our Athens? Many charms hath she,
But she hath kings. Accursed be the race!
  Æschylos. But where kings honor better men than they
Let kings be honored too.
                The laurel crown
Surmounts the golden; wear it, and farewell.

ACON AND KEPOS

ACON

KEPOS! what brings thee from the market-place?

KEPOS

What drove me from it, rather ask.

ACON
Well, what?

KEPOS

There was a scramble round about my stall,
And two unlucky boys were fighting hard
Which of them should sweep off the fruit; at last
They overturn'd the board: 'twas time to run.

ACON

And were the people then indifferent?

KEPOS

At first they were not; presently they laught
To see a split pomegranate's slippery fruit
Drop from the fingers of the foremost two,
With nothing left between them but hard rind
And deeply-dyed and ever-during stain.

ACON

Children of Hellas! learn your lesson here,
Nor touch pomegranate in the market-place.

LEONTION, ON TERNISSA'S DEATH
(EPICUROS ALSO DEPARTED)

BEHOLD, behold me, whether thou
Art dwelling with the Shades below
    Or with the Gods above:
With thee were even the Gods more blest . .
I wish I could but share thy rest
    As once I shared thy love.

'Twas in this garden where I lean
Against thy tombstone, once the scene
    Of more than mortal bliss,
That loiter'd our Ternissa; sure
She left me that her love was pure;
    It gave not kiss for kiss.

Faint was the blush that overspred
Thro' loosen'd hair her dying head;

One name she utter'd, one
She sigh'd and wept at; so wilt thou,
If any sorrows reach thee now . .
   'Twas not *Leontion*.

Wert thou on earth thou wouldst not chide
The gush of tears I could not hide
   Who ne'er hid aught from thee.
Willing thou wentest on the way
She went . . and am I doom'd to stay?
   No; we soon meet, all three.

The flowers she cherisht I will tend,
Nor gather, but above them bend
   And think they breathe her breath.
Ah, happy flowers! ye little know
Your youthful nurse lies close below,
   Close as in life in death.

PINDAR AND HIERO

Hiero. Pindar! no few are there among my guests
Who lift up eyebrows archt and rounded eyes
To hear thee talk as they do. Poets grin
And whisper,
      He is one of us, not more,
Tho' higher in . . I think they also add
Our foolish king's esteem.
   Pindar.   In verse I sing
Not always dithyrambics. I may lift
A mortal over an admiring crowd,
And I may hear and heed not their applause,
A part whereof is given to him who fed
The steeds, a part to him who drove, a part
At last to me.
   Hiero.   My friend! the steeds are gone,
The charrioteers will follow: Death pursues
And overtakes the fleetest of them all:
He may pant on until his ribs are crackt,
He never shall reach thee. Believe one word
A king hath spoken . . Ages shall sweep off
All lighter things, but leave thy name behind.
   Pindar. I was amused at hearing the discourse
Of our wise judges, when their maws were fill'd,
About some poets of the present day.
   Hiero. I did not hear it. I would not surcharge
Thy memory, 'twere unfriendly; but perchance

A tittle of the tattle may adhere
Stil to thy memory, as on amber hairs
That some loose wench hath combed into the street:
If so, pray let me have it.
    Pindar.   An old friend
Of mine had represented the grave sire
Of poets, in the ile of Ithaca,
Conversing with Laertes.
    Hiero.   He was wrong.
Homer lived some time after him.
    Pindar.   Who knows?
Howbeit, the worst complaint was that a king
Spoke of stale bread, and offered it his guest.
    Hiero. Ithaca is not Sicily: the rocks
Of that poor iland bear no crops of wheat;
Laertes might not every day have spared
The scanty brushwood for the oaten cake.
Wine, I will wager, your old friend hath jogg'd
The generous host to lay upon the board.
    Pindar. And both converst as other men converse.
The poet is no poet at all hours,
The hero is no hero with a friend.
    Hiero. The virtuous, the valiant, and the wise,
Have ever been thy friends, and they alone.
    Pindar. Few have I found, and fewer have I sought.
Apart I chose to stand. The purest air
Breathes o'er high downs on solitary men.
Thou smilest, O king Hiero, at my words,
Who seest me in thy court.
    Hiero.   No, no, my friend!
    Pindar. We must not penetrate the smile of kings,
There may be secrets in it.
    Hiero.   Open mine;
There is but one for thee; and it is this;
'Tis written on no scroll, but on my heart;
Command I dare not call it, though I would . .
Pindar is Pindar, Hiero is but king.
    Pindar. Embolden'd when I ought to be abasht,
I venture now to question thee.
    Hiero.   Obey.
Sprinkle a drop of Lethe on the fount
Of sparkling Dirce, nor remember Thebes,
Or him alone remember, him whose harp
Rais'd up her walls, which harp thou strikest now
With hand more potent than Amphion's was.
Here shalt thou dwell in honor, long thy due,
And sing to us thy even-song of life.

PTOLEMY AND THEOCRITOS

Ptolemy. Pleasant art thou, Theocritos! The pair
Thou broughtest forward to our festival
Of yesterday, Praxinoe and Gorgo,
Are worthy pair for Aristophanes,
Had he been living, to have brought on stage:
Even grave Menander, wittiest of the wise,
Had smiled and caught thee by the hand for this.
    Theocritos. Ah! to be witty is hard work sometimes.
'Tis easier to lie down along the grass.
Where there is any, grass there none is here.
    Ptolemy. But here are couches where we may repose
And dream as easily. Thy dreams were all
For Sicily, about the Nymphs and swains.
    Theocritos. It seems an easier matter to compose
Idyls of shepherds and of little Gods
Than great heroic men.
    Ptolemy.   Thou hast done both.
    Theocritos. Neither is easy. Grass in Sicily
Is slippery, scant the turf and hard to tread.
The sheep oft wonder, and crowd close, at sight
Of venturous shepherd, putting pipe to lip
And, ere he blow it, sprawling heels in air.
I have sung hymns; but hymns with fuller breath
Are chaunted by my friend Kallimakos.
    Ptolemy. Friend! O strange man! poet call poet *friend!*
If my good genius brought thee hither, thanks
We both may pay him.
    Theocritos.   Well indeed may I.
    Ptolemy. What! for disturbing dreams of Nymphs and swains,
And whispering leaves of platan and of pine?
Sweet whispers! but with sweeter underneath.
    Theocritos. No; but for banishing far different ones,
Such as were facts in our fair Sicily.
Had kings like Ptolemy been living then,
However far removed this empire lies,
Phalaris never had shut up within
His brazen bull the bravest and the best.
    Ptolemy. Kings have their duties: it concerns them all
To take good heed that none betray their trust,
Lest odious be the name, and they themselves
Fall thro the crime of one: the crowns they wear
Make some hot-headed, nearly all weak-eyed.
'Tis written how this bull went close behind,
Bellowing his thunders, belching smoke and flame,
Wherever that king went.

Theocritos. No fiction, sire,
Of poets, or historians, who feign more.
Ptolemy. Pleasanter in our Ægypt be thy dreams!
Come, let me hear the latest; speak it out.
Theocritos. Last night, beneath the shadow of a sphynx
I fancied I was lying, and I dream'd
Only of placid Gods and generous kings.
Ptolemy. Knave! knave! on neither shall thy dream be vain.

MARCUS AURELIUS AND LUCIAN

Marcus Aurelius. Lucian! in one thing thou art ill-advised.
Lucian. And in one only? tell me which is that.
Marcus Aurelius. In scoffing, as thou hast done openly,
At all religions: there is truth in all.
Lucian. Ah! could we see it! but the well is deep.
Each mortal calls his God inscrutable;
And this at least is true: why not stop there?
Some subdivide him; others hold him close,
Forcing the subdivisions to unite.
The worshiper of Mithras lifts his eyes
To hail his early rising, for he knows
Who gives the fruits of earth to nourish him;
Olympus and the Alps are hills alike
To him, and goats their best inhabitants.
  Did Epictetus take our rotten staves
To walk with uprightly? did Cicero
Kneel down before our urban deities?
He carried in his mouth a Jupiter
Ready for Senates when he would harangue,
Then wiped him clean and laid him down again.
Marcus Aurelius. Religions, true or false, may lend support
To man's right conduct: some deterr from ill
Thro' fear, and others lead by gentleness,
Benevolence in thought, beneficence
In action, and at times to patriotism
And gallant struggles for their native land.
Lucian. So much the worse for these. Did Julius spare
The Druid in his grove? no; he wrencht off
The golden sickle from the misleto,
And burnt the wicker basket ere it held
Aloft on sacred oak the wretch within.
Marcus Aurelius. I doubt it: he knew well the use of priests.
Scoffing was not his fault, ambition was;
Yet clemency could over-rule ambition.
Lucian. This of all vices is the very worst
Where the best men are made the sacrifice.

U

278

Marcus Aurelius. I am accused, I hear, of wanting it.
   Lucian. Yet thou too, Marcus, art ambitious; thou
Wouldst conquer worlds .. with kindness, wouldst instruct
The unwise, controll the violent, and divert
From battle-field to corn-field.
   Marcus Aurelius.   This I would,
But never irritate weak intellects
Clinging to a religion learnt by heart
From nurse and mother, thence most justly dear.
   Lucian. Founded on falsehood are not all religions,
All copies, more or less, from older ones?
Some by transfusion purified, and some
Weaken'd, and pour'd again upon the dregs,
Until they first ferment and then turn sour.
   Marcus Aurelius. Yet, Lucian, there is truth in one religion,
Truth in that one which rises from a heart
With sweet and silent gratitude o'erflowing.
   Lucian. Weakest of orders is the composite,
Such is the fabric folks walk under here,
Already we have seen part after part
Crack off, and terrify bare scalps below.
   Marcus Aurelius. Leave Rome her quiet Gods.
   Lucian.   Not Saturn though.
Who would have eaten every God ere teetht,
But his first-born disabled him, and made
The little Venus laugh at granpapa.
   Marcus Aurelius. We are not going up so far as him.
   Lucian. Fain would I stop at Venus and her son;
It were ungrateful in me to malign
Such gentle Deities; to laugh at them
They now, alas! have left me little power;
Juno has helpt in my discomfiture.
   Marcus Aurelius. Into your Lares I will not intrude:
Temples I enter rarely; not a God
Minds me above those atoms of the earth
Whereof we, low and lofty, are composed.
Such is the surest doctrine to uphold,
But to divulge even this may be unsafe.
Have not we known the Sage of Palestine
Derided, persecuted, crucified?
Have we not seen his simple followers
Slaughter'd in this our city, this our Rome,
Some burnt alive, some thrown among wild beasts?
   Lucian. Woefully true! and thieves and murderers
Have sprung up from the ground whereon they bled;
No wicker-basket men, men calling Heaven
To help them in their vengeance on a foe
Who puts the left leg where he should the right,

And will not draw it back, but walk strait on.
Marcus Aurelius. Woefully true this also, but unwise,
Because unsafe, to utter.
Lucian.   Truth is more
Unsafe than falsehood, and was ever so.
Marcus Aurelius. Well, I would not exasperate by wit's
Sharp point the robb'd and bleeding; stoop thou rather
To heal them.
Lucian.   They would kick me in the face
If for such office I bend over them.
Better to strip the sophists of their rings
And trailing trappings, chaunting boys before,
Waving fat incense up against their beards
Ere they parade in them through every street,
And at the end of Via Sacra halt
To choose an Imperator of their own.
Marcus Aurelius. Friend Lucian! thou art more jocose than ever.
Why not imagine they may take my horse
From under me, then round men's shoulders strap
The curule chair and hoist a priest thereon?
Lucian. Thy depth of wisdom, Marcus, long I knew,
But never knew thee poet til this hour.
Homer feign'd Polypheme, Calypso, Circe,
Imagination left him on the strand
With these; he never saw, even in a dream,
So strange a rider mount a curule chair.

The sentiments of M. Aurelius and of Lucian are here exhibited. That Lucian was an honest man (if such a scoffer as he and Rabelais, and Cervantes and Dean Swift, are allowed to be) is probable by so sagacious and virtuous a prince as M. Aurelius appointing him to an important office in Egypt. There is more of banter than of wit in his Dialogues. In wit he is far inferior to Molière, Voltaire, Congreve, Swift, Hood, and some now living.

APPENDED TO THE *HELLENICS*

A heartier age will come; the wise will know
If in my writings there be aught of worth,
Said ardent Milton, whose internal light
Dispel'd the darkness of despondency,
Before he with imperishable gold
Damaskt the hilt of our Protector's blade.
Wonder not if that seer, the nighest to heaven
Of all below, could have thus well divined.
   I, on a seat beneath, but on his right,
Neither expect nor hope my verse may lie
With summer sweets, with albums gaily drest,
Where poodle snifts at flower between the leaves.
A few will cull my fruit, and like the taste,

And find not overmuch to pare away.
The soundest apples are not soonest ripe,
In some dark room laid up when others rot.
  Southey and Hare and, on his deathbed, Ward,
And others of like stamp, have nodded praise.
Unchallenged I have crost the Argive tents,
Alone; and I have wrestled with the prime
Of shepherds on the plains of Sicily,
And her young maidens placed me by their side,
And bade my rival listen while I sang.
Meanwhile not querulous nor feverish
Hath been my courtship of the passing voice,
Nor panted for its echo. Time has been
When Cowley shone near Milton, nay, above!
An age roll'd on before a keener sight
Could separate and see them far apart.
Thus in our day hath Ireland's noble sage
Brought down to human ken and shown how vast
The space between two stars, which few had seen,
And none seen separate.
                              We upon earth
Have not our places and our distances
Assign'd, for many years; at last a tube,
Rais'd and adjusted by Intelligence,
Stands elevated to a cloudless sky,
And place and magnitude are ascertain'd.
  If I extoll'd the virtuous and the wise,
The brave and beautiful, and well discern'd
Their features as they fixt their eyes on mine;
If I have won a kindness never wooed;
Could I foresee that . . fallen among thieves,
Despoil'd, halt, wounded . . tramping traffikers
Should throw their dirt upon me, not without
Some small sharp pebbles carefully inclosed?
However, from one crime they are exempt;
They do not strike a brother, striking *me*.
  This breathes o'er me a cool serenity,
O'er me divided from old friends, in lands
Pleasant, if aught without old friends can please,
Where round their lowly turf-built terraces
Grey olives twinkle in this wintery sun,
And crimson light invests yon quarried cliff,
And central towers from distant villas peer
Until Arezzo's ridges intervene.
  Festival I would keep before I leave
The land where I am tarrying; to this end
Muses! who often heard me, hear me now!
Come, and invite my neighbours on the marsh

To lay aside the homely bowl for once;
Come, tell them, at my table they may taste
The generous wines of Cypros and of Crete,
And hear the chaunt in honor of that God
Who gave the mask and buskin to the stage,
Which the wise Goddess from her fane aloft
Surveyed with stedfast eyes, nor disapproved.
Let me look back upon the world again!
Ah! let me look upon the graves of friends
Departed; let me rest my eyes at last
Upon one happy mansion, hers whose pure
And holy light fell down on me when first
It dawned, and few had ever gazed at mine.
Quitting our poplars and our cypresses,
And the secluded scene they overhang,
Run glibly on, my little Affrico,
Content to cool the feet of weary hind
On thy smooth pavement, strown for him with moss;
Regretting not thy vanisht lake, and maids
Aside its bank, each telling tale for tale;
Revert thee rather, and with pride record
Here blythe Boccaccio led his *Fair Brigade*,[1]
Here Galileo with the stars converst,
And Milton soar'd above them to his God.

HIPPOMENES AND ATALANTA

Hippomenes and Atalanta strove
To win a race: he lov'd her; but she shunn'd
All lovers, and her royal sire had sworn
That none should marry her unless the one
Swifter of foot, believing none could match
His girl in fleetness, and decreed that all
Should surely die who fail'd in such attempt.
Courageously came forth Hippomenes.
She once beheld him, and she pitied him,
For she had made a vow to Artemis
That she would never violate a word
Her father had exacted.
                              Now the hour
Had come to prove her faith; the venturous youth
Stood now before her. Down she cast her eyes,
And cried in broken words, 'Rash youth! depart,
The Fates (thou seest them not) are close behind;

[1] Called *La bella Brigata* by him.

Seven brave youths, hardly less brave than thou,
Have fallen for contending in the race
With wretched Atalanta . . . Go.'

   Hippomenes.   To live
For Atalanta is the first of glory,
To die for her the next: this they enjoyed
In death, the better they bequeathe to me.
   Atalanta. Pity I gave them, do not ask for more,
Nor for such cause; let me not weep again,
Let that be the last time.
   Hippomenes.   So may it be!
So shall it; for the Gods have given me strength
And confidence: one name for victory.
Certain I am to win.
   Atalanta.   No, thou rash boy!
If thou must try such hazard . . if thou must . . .
Must? what impels thee? madness! There is time
Yet to turn back; I do implore thee . . go.
Artemis sees me.
   Hippomenes.   Aphrodite sees
Me, and smiles on me, and instructs me how . .
   Atalanta.   Cease, cease, this instant: I abhor the name;
My Goddess hates her, should not I? I do.
   Hippomenes. I love all Goddesses, the kindest most,
And I beseech her now to make me grateful.
   Atalanta. All I can hope for is thy swift escape;
Be prompt: I see white sails below the cliff;
My father soon shall know 'twas my command,
He wills obedience, he shall value thine,
And send thee gifts.
   Hippomenes.   I want but one, which one
The king shall give me.
   Atalanta.   What is that?
   Hippomenes.   This hand.
   Atalanta. And snatchest thou my hand? audacious creature!
No man hath dared to touch it until now,
Nor I converst with any half so long.
   Hippomenes. Not half so long have any loved as I.
   Atalanta. Insane! it was but yesterday we met.
   Hippomenes. In yesterday, its day and night, lay years.
   Atalanta. I never was dissembler. I will pass
Unyoked thro' life.
   Hippomenes.   O Atalanta! love
No yoke imposes, he removes the heaviest
The Destinies would throw around the neck
Of youth, who wearies in the dismal way
Of lonely life.

Atalanta.   I do not comprehend
Those flighty words, they sound like idle song.
    Hippomenes. Scoff not, add not another to the seven,
Without a race for it; my breath is failing.
    Atalanta. O perfidy! to make me weep again!
Others too may have loved.
    Hippomenes.   But not like me;
Else would the Gods have rais'd them to themselves,
Ay, and above themselves, in happiness,
Crowning the best of them with amaranth.
    Atalanta. Zeus holds the scales of weal and woe.
    Hippomenes.   Zeus holds them,
But little Eros with light finger stoops
The balance-bowl: Zeus shakes his head and smiles.
    Atalanta. What wouldst thou?
    Hippomenes.   Thee; thee only; no rich ile,
No far dominion over land and sea.
    Atalanta. Easier to win than what thou seekest here.
Remember last year's fruit; it lies beneath
The seven hillocks of yon turf, ill-squared
And disunited yet, on the left hand.
Shame! thus to weaken me in my resolve,
And break my father's heart! no, thou shalt not.
    Hippomenes. I blame not tears for those who bravely fell.
    Atalanta. I never did shed tears, and never will.
Come, let us lose no time, if strive we must.
The sward is level here and sound and soft;
Throw off thy sandals, I will throw off mine.
Start.

        They both started; he, by one stride, first,
For she half pitied him so beautiful,
Running to meet his death, yet was resolved
To conquer: soon she near'd him, and he felt
The rapid and repeated gush of breath
Behind his shoulder.
                    From his hand now dropt
A golden apple: she lookt down and saw
A glitter on the grass, yet on she ran.
He dropt a second; now she seem'd to stoop:
He dropt a third; and now she stoopt indeed:
Yet, swifter than a wren picks up a grain
Of millet, rais'd her head: it was too late,
Only one step, only one breath, too late.
Hippomenes had toucht the maple goal
With but two fingers, leaning pronely forth.
She stood in mute despair; the prize was won.

Now each walkt slowly forward, both so tired,
And both alike breathed hard, and stopt at times.
When he turn'd round to her, she lowered her face
Cover'd with blushes, and held out her hand,
The golden apple in it.
      'Leave me now,'
Said she, 'I must walk homeward.'
         He did take
The apple and the hand.
       'Both I detain,'
Said he, 'the other two I dedicate
To the two Powers that soften virgin hearts,
Eros and Aphroditè; and this one
To her who ratifies the nuptial vow.'
 She would have wept to see her father weep;
But some God pitied her, and purple wings
(What God's were they?) hovered and interposed.

THESEUS AND HIPPOLYTA

Hippolyta. Eternal hatred I have sworn against
The persecutor of my sisterhood;
In vain, proud son of Ægeus, hast thou snapt
Their arrows and derided them; in vain
Leadest thou me a captive; I can die,
And die I will.
 Theseus. Nay; many are the years
Of youth and beauty for Hippolyta.
 Hippolyta. I scorn my youth, I hate my beauty. Go!
Monster! of all the monsters in these wilds
Most frightful and most odious to my sight.
 Theseus. I boast not that I saved thee from the bow
Of Scythian.
 Hippolyta. And for what? to die disgraced.
Strong as thou art, yet thou art not so strong
As Death is, when we call him for support.
 Theseus. Him too will I ward off; he strikes me first,
Hippolyta long after, when these eyes
Are closed, and when the knee that supplicates
Can bend no more.
 Hippolyta. Is the man mad?
 Theseus.   He is.
 Hippolyta. So, thou canst tell one truth, however false
In other things.
 Theseus. What other? Thou dost pause,
And thine eyes wander over the smooth turf
As if some gem (but gem thou wearest not)
Had fallen from the remnant of thy hair.

Hippolyta! speak plainly, answer me,
What have I done to raise thy fear or hate?

Hippolyta. Fear I despise, perfidy I abhor.
Unworthy man! did Heracles delude
The maids who trusted him?

  Theseus.   Did ever I?
Whether he did or not, they never told me:
I would have chided him.

  Hippolyta.   Thou chide him! thou!
The Spartan mothers well remember thee.

 Theseus. Scorn adds no beauty to the beautiful.
Heracles was beloved by Omphalè,
He never parted from her, but obey'd
Her slightest wish, as Theseus will Hippolyta's.

 Hippolyta. Then leave me, leave me instantly; I know
The way to my own country.

  Theseus.   This command,
And only this, my heart must disobey.
My country shall be thine, and there thy state
Regal.

 Hippolyta. Am I a child? give me my own,
And keep for weaker heads thy diadems.
Thermodon I shall never see again,
Brightest of rivers, into whose clear depth
My mother plunged me from her warmer breast,
And taught me early to divide the waves
With arms each day more strong, and soon to chase
And overtake the father swan, nor heed
His hoarser voice or his uplifted wing.
 Where are my sisters? Are there any left?

 Theseus. I hope it.

 Hippolyta.   And I fear it: theirs may be
A fate like mine; which, O ye Gods, forbid!

 Theseus. I pity thee, and would assuage thy grief.

 Hippolyta. Pity me not; thy anger I could bear.

 Theseus. There is no place for anger where thou art.
Commiseration even men may feel
For those who want it: even the fiercer beasts
Lick the sore-wounded of a kindred race,
Hearing their cry, albeit they may not help.

 Hippolyta. This is no falsehood: and can he be false
Who speaks it?
       I remember not the time
When I have wept, it was so long ago.
Thou forcest tears from me, because . . because . .
I can not hate thee as I ought to do.

THE TRIAL OF ÆSCHYLOS

Judge. Bring into court the culprit, him accused
Of having, and deliberately, betray'd
The mysteries of Eleusis.
  Æschylos.   Here I stand,
No culprit, and no jailer brings me forth.
  Judge. Hast thou not, Æschylos, divulged the rites
Taught by Demeter?
  Æschylos.   What have I divulged
Beside the truths the Gods to men impart,
And none beside the worthy do they trust.
The human breast they open and they close,
And who can steal their secrets? who shall dare
Infringe their laws, or who arraign their will?
Ye men of Athens! before *you* I stand,
Known to ye long ago, nor only here,
But on the plain of Marathon: who flincht
In that fierce fray? did I? and shall I now?
The brave man venerates, the base man fears,
I scorn to supplicate, or even to plead,
For well I know there is a higher court,
A court of last appeal.
  Judge.   We know it not;
Where is it situated?
  Æschylos.   In man's heart.
In life it may be barr'd, so dark that none
See into it, not he himself; Death comes,
And then the Furies leave their grove and strike.
  Citizen. He spake no wiser words upon the stage,
Where all men speak their wisest and their best.
  Another Citizen. I wish he had not said a word about
Those Furies; Death is bad enough.
  First Citizen.   Hush! hush!
The Arkon rises up and waves his hand.
  Judge. What say ye, men of Athens, to the charge
Ye heard denounced this morning? Are ye mute?
Sadness I see in some, in others wrath,
Wrath ill becomes the seat I occupy;
And even sadness I would fain suppress.
But who can bear irreverence to his Gods?
Their profanation (by your laws) is death.
  Amyntos. (*Rushes forward and bares his brother's scars.*) What have
    these merited? These wounds he won
From Persia, nothing else. Let others show
The purple vestures, stript from satraps slain,
He slew them, and left those for weaker hands
To gather up, and to adorn their wives.

Æschylos. Amyntos is my brother, so are ye,
But why display my ragged white-faced scar?
Why show the place where one arm *was,* if one
Keeps yet its own? this left can wield the sword.

   Amyntos. Fling not thy cloak about thee, nor turn round,
Nay, brother, thou shalt not conceal the scars
With that one hand yet left thee.
                    Citizens!
Behold the man, that impious man, who smote
Those who defiled the altars of your Gods.
Look up: is Pallas standing on yon hill?
She would not have been standing there unless
Men like the man before ye had well fought
At Marathon, not braver than some here
Who fought with him and bound his shattered limb.
If Æschylos your comrade had profaned
Her mysteries, would Demeter since have blest
Your fields with what we call the staff of life,
To give ye strength and courage to protect
Your country, wives, and friends.
                      Ye want him not,
But ye may miss him in the hour of need.
If irreligious wretch hath violated
What all hold sacred, Æschylos not least,
To death condemn him.
                   Weep not thou, whoe'er
Thou art, nor stamp thou other, no, nor shout,
Impatient men! impatient as for battle.
If there be any here who deem him guilty,
To death condemn him, or to worse than death,
Drive him from Athens, bid him raise no more
Your hearts and souls, for he no more can fight
To save our country, nor call heroes down
To stand before ye, not more brave than he,
Alas! alas! nor more unfortunate.

   Citizen. Truth, by the Gods! thou speakest.
   Judge.   Speak ye too,
Judges who sit beside me.
   Judges.   Thou art absolved
By all the people; we confirm the voice.
Æschylos, go in peace.
   Citizen.   In glory go.
Are there no clarions nigh, to waft him home
With their strong blast? no harp to ring before?
   Another Citizen. No olive? none there had been but for him
In all this land.

Another Citizen. At least we can raise up
Our voices to the hymn they have begun,
And call our children to come forth and kiss
The threshold that our Æschylos hath crost.

A FRIEND TO THEOCRITOS IN EGYPT

Dost thou not often gasp with longdrawn sighs,
Theocritos, recalling Sicily?
Glorious is Nile, but rather give me back
Our little rills, which fain would run away
And hide themselves from persecuting suns
In summer, under oleander boughs,
And catch its roses as they flaunt above.
Here are no birds that sing, no sweeter flower
Than tiny fragile weak-eyed resida,
Which faints upon the bosom it would cool.
Altho' the royal lotos sits aloof
On his rich carpet, spred from wave to wave,
I throw myself more gladly where the pine
Protects me, loftier than the palace-roof,
Or where the linden and acacia meet
Across my path, in fragrance to contend.
Bring back the hour, Theocritos, when we
Shall sit together on a thymy knoll,
With few about us, and with none too nigh,
And when the song of shepherds and their glee
We may repeat, perchance and gaily mock,
Until one bolder than the rest springs up
And slaps us on the shoulder for our pains.
Take thou meanwhile these two papyrus-leaves,
Recording, one the loves and one the woes
Of Pan and Pitys, heretofore unsung.
Aside our rivers and within our groves
The pastoral pipe hath dropt its mellow lay,
And shepherds in their contests only try
Who best can puzzle.
                    Come, Theocritos,
Come, let us lend a shoulder to the wheel
And help to lift it from this depth of sand.

PAN

Pan led me to a wood the other day,
Then, bending both hoofs under him, where moss
Was softest and where highest was the tuft,
Said he, 'sit thou aside me; there is room

Just for us two; the tinklers are below
To catch the little birds and butterflies,
Nor see us nor would heed us if they saw.
I minded thee in Sicily with one
I dearly love; I heard thee tell my loss
Of Pitys; and he swore that none but thou
Could thus contend with him, or ever should.
Though others had loud lyres and struck them well,
Few could bring any harmony from reeds
By me held high, and higher since thou hast breath'd
Thy gentle breath o'er Pitys and her Pan.'

THE GARDENER AND THE MOLE

A GARDENER had watcht a mole
And caught it coming from its hole.
'Mischievous beast!' he cried, 'to harm
The garden as thou dost the farm.
Here thou hast had thy wicked will
Upon my tulip and jonquil.
Behold them drooping and half dead
Upon this torn and tumbled bed.'
   The mole said meekly in reply,
'My star is more to blame than I.
To undermine is mole's commission,
Our house stil holds it from tradition.
What lies the nearest us is ours.
Decreed so by the higher Powers.
We hear of conies and of hares.
But when commit we deeds like theirs?
We never touch the flowers that blow,
And only bulbs that lurk below.
'Tis true, where we have run, the ground
Is rais'd a trifle, nor quite sound,
Yet, after a few days of rain,
Level and firm it lies again;
Wise men, like you, will rather wait
For these than argue against fate,
Or quarrel with us moles because
We simply follow Nature's laws.
We raise the turf to keep us warm,
Surely in this there is no harm.
Ye break it up to set thereon
A fortress or perhaps a throne,
And pray that God cast down his eyes
Benignly on burnt sacrifice,

The sacrifice of flesh and bone
Fashioned, they tell us, like His own,
Ye in the cold lie all the night
Under thin tents, at morn to fight.
Neither for horn'd nor fleecy cattle
Start we to mingle in the battle,
Or in the pasture shed their blood
To pamper idleness with food.
Indeed we do eat worms; what then?
Do not those very worms eat men,
And have the impudence to say
Ye shall ere long be such as they?
We never kill or wound a brother,
Men kill by thousands one another,
And, though ye swear ye wish but peace,
Your feuds and warfares never cease.'
   Such homebrought truths the gardener,
Though mild by nature, could not bear,
And lest the mole might more have said
He chopt its head off with the spade.

MEMORY

THE mother of the Muses, we are taught,
Is Memory: she has left me; they remain,
And shake my shoulder, urging me to sing
About the summer days, my loves of old.
Alas! alas! is all I can reply.
Memory has left with me that name alone,
Harmonious name, which other bards may sing,
But her bright image in my darkest hour
Comes back, in vain comes back, call'd or uncall'd.
Forgotten are the names of visitors
Ready to press my hand but yesterday;
Forgotten are the names of earlier friends
Whose genial converse and glad countenance
Are fresh as ever to mine ear and eye;
To these, when I have written, and besought
Remembrance of me, the word *Dear* alone
Hangs on the upper verge, and waits in vain.
A blessing wert thou, O oblivion,
If thy stream carried only weeds away,
But vernal and autumnal flowers alike
It hurries down to wither on the strand.

AN OLD POET TO SLEEP

No God to mortals oftener descends
Than thou, O Sleep! yet thee the sad alone
Invoke, and gratefully thy gift receive.
Some thou invitest to explore the sands
Left by Pactolos, some to climb up higher,
Where points Ambition to the pomp of War;
Others thou watchest while they tighten robes
Which Law throws round them loose, and they meanwhile
Wink at the judge, and he the wink returns.
Apart sit fewer, whom thou lovest more
And leadest where unruffled rivers flow,
Or azure lakes neath azure skies expand.
These have no wider wishes, and no fears,
Unless a fear, in turning, to molest
The silent, solitary, stately swan,
Disdaining the garrulity of groves
Nor seeking shelter there from sun or storm.
    Me also hast thou led among such scenes,
Gentlest of Gods! and Age appear'd far off
While thou wast standing close above the couch,
And whispered'st, in whisper not unheard,
'I now depart from thee, but leave behind
'My own twin-brother, friendly as myself,
'Who soon shall take my place; men call him Death.
'Thou hearest me, nor tremblest, as most do,
'In sooth why shouldst thou? what man hast thou wrong'd
'By deed or word? few dare ask this within.'
    There was a pause; then suddenly said Sleep
'He whom I named approacheth, so farewell.'

[PREFERENCES OF THE HERD]

Jonson to Shakespeare was preferr'd
By the bell-jingling low-brow'd herd,
Cowley to Milton. Who would mind
The stumbles of the lame and blind?
We may regret their sad estate,
But can not make them amble strait.

PROPHECY

The Mexicans will flay the Spaniards
And throw their skins into the tanyards;
The tawny tribes around will wrench
Their beards and whiskers off the French,
And, after a good hearty scourging,
Devote them to the Blessed Virgin.

IRONY

IRONY is the imp of wit,
The truly witty banish it.
Where are the mountebank and clown
Who can not turn things upside down?
When one has fail'd in his endeavour
The other cries, *Zooks!* thou art clever.

ON SOUTHEY'S TOMB

FEW tears, nor those too warm, are shed
By poet over poet dead.
Without premeditated lay
To catch the crowd, I only say,
As over Southey's slab I bend,
The best of mortals was my friend.

TRASH

I HAVE thrown more behind the grate
Than would have bought a fair estate.
And I might readily have sold
My drops of ink for grains of gold.
A bladder sounds with peas within,
Boys shake it and enjoy the din:
There is some poetry that bears
Its likeness, made for boyish ears.

[BY TIME CUT DOWN]

THEY smile on us by Time cut down
    Who always while we lived lookt sour,
So grass smells sweeter when it's mown
    Than fresh and waving in full flower.

TO CHAUCER

CHAUCER, O how I wish thou wert
Alive and, as of yore, alert!
Then, after bandied tales, what fun
Would we two have with monk and nun.
Ah, surely verse was never meant
To render mortals somnolent.

In Spenser's labyrinthine rhymes
I throw my arms o'erhead at times,
Opening sonorous mouth as wide
As oystershells at ebb of tide.
Mistake me not: I honour him
Whose magic made the Muses dream
Of things they never knew before,
And scenes they never wandered o'er.
I dare not follow, nor again
Be wafted with the wizard train.
No bodyless and soulless elves
I seek, but creatures like ourselves.
If any poet now runs after
The Faeries, they will split with laughter,
Leaving him in the desert, where
Dry grass is emblematic fare.
Thou wast content to act the squire
Becomingly, and mount no higher,
Nay, at fit season to descend
Into the poet with a friend,
Then ride with him about thy land
In lithesome nutbrown boots well-tann'd,
With lordly greyhound, who would dare
Course against law the summer hare,
Nor takes to heart the frequent crack
Of whip, with curse that calls him back.
    The lesser Angels now have smiled
To see thee frolic like a child,
And hear thee, innocent as they,
Provoke them to come down and play.

REMONSTRANCE AND ADVICE

TO BYRON

SAY, Byron, why is thy attar
Profusely dasht with vinegar?
Each of them in its place is good,
But neither fit for daily food.
Open thy latticed window wide
For breezes from the Ægæan tide;
And from Hymettus may its bee
Bear honey on each wing to thee:
But keep apart these two perfumes
For hospitals and drawing-rooms.
    Now one more counsel: let alone
The fatty that outflanks the throne,
Nor fancy you can cure a leper
With poultices of cayenne-pepper.

PRAYER OF WALTER MAPES TO HIS
HOLINESS THE POPE

BEATITUDE! we humbly ask
For each poor priest his second flask.
Hourly we pray for daily bread.
Take half, and give us wine instead.
Thou keepest, as we know, the keys
Of heaven and earth; now, one of these
Can ope the cellar as thou wilt;
Trust us, no drop shall there be spilt.
If ever should a vintage fail
(God help us!) we must come to ale.
In sooth our sins deserve it all,
Yet never may such evil fall
Upon the priesthood and the grapes
Most fervently prays Walter Mapes.

DICKENS

You ask me what I see in Dickens . .
A game-cock among bantam chickens.

[OUR ENEMIES]

Pardon our enemies, we pray
Devoutly every sabbath-day;
Ere the next morn we change our notes,
And blow them up or cut their throats.
Above us and below meanwhile
The Angels weep, the Devils smile.

[LOVE AND FRIENDSHIP]

UNHAPPY he whom Love beguiles
With wavering and insidious smiles;
Unhappier, who has lived to prove
That Friendship is as frail as Love.

[MALICE]

SNAP at me, Malice! snap; thy teeth are rotten
And hurt me not: all know thee misbegotten!
The cureless evil runs throughout thy race,
And from Cain downward thy descent we trace.

THERE are a hundred now alive
Who buz about the summer hive,
Alas! how very few of these
Poor little busy poet bees
Can we expect again to hum
When the next summer shall have come.

THE SQUIRE

A VILLAGE church one Sabbath-day,
Many had entered there to pray.
Some knelt along the flagstone floor,
Old men, old women, halt and poor.
Piously in response they said
'*Give us this day our daily bread.*'
Whether they got it, I don't know,
But twice or thrice they pleaded so.
Those words the squire repeated too
Above his cushion'd giltnail'd pew.
Sudden a distant shot he heard,
And up his portly girth was reared.
'*Jim!*' cried he, '*drowsy devil! run,
Tell keeper . . . by the Lord! . . . a gun!
Zounds! I am always in bad luck . . .
Perhaps there goes my fattest buck!*'

A FUNERAL

A HEARSE is passing by in solemn state,
Within lies one whom people call the great.
Its plumes seem nodding to the girls below
As they gaze upward at the raree-show,
Boys from the pavement snatch their tops, and run
To know what in the world can be the fun.

FRIENDS

THE heaviest curse that can on mortal fall
Is 'who has friends may he outlive them all!'
This malediction has awaited me
Who had so many . . . I could once count three.

[DANTE ALIGHIERI]

With frowning brow o'er pontif-kings elate,
Stood Dante, great the man, the poet great.
Milton in might and majesty surpast
The triple world, and far his shade was cast.
On earth he sang amid the Angelic host,
And Paradise to him was never lost.
But there was one who came these two between
With larger light than yet our globe had seen.
Various were his creations, various speech
Without a Babel he bestow'd on each.
Raleigh and Bacon towered above that earth
Which in their day had given our Shakespeare birth,
And neither knew his presence! they half-blind
Saw not in him the grandest of mankind.

[PAN AND HOMER]

Flies have alighted on the shanks of Pan,
And some have settled upon Homer's head;
We whisk them off with jewel-studded fan
Till few escape and many more lie dead.

[YE WHO HAVE TOILED]

Ye who have toil'd uphill to reach the haunt
Of other men who lived in other days,
Whether the ruins of a citadel
Rais'd on the summit by Pelasgic hands,
Or chamber of the distaff and the song . . .
Ye will not tell what treasure there ye found,
But I will.
              Ye found there the viper laid
Full-length, flat-headed, on a sunny slab,
Nor loth to hiss at ye while crawling down.
Ye saw the owl flap the loose ivy leaves
And, hooting, shake the berries on your heads.
   Now, was it worth your while to mount so high
Merely to say ye did it, and to ask
If those about ye ever did the like?
Believe me, O my friends, 'twere better far
To stretch your limbs along the level sand
As they do, where small children scoop the drift,
Thinking it must be gold, where curlews soar
And scales drop glistening from the prey above.

[YOUTH TO AGE]

FROM Youth's bright wing the soonest fall
The brightest feathers of them all:
Few of the others that remain
Are there without some darker stain;
Youth, when at these old Age looks grim,
Cries, '*Who the devil cares for him?*'

WRITTEN IN A CATULLUS

AMONG these treasures there are some
That floated past the wreck of Rome;
But others, for their place unfit,
Are sullied by uncleanly wit.
So in its shell the pearl is found
With rank putridity around.

[SCORN OF THE CROWD]

'CALL me not forth,' said one who sate retired,
Whom Love had once, but Envy never, fired.
'I scorn the crowd: no clap of hands he seeks
Who walks among the stateliest of the Greeks.'

[POETS PREFERRED]

SQUIBS, crackers, serpents, rockets, Bengal lights,
Lead thousands running to the Dardanelles,
Where girls by sackfuls bubble thro' the wave;
I, leaving good old Homer, not o'erlong,
Enjoy the merriment of Chaucer's tales
Or louder glee of the large-hearted Burns,
And then partaking Southey's wholesome fare,
Plenteous, and savoury, without spice, I turn,
To my own sofa, where incontinent
Wordsworth's low coo brings over me sound sleep.

[WHELPS OF THEMIS]

RANCOUR is often the most bitter
Between two mongrels of one litter.
The old bitch Themis grins to teach
Her whelps where lies the prey for each.
They crack the hard, they tear the tough,
And never think they gorge enough.
From Death alone would they crouch back,
For Death shows bones they can not crack.

[SCRIBBLERS]

WHY should the scribblers discompose
Our temper? would we look like those?
There are some curs in every street
Who snarl and snap at all they meet:
The taller mastif deems it aptest
To lift a leg and play the baptist.

[BURIED AT ROME]

THOU hast not lost all glory, Rome!
With thee have found their quiet home
Two whom we followers most admire
Of those that swell our sacred quire;
And many a lowered voice repeats
Hush! here lies Shelley! here lies Keats!

A FOREN RULER

HE says, *My reign is peace,* so slays
A thousand in the dead of night.
Are you all happy now? he says,
And those he leaves behind cry *quite.*
He swears he will have no contention,
And sets all nations by the ears;
He shouts aloud, *No intervention!*
Invades, and drowns them all in tears.

[CRITICS OF VOLTAIRE]

OF those who speak about Voltaire
The least malicious are unfair.
The groundlings neither heed nor know
The victories of Apollo's bow;
What powers of darkness he withstood
And stampt upon the Python's blood.
Observing stil his easy pace,
They call it levity, not grace.

REPLY TO AN INVITATION

Will you come to the bower I have shaded for you?
Our couch shall be roses all spangled with dew.
Tommy Moore, Tommy Moore, I'll be hang'd if I do,
It would give me a cough, and a rheumatise too.

The girl who is prudent, I take it would rather
Repose (tho' alone) upon horsehair or feather.
Poor Peggy O'Corcoran listened to some
Who sang in her ear, *Will you come? Will you come?*
She swells and she squaddles . . so what I suppose is
She must have been lying one day upon roses.

[JERROLD AND WORDSWORTH]

Come lads, the day is all before ye,
Jerrold will tell a merry story,
And ere ye go to bed ye may
Regale on Wordsworth's curds and whey.
I can not join you, for I question
If such things suit with my digestion.

[PEGASUS]

Oft, when the Muses would be festive,
Unruly Pegasus runs restive,
And, over the Pierian fount
Flies upward to their sacred mount;
Aware that marshes rot the hoof
He proudly wings his way aloof.
He loves the highest ground the best,
And takes where eagles soar his rest.

EXCOMMUNICATION, DENOUNCED ON January 30, 1850

Cursed be the wretch who snarls
At the blessed martyr Charles,
And who traitorously opposes
Slitting ears and shortening noses.
Fifty thousand Devils scourge
The blasphemers of Saint George.
Let our Church with annual rites
Celebrate the first of knights,
While the choir more loudly sings
Glory to the best of kings!

Cursing Milton, Hampden, Sidney,
And all others of their kidney,
Satan's sons, who drew the sword
'Gainst the anointed of our Lord,
Whence this day hath been appointed,
Sacred to our Lord's anointed,

We will close it with a prayer
Such as He may deign to hear.
Short prayer after long banning.
'Ever be there worshipt by us
Kings as merciful and pious!'

[THE GATE OF DEATH]

THE pathway to the gate of Death
    Grows darker at each step we take,
And when we reach it, out of breath,
    Our bones, before we rest them, ache:
But suddenly, as if a spell
    Came over us, we fall asleep.
In Earth's warm bosom cuddled well
    Her children never toss and weep.

[LOVE'S TEACHING]

THERE are who say we are but dust,
    We may be soon, but are not yet,
Nor should be while in Love we trust
    And never what he taught forget.

[THREAD AND ROPE]

A SAGE of old hath gravely said
Man's life is hung upon a thread
* * *! the cheated tradesmen hope
That thine may hang upon a rope.

[THE HAY OF LOVE]

LOVE-MAKING is like haymaking, soon over,
    And both are mutable throughout their season.
Haymaker! hear me; thou too hear me, lover,
    Nor scorn experience nor be deaf to reason.
Be quick at work; the sunny hours won't last,
And storms may come before they half are past.

[DEVILS UNASSISTED]

THE Devils in the herd of swine
    May madly run down hill,
Hallooed by never shout of mine,
    Shall they be, shout who will.
Let them with grunts each other shove,
Their grunts molest not me above.

[UPON THE PINDAN TURF]

Upon the Pindan turf our horse
Beats other breeds in wind and force:
He shows activity, and yet
No groom can teach him to curvet:
Young riders twitch him, but in vain,
He plunges, and trots home again.

[TRUE FRIENDS]

By our last ledger-page we ascertain
What friends have fail'd and fled, and what remain.
Content, in summing up, to find how few
Are scored for false, how many starr'd for true.

TO YOUNG POETS

FROM AN OLDER

Children! why pull ye one another's hair?
May not Callimachus or Bion wear
A sprig of bay or myrtle they have found
Lying since nightfall on neglected ground?

[TO MY NINTH DECAD]

To my ninth decad I have tottered on,
  And no soft arm bends now my steps to steady;
She, who once led me where she would, is gone,
  So when he calls me, Death shall find me ready.

ON SOME OBSCURE POETRY

In vain he beats his brow who thinks
To get the better of a Sphynx.

TO IANTHE

A voice I heard and hear it yet,
  We meet not so again;
My silly tears you must forget,
  Or they may give you pain.

The tears that on two faces meet
  My Muse forbids to dry,
She keeps them ever fresh and sweet
  When hours and years run by.

[ENGLISH MEN AND POETS]

BOTH men and poets of the Saxon race
Excell in vigour, none excell in grace.

[PRUDENCE]

LET fools place Fortune with the Gods on high,
Prudence, be thou my guardian deity.
I have neglected thee, alas, too long!
But listen now and hear life's evensong.

[HANDS LESS COLD]

I LIE upon my last made bed,
About to share it with the dead.
Death's cold hand makes me think the more
Of other hands less cold before.
I will not press too close; no fear
Of finding any rival near;
Nor will ye turn your heads away
From the fond things I used to say,
Nor shall I hear. *Now, I declare,*
You jealous man! how changed you are.
Too true indeed is that remark,
And ye may see it in the dark.

[LOVE AND FAME]

IANTHE took me by both ears and said
You are so rash, I own I am afraid.
Prop, or keep hidden in your breast, my name,
But be your love as lasting as your fame.

TO PORSON

LET alone, my old friend, our best poet; ask Parr
If I keep not stout harness well buckled for war.
Of the birch in my field I have wasted no twig
On a petulant Jeffrey or any such prig;
But run not *you* foul on the wise and the kind,
Or you'll soon have to clap your ten fingers behind.

[FRIENDSHIP]

WE may repair and fix again
A shatter'd or a broken pane,
Not friendship so: it lies beyond
Man's wit to piece a diamond.

[FAME AND THE GRAVE]

O IMMORTALITY of fame!
What art thou? even Shakespeare's name
Reaches not Shakespeare in his grave.
The wise, the virtuous, and the brave,
Resume ere long their common clay,
And worms are longer lived than they.
At last some gilded letters show
What those were call'd who lie below.

[PLAIN DISHES]

I OWN I like plain dishes best,
And those the easiest to digest.
Take in the fresher, tougher, harder,
But hook them longer in the larder.
Show me that humble village inn
Where Goldsmith tuned his violin,
Then leave me, at the close of day,
To muse in the churchyard with Gray.

[EMBLEM OF TIBULLUS]

A SPARROW was thy emblem, O Catullus!
A dove was thine, tender and true Tibullus!
No truer and no tenderer was the dove
Whom Noe chose all other birds above
To be the parent inmate of his ark,
When earth was water and the sun was dark.

[YOUR NAME UPON THE SAND]

WELL I remember how you smiled
    To see me write your name upon
The soft sea-sand . . . '*O! what a child!*
    You think you're writing upon stone!'
I have since written what no tide
    Shall ever wash away, what men
Unborn shall read o'er ocean wide
    And find Ianthe's name agen.

[WANING OF LOVE]

How often, when life's summer day
   Is waning, and its sun descends,
Wisdom drives laughing wit away,
   And lovers shrivel into friends!

[ON PLATO]

Doctor'd by Bacon and Montaigne
My eyebrows may sprout forth again,
Worne by hard rubbing to make out
Plato's interminable doubt.
Around him were some clever folks
Until they stumbled into jokes;
Incontinent I quitted these
To stroll with Aristophanes.
I'd rather sup on cold potato,
Than on a salmi cookt by Plato,
Who, always nice but never hearty,
Says Homer shall not join the party.

[THE EYES OF DEATH]

Death indiscriminately gathers
The flowering children and rough-rinded fathers:
His eyes are horny, thus he knows
No different color in the dock and rose.

SHAKESPEARE IN ITALY

Beyond our shores, past Alps and Appennines,
   Shakespeare, from heaven came thy creative breath,
Mid citron groves and over-arching vines
   Thy genius wept at Desdemona's death.
In the proud sire thou badest anger cease
And Juliet by her Romeo sleep in peace;
Then rose thy voice above the stormy sea,
And Ariel flew from Prospero to thee.

[THE HONEST NAME]

Give me for life the honest name,
Then take my due arrears of fame.
I am grown deaf, and shall become
A trifle deafer in the tomb.

[CRITICS OF GIBBON]

GIBBON! tho' thou art grave and grand
And Rome is under thy command,
Yet some in cauliflower-white wigs,
Others put lately into brigs,
Instead of bending back and knee,
Would pull thy chair from under thee.

[TRIFLING WITH EPIGRAMS]

YOU ask how I, who could converse
With Pericles, can stoop to worse:
How I, who once had higher aims,
Can trifle so with epigrams.
    I would not lose the wise from view,
But would amuse the children too;
Beside, my breath is short and weak,
And few must be the words I speak.

INVITATION OF PETRONIUS TO GLYCON

TRYPHŒNA says that you must come
To dine with us at Tusculum.
She has invited few to share
Her delicate but frugal fare.
Contrive the dinner to make out
With venison, ortolans, and trout;
These may come after haunch of boar,
Or neck, which wise men relish more;
And, Glycon, 'twould not be unpleasant
To see among them spring a pheasant.
I voted we should have but two
At dinner, these are quite enow.
One of them, worth half Rome, will meet us,
Low-station'd high-soul'd Epictetus.
He told his mind the other day
To ruby-finger'd Seneca,
Who, rich and proud as Nero, teaches
The vanity of pomp or riches.
Just Epictetus can assure us
How continent was Epicurus,
How gorged and staggering Romans claim
With hiccups that immortal name.

[GAMECOCK OF THE CHURCH]

I saw upon his pulpit-perch
A well-fed gamecock of the church
Spread out his plumes, and heard him crow
To his lean pullets croucht below.
'Wretches! ye raise your throats to men
Who pry into your father's pen;
Look at your betters, do as they do,
And be content to chant a *credo*.'

[PORSON DRUNK]

'Twas far beyond the midnight hour
   And more than half the stars were falling,
And jovial friends, who lost the power
   Of sitting, under chairs lay sprawling;

Not Porson so; his stronger pate
   Could carry more of wine and Greek
Than Cambridge held; erect he sate;
   He nodded, yet could somehow speak.

' 'Tis well, O Bacchus! they are gone,
   Unworthy to approach thy altar!
The pious man prays best alone,
   Nor shall thy servant ever falter.'

Then Bacchus too, like Porson, nodded,
   Shaking the ivy on his brow,
And graciously replied the Godhead,
   'I have no votary staunch as thou.'

[TO JULIUS HARE]

Julius, dear Julius, never think
My spirits are inclined to sink
Because light youths are swimming by
Upon their bladders; so did I.
When in our summer we swam races
I splasht the water in their faces;
And little hands, now only bone,
Clapt me, and call'd the prize my own.

[ON SWIFT]

WILL nothing but from Greece or Rome
Please me? is nothing good at home?
Yes; better; but I look in vain
For a Molière or La Fontaine.
Swift in his humour was as strong
But there was gall upon his tongue.
Bitters and acids may excite,
Yet satisfy not appetite.

[ON CHRISTMAS-DAY]

THERE is a tribute all must pay,
Willing or not, on Christmas-day.
I would be generous, nor confine
Within too narrow limits mine.
For such warm wishes, and such true
Assurances as come from you,
I almost doubt I send enough
In sending a full pinch of snuff.

TO A POET

I NEVER call'd thy Muse splayfooted,
Who sometimes wheez'd, and sometimes hooted,
As owls do on a lonely tower,
Awaiting that propitious hour
When singing birds retire to rest,
And owls may pounce upon the nest.
I only wish she would forbear
From sticking pins into my chair,
And let alone the friends who come
To neutralize thy laudanum.

A GREEK TO THE EUMENIDES

YOUR lips, old beldames, will get dry,
'Tis time to lay the spindle by.
With that incessant hum ye make
Ye will not let me lie awake,
Or, what is better, fall asleep . .
Ah! what a doleful din ye keep!
Unvaried all the year around
The tiresome tune; its tremulous sound
By fits and starts makes tremble too
Me who would fain get rid of you.

Maids are ye! maids whom Love derides
Until he almost cracks his sides.
He points at you, all skin and bones,
And stiff as horn and cold as stones.
I can not bear your nearer breath,
A pleasanter is that of Death.

[A RESTLESS MORTAL]

THERE is a restless mortal who
Feeds on himself, and eats for two.
Heartburn all day and night he feels
And never tries to walk but reels.
Boy! on the table set the taper
And bring your lucifer; this paper
I must without delay set fire on
Or folks may fancy I mean Byron.
Be petty larcenies forgiven,
The fire he stole was not from heaven.

ON ENGLISH HEXAMETERS

PORSON was askt what he thought of hexameters written in English:
'Show me,' said he, 'any five in continuance true to the meter,
Five where a dactyl has felt no long syllable puncht thro' his midrif,
Where not a trochee or pyrric has stood on one leg at the entrance
Like a grey fatherly crane keeping watch on the marsh at Cayster.
Zounds! how they hop, skip, and jump! Old Homer, uplifting his
    eyebrows,
Cries to the somnolent Gods . . 'O ye blessed who dwell on Olympos!
What have I done in old-age? have I ever complain'd of my blind-
    ness?
Ye in your wisdom may deem that a poet sings only the better
(Some little birds do) for *that*; but why are my ears to be batter'd
Flat to my head as a mole's or a fish's, if fishes have any?
Why do barbarians rush with a fury so headstrong against me?
Have they no poet at home they can safely and readily waylay?'
    Then said a youth in his gown, 'I do humbly beg pardon,
        Professor,
But are you certain that you, to whom all the wide Hellas is open,
Could make Homer, who spoke many dialects with many nations,
Speak, as we now have attempted to teach him, our pure Anglo-
    saxon?'

Then the Professor, 'I wager a dozen of hock or of claret,
Standing on only one foot I can throw off more verses and better
Than the unlucky, that limp and halt and have '*no foot to stand on.*'
' 'Pon my word, as I live!' said a younger, 'I really think he has
    done it,
Every soul of us here, by a score of hexameters, quizzing.'[1]

TIBULLUS

ONLY one poet in the worst of days
Disdain'd Augustus in his pride to praise.
Ah, Delia! was it wantonness or whim
That made thee, once so tender, false to him?
To him who follow'd over snows and seas
Messala storming the steep Pyrenees.
But Nemesis avenged him, and the tear
Of Rome's last poet fell upon his bier.

[LAUREL AND THORN]

LATELY our poets loiter'd in green lanes,
Content to catch the ballads of the plains;
I fancied I had strength enough to climb
A loftier station at no distant time,
And might securely from intrusion doze
Upon the flowers thro' which Ilissus flows.
In those pale olive grounds all voices cease,
And from afar dust fills the paths of Greece.
My slumber broken and my doublet torn,
I find the laurel also bears a thorn.

[THE BAYS]

THE scentless laurel a broad leaf displays,
Few and by fewer gather'd are the bays;
Yet these Apollo wore upon his brow . .
The boughs are bare, the stem is twisted now.

---

[1] It is to be hoped that Milton may escape this profanation. Dryden, the
master of rhyme, would have violated the Muse of Zion. That poet's ears must
be stiff with indurated wax which receive not at least an equal pleasure from the
cadences of Milton's verse as from Homer's. Every people has its pet poet; one
unwieldy like Dante, another skittish like Voltaire; but Homer and Milton
have been venerated wherever have been prominent the organs of veneration.
May no iconoclast prevail against them.

DISTRIBUTION OF HONOURS FOR LITERATURE

THE grandest writer of late ages
Who wrapt up Rome in golden pages,
Whom scarcely Livius equal'd, Gibbon,
Died without star or cross or ribbon.

TO SCOTCH CRITICS

WHY should ye sourly criticise
A poet more profuse than wise?
The gentle Muse would not send from her
Her Ovid, tho' preferring Homer.
Mind, wise was gentle Ovid too,
And equal'd in his art by few.
Sirs, malice is a worse disease
Than all your itch and all your fleas.

GIBBON

GIBBON has planted laurels long to bloom
Above the ruins of sepulchral Rome.
He sang no dirge, but mused upon the land
Where Freedom took his solitary stand.
To him Thucydides and Livius bow,
And Superstition veils her wrinkled brow.

[NEVER A SONNET]

No, I will never weave a sonnet,
Let others wear their patience on it;
A better use of time I know
Than tossing shuttles to an fro.

FOR A GRAVESTONE IN SPAIN

SAY thou who liest here beneath,
To fall in battle is not death.
You, tho' no pall on you was cast,
Heard the first trump nor fear'd the last.

[PARROT AND DOVE]

PARROTS have richly color'd wings,
Not so the sweetest bird that sings;
Not so the lonely plaintive dove;
In sadder stole she mourns her love,
And every Muse in every tongue
Has heard and prais'd her nightly song.

[DECEIVER]

A MAN there is who was believ'd
By many; all he has deceiv'd;
To one on earth may he prove true,
O lady, and that one be you.

BID TO THINK OF FAME

RATHER than flighty Fame give me
A bird on wrist or puss on knee.
Death is not to be charm'd by rhymes
Nor shov'd away to after-times.
Of maiden's or of poet's song
Did anything on earth sound long?
Why then should ever mortal care
About what floats in empty air?
All we devise and all we know
Is better kept for use than show.
Perhaps we deem ourselves the wise,
Other may see with clearer eyes.
Little I care for Fame or Death,
Or groan for one gasp more of breath.
Death, in approaching me looks grim,
I in return but smile at him.

[NEVER MUST MY BONES BE LAID]

NEVER must my bones be laid
Under the mimosa's shade.
He to whom I gave my all
Swept away her guardian wall,
And her green and level plot
Green or level now is not.

[A POET'S LEGACY]

ABOVE all gifts we most should prize
The wisdom that makes others wise:
To others when ourselves are dust
We leave behind this sacred trust.
We may not know, when we are gone,
The good we shall on earth have done;
Enough in going is the thought
For once we acted as we ought.

ON THE HEIGHTS

THE cattle in the common field
   Toss their flat heads in vain,
And snort and stamp; weak creatures yield
   And turn back home again.

My mansion stands beyond it, high
   Above where rushes grow;
Its hedge of laurel dares defy
   The heavy-hooft below.

NOTES

P. 1. [LADY GODIVA]. Possibly written by Landor when at school at Rugby.

P. 3. [ROSE AYLMER]. The text is the revised version from Landor's *Works*, 1846. The Hon. Rose Whitworth Aylmer, whom Landor knew at Laugharne, in Carmarthenshire, 1796-1799. She died in India in 1800. Landor said that he made up the poem 'when I was cleaning my teeth before going to bed' (R. H. Super. *Walter Savage Landor*, 1954, p. 37).

P. 3. [FROM SAPPHO]. Suggested by a two line fragment of Sappho

Γλύκεια μᾶτερ, ού τοι δύναμαι κρέκην τὸν ἴστον,
Πόθῳ δάμεισα πάιδος βραδίναν δι' 'Αφρόδιταν

Sweet mother, I cannot strike the web,
Overcome by tender Aphrodite with longing for a boy.

P. 4. TO IANTHE, WITH PETRARCH'S SONNETS. Ianthe, the illumination of Landor's emotional being, was the Irish girl, Jane Sophia Swift. He came to know her at Bath, *c.*1798. 'One loved me at twenty, another at twenty-five—none between, and none wanted I,' Landor wrote in his old age (Super, op. cit., p. 58). Ianthe was this second girl. She rejected him, returned to Ireland, soon married her cousin Godwin Swift, and was left a widow with seven children in 1814. By her second marriage she became the Countess Molandé. Landor and Ianthe remained friendly until her death in 1851.

P. 6. TO ZOË, and FROM THE BAY OF BISCAY. Both poems, though published long after, were presumably written in 1808, when Landor was on his way to Corunna to join the Spanish insurgents. If Malcolm Elwin's theory (in his *Savage Landor*, 1941) is true, that Landor continued an intermittent liaison with Ianthe for some time after her marriage, the date of which is given as 1803, then the poems may have been written to her. 'Zoë' was 'Psyche' when the longer poem was first published in 1838. Landor's revision of 1842, here given, improved the poem considerably.

P. 7. GEBIR. Substantially the revised text of 1803, though Landor's footnotes are omitted. In Book I the first eleven lines are retained from 1798 (the later versions began 'I sing the fates of Gebir! how he dwelt'). In Book IV, lines 1-10 and lines 217-221 have been added from the text of 1831.

P. 56. [ON THE DEATH OF GEORGE HANGER, LORD COLERAINE]. Lord Coleraine (1751?-1824), Gloucestershire eccentric, sportsman, and soldier, whose *Life, Adventures and Opinions* were published in 1801. See the Imaginary Conversation (1828) 'Lord Coleraine, Rev. Mr. Bloombury, and Rev. Mr. Swan.'

P. 58. [ACROSS THE SEA]. Text of 1846.

P. 58. [FIESOLAN MUSINGS]. Text of 1846. Landor moved to Florence in 1821, and settled in a villa at Fiesole, above the city, in 1829, abandoning it to his wife and children in 1835.

P. 62. [ON VISCOUNT MELVILLE]. Henry Dundas, 1st Viscount Melville (1742-1811), Scotch lawyer and politician. As Home Secretary under Pitt responsible for the savage laws against Jacobinism and sedition during the wars against France. Impeached in 1806 for corrupt use of public funds during earlier service as treasurer of the Admiralty; but acquitted. See Landor's *Moral Epistle to Earl Stanhope*, 1795.

P. 62. EPISTLE TO A BARRISTER. William Elias Taunton acted for Charles Betham, tenant of one of Landor's farms at Llanthony, with whom Landor quarrelled. See R. H. Super's *Walter Savage Landor*.

l. 93 Lord Kenyon, Lord Chief Justice from 1788-1802.

l. 97 John Scott, Earl of Eldon (1751-1838), Lord Chancellor, and William Scott, Baron Stowell (1745-1836), judge of the high court of Admiralty.

l. 100 Lord Thurlow (1731-1806), Lord Chancellor.

l. 259 Frederick Betham, younger brother of Charles Betham. He was accused of uprooting Landor's trees, and sued Landor for libel in 1814. See Super, op. cit., p. 120.

P. 72. ON A POET IN A WELSH CHURCH-YARD. Wheeler, *Poetical Works*, (III, p. 166) suggests that Landor refers to the grave of Henry Vaughan (1621-1695) in the churchyard of Llansantfraed, in Breconshire, not far from Llanthony.

P. 72. FOR AN EPITAPH AT FIESOLE. See Forster's *Landor*, ii 266, for these mimosas planted at Landor's home by Ianthe, on a visit. Also Super, op. cit., p. 463.

P. 74. [TO THE POET T. J. MATHIAS]. Thomas John Mathias (?1754-1835), poet, Italian scholar, translator of English poetry into Italian, disliked by Landor especially for his popular satirical poem *The Pursuits of Literature or What You Will*, 1794-1797. Landor attacked him first in his prose *Post-script to Gebir*, printed in 1800, but not published (Wheeler, *Poetical Works*, vol. I, p. 480), then laughed at him in epigrams. The two poets met in Naples, in 1827.

P. 79. TO LYSIS. See Landor's *Pericles and Aspasia*, 1836, (*Aspasia to Cleone*).

P. 81. THE DEATH OF ARTEMIDORA. ibid.

P. 82. (NICONÖE AND PRIAPOS). ibid.

P. 86. A SATIRE ON SATIRISTS.

l. 66 Ebenezer Elliott (1781-1849), who published his *Corn-Law Rhymes*, 1831.

l. 67 *Paracelsus*, by Robert Browning, 1835.

l. 77 Mathias. See note above on TO THE POET T. J. MATHIAS.

l. 81 'Peter Porcupine' was William Cobbett's pen-name in America, 1793-1800.

l. 82 John Wilson (1785-1854), Professor of Moral Philosophy, Edinburgh, 1820. Wrote for Blackwood's as 'Christopher North'.

l. 142 William Burke, hanged 1829, the murderer who sold corpses to Edinburgh surgeons.

l. 223 *Ion*, Greek tragedy by Sir Thomas Talfourd, 1835.

l. 240-1 See Wordsworth's abysmal *Thanksgiving Ode*, 1816.

l. 302. Kalgarth-flat, i.e. Calgarth, on the east shore of Windermere, in the Lake District.

l. 323 Rev. George Croly (1780-1860), poet, novelist, contributor to Blackwood.

P. 96. ESPOUSALS OF H.M. OF PORTUGAL—i.e. of Maria II, the young Queen of Portugal, who married Prince Ferdinand of Saxe-Coburg-Gotha in April 1836.

P. 97. EPITAPH [ON FRANCIS IST]. Francis 1st (1768-1835), first Emperor of Austria and oppressor of the Italians. See Imaginary Conversation (1824) 'Andrew Hofer, Count Metternich and the Emperor Francis.'

P. 98. [TRELAWNY], i.e. Edward John Trelawny (1792-1881), tempestuous friend of Shelley and Byron, whose autobiographical (and fictional) *Adventures of a Younger Son* appeared in 1831.

P. 116. TO IANTHE (IN VIENNA). Text of Nicoll and Wise, *Literary Anecdotes*, 1895, as sent to the Countess of Blessington in 1838. Lines 17-18 are retained from the first printed version.

P. 117. [DR. WORDSWORTH]. Wordsworth, old, accepted and reactionary, was given the honorary degree of D.C.L. by the University of Oxford at the Commemoration of 1839.

P. 125. ON READE's *CAIN*. John Edmund Reade (1800-1870), whose residence at Bath made him known to Landor, published *Cain the Wanderer* in 1830, an undramatically dramatic poem in his flattest mode. He modelled himself on Byron (no recommendation to Landor), Rogers, etc., and feebly lifted from other poets. 'Never was poet so hot for celebrity. It has made him very ill. He is now about to publish a drama of the Deluge, in which he tells me he has been employed for twenty years. You cannot be surprised that he is grievously and hopelessly afflicted, having had water on the brain so long.' Landor to Lady Blessington, quoted Super, p. 299.

P. 126. [TO SIR SAMUEL MEYRICK]. Sir Samuel Rush Meyrick (1783-1848,) lawyer, antiquary, local historian, of Goodrich Court, Herefordshire, which Meyrick built 1828-1831 as a baronial castle, and filled with a splendid collection of armour.

P. 126. TO MY DAUGHTER. Julia Landor, born at Pisa, 1820.

P. 128. [AN IMAGINARY CONVERSATION]. Kenyon—Landor's friend John Kenyon, minor poet (1784-1856), friend also of Southey, Wordsworth, and Browning.

P. 152. [FOR A TOMB IN WIDCOMBE CHURCH-YARD]. Landor hoped to lie in Widcombe churchyard, not far from Bath, where he had bought a plot, near the church-tower. See Super, op. cit., p. 453, quoting a letter of May 29th, 1858. 'Sixty years ago, in this season, I promised a person I dearly loved'—i.e. Ianthe —'it should be here. We were sitting under some old elders, now supplanted by a wall of the churchyard.' In fact, he was buried in Florence.

P. 152. SENT WITH POEMS. Landor presumably meant T. J. Mathias (see note on p. 314), indicating him by the similarly named victim of the satire of Martial and Juvenal.

P. 154. [ON THE POET MATHO]. See previous note.

P. 155. [ON SPENCER PERCEVAL, IRVINGITE]. Tory M.P., and son of the Prime Minister of the same name assassinated by a madman in the Palace of Westminster in 1812. He fervently supported Edward Irving's religious extremism, and was an Apostle in the Catholic Apostolic Church which the Irvingites founded. Carlyle mentions him among the guests at an Irvingite dinner given by the banker and student of the Second Coming, Henry Drummond, in 1831—'all prophetical, Toryish, ultra-religious.'

P. 164. PAN AND PITYS. Text from the 2nd edition of Landor's *Hellenics*, 1859.

P. 169. GUIZOT's DISGUISE. Guizot, anti-liberal foreign minister under Louis-Philippe, came to England in disguise when Louis-Philippe abdicated after the revolution of 1848.

P. 172. DYING SPEECH OF AN OLD PHILOSOPHER. Written at Bath on the night of Landor's 74th birthday, January 30th, 1849. See introduction, p. 17.

P. 173. TO THE AUTHOR OF *FESTUS*, etc., i.e. the poet Philip James Bailey (1816-1902), whose *Festus* was published in 1839.

P. 181. REPROOF OF THANKS. As printed in *Landor's Last Fruit off an Old Tree*, 1853.

P. 181. NIL ADMIRARI, ETC. As printed in *Last Fruit Off an Old Tree*, 1853.
The root of the poem is No. 6 in Horace's first book of Epistles, beginning

> Nil admirari prope res est una, Numici,
> solaque, quae possit facere et servare beatum.

The epistle was translated by Thomas Creech (*The Odes*, Satyrs, and Epistles of
Horace, 1684), and imitated by Pope.

P. 185. PARAPHRASE OF HORACE'S PYRRHA. Based on Horace, Odes I, V.

P. 188. [CRITICS AND POETS]. For Mathias, see above, p. 314.

P. 190. THE DUKE OF YORK'S STATUE. Sir Richard Westmacott's statue of
the Duke (1834), surmounting the Duke of York's Column in Waterloo Place,
London.

P. 191. TO JOHN FORSTER. John Forster (1812-1876), first biographer of
Landor.

P. 197. [O PLAINS OF TOURS]. In the summer of 1852, the town council of
Tours gave its support to Louis Napoleon, after the *coup d'état* of the previous
December, which led to his elevation as Napoleon III. Between Poitiers and
Tours, Charles Martel had defeated the advancing Arabs in 732.

P. 197. EXPOSTULATION. The scene is Wastwater (in the Lakes), visited by
Landor in company with Wordsworth in 1832.

P. 203. APOLOGY FOR GEBIR. Fidler: Landor's Welsh pony. Cardigan,
Somerset, Dundas: trio of the Crimean War—Lord Cardigan, of the Charge of
the Light Brigade; Fitzroy Somerset, 1st Lord Raglan, Commander-in-Chief;
Admiral Sir James Dundas, chief of naval operations.

P. 205. [LORD ABERDEEN]. Prime Minister during the Crimean War, the
dismal conduct of which led to his resignation in 1855, whereupon Queen Victoria
gave him the Order of the Garter.

P. 206. LEADERS AND ASPIRANTS. Little John: Lord John Russell. Jim Crow:
Sir James Graham, by whose authority as Home Secretary in 1844 refugees'
letters had been impounded and opened. He was First Lord of the Admiralty
under Lord Aberdeen, during the Crimean War, but soon had to resign under
Palmerston, Aberdeen's successor.

P. 247. GEORGE THE THIRD'S STATUE. The statue of George III with a pig-
tail on horseback, by the much criticized Mathew Cotes Wyatt, in Cockspur
Street, London, unveiled 1836.

P. 249. PEOPLE AND PATRIOTS. See note above on LEADERS AND ASPIRANTS.

P. 250. HEROICS OR DACTYLICS. See note on LEADERS AND ASPIRANTS.

P. 253. A SENSIBLE GIRL'S REPLY. See also REPLY TO AN INVITATION, p. 298.

P. 253. ACCUSED OF INDIFFERENCE TO PRAISE. TO SOPHIA.—i.e. to Ianthe,
Jane Sophia Swift.

P. 253. THERMOMETER. See note above (p. 315) on the epigram ON READE'S
CAIN.

P. 254. TRIPOS. Andrew Crosse (1784-1855), scientific amateur, and re-
searcher into electrical phenomema, of Fyne Court, in the Quantocks, Somerset.
For Crosse, insects, and electricity, see the D.N.B.

P. 259. [PARADISE LOST]. See Super, op. cit., p. 472, where it is explained,
on the evidence of a letter from Browning now in the Boston Public Library,

that Landor at Marciano in 1859 brought Browning two unrhyming lines about his wife's conduct, which had made him leave his villa at Fiesole:

> Out of his Paradise an Angel drove
> Adam, a Devil now drives me from mine.

Mrs. Browning said that rhyme was needed, and Browning thereupon refashioned the lines as we know them.

P. 273. LEONTION, ON TERNISSA'S DEATH. For the characters, see Landor's Imaginary Conversation of 1829, *Epicurus, Leontion, and Ternissa*.

P. 279. [APPENDED TO *THE HELLENICS* 1859]. l. 30. Ireland's noble sage: Sir William Rowan Hamilton (1800-1865), Astronomer Royal Of Ireland.

P. 291. AN OLD POET TO SLEEP. This is the second of two versions both printed in Landor's last book of verse, *Heroic Idyls*, 1863.

P. 294. PRAYER OF WALTER MAPES, etc. An edition of *De Nugis Curialium*, the collection of anecdotes, folk stories about Wales and the Marches, etc., by the witty 12th century ecclesiastic Walter Map or Mapes, had appeared in 1850, and a collection of Latin poems once ascribed to him (including the famous drinking song of the Arch Poet) in 1841. Map's association with Herefordshire and the Marches, near Llanthony, no doubt increased his attraction for Landor.

P. 298. REPLY TO AN INVITATION. See also A SENSIBLE GIRL'S REPLY, p. 253.

P. 299. EXCOMMUNICATION. January 30th—Landor's birthday and the day on which Charles I was executed. The last eleven lines were printed in *Heroic Idyls*, 1863,—apparently in error—as a separate poem.

P. 302. TO PORSON—Richard Porson (1759-1808), classical scholar and textual critic of formidable personality and power, and head for liquor (see *Porson Drunk*, p. 306), made by Landor a protagonist of the excellent Imaginary Conversation, *Southey and Porson* (1824).

Samuel Parr (1747-1825), scholar, Whig (like Porson), literary and political controversialist and friend of writers. Landor first knew him in his Warwickshire childhood, and remained a friend till Parr's death.

P. 310. FOR A GRAVESTONE IN SPAIN. Landor went to Spain in 1808, with the intention of fighting for the Spaniards in their rising against Napoleon.

INDEX OF TITLES

322

INDEX OF FIRST LINES

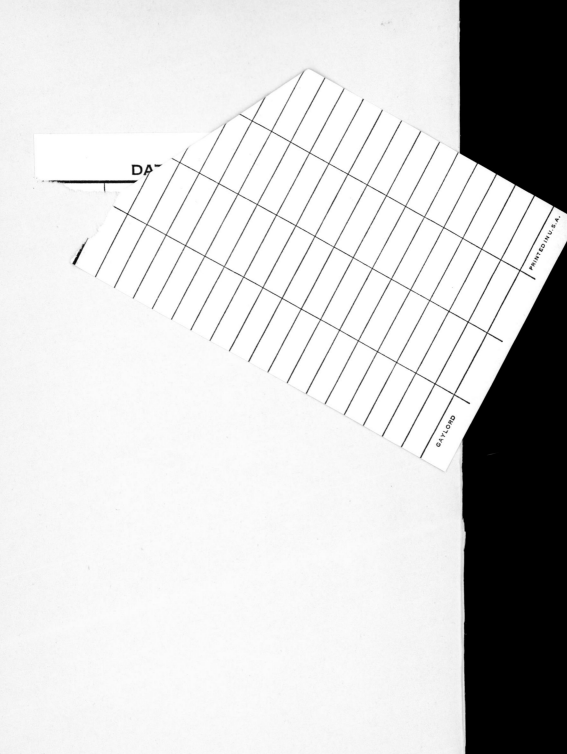

DATE

GAYLORD

PRINTED IN U.S.A.